10/05/24
23/05/24

KT-416-466

Please return or renew this item
by the last date shown. You may
return items to any East Sussex
Library. You may renew books
by telephone or the internet.

BAT **East Sussex**
County Council

0345 60 80 195 for renewals
0345 60 80 196 for enquiries

Library and Information Services
eastsussex.gov.uk/libraries

EAST SUSSEX COUNTY COUNCIL
WITHDRAWN

23 MAY 2024

04515596

BY THE SAME AUTHOR

*The Man Who Broke Out of the Bank
and Went for a Walk in France*

COBRA IN THE BATH

Adventures in Less Travelled Lands

Miles Morland

BLOOMSBURY
LONDON • OXFORD • NEW YORK • NEW DELHI • SYDNEY

Bloomsbury Paperbacks
An imprint of Bloomsbury Publishing Plc

50 Bedford Square   1385 Broadway
London   New York
WC1B 3DP   NY 10018
UK   USA

www.bloomsbury.com

BLOOMSBURY and the Diana logo are trademarks of Bloomsbury Publishing Plc

First published in Great Britain 2015
This paperback edition first published in 2016

© 2015 by Miles Morland

Miles Morland has asserted his right under the Copyright,
Designs and Patents Act, 1988, to be identified as Author of this work.

Photographs are from the author's personal collection.

All rights reserved. No part of this publication may be reproduced or transmitted in
any form or by any means, electronic or mechanical, including photocopying,
recording, or any information storage or retrieval system, without prior permission
in writing from the publishers.

No responsibility for loss caused to any individual or organization acting on or
refraining from action as a result of the material in this publication
can be accepted by Bloomsbury or the author.

British Library Cataloguing-in-Publication Data
A catalogue record for this book is available from the British Library.

Library of Congress Cataloguing-in-Publication Data has been applied for.

ISBN: HB: 978-1-4088-6367-1
PB: 978-1-4088-6368-8
ePub: 978-1-4088-6369-5

2 4 6 8 10 9 7 5 3 1

Typeset by Newgen Knowledge Works (P) Ltd., Chennai, India
Printed and bound in Great Britain by CPI Group (UK) Ltd, Croydon CR0 4YY

To find out more about our authors and books visit www.bloomsbury.com.
Here you will find extracts, author interviews, details of forthcoming events and
the option to sign up for our newsletters.

To Georgia, for whom the adventure never ended

Yet all experience is an arch wherethrough
Gleams that untravelled world, whose margin fades
For ever and for ever when I move.
How dull it is to pause, to make an end,
To rust unburnished, not to shine in use!

'Ulysses', Alfred, Lord Tennyson

Contents

PART I

COBRA IN THE BATH

I

Cobra in the Bath

There is a cobra in the bath. It is coiled round the big square plughole that drains through the wall into the garden; it has slithered up there looking for shade in the heat of the Delhi afternoon. Its head wavers up to look at the small freckly English boy who has come into the bathroom and disturbed its sleep. For a very short time boy and snake look at each other motionless.

Then with a scream so loud that it starts the crows from the dunghill, the boy runs from the room, slamming the door behind him. 'Cobra, cobra. Cobra in bath,' he cries. Turmoil. Ma comes running; the ayah comes clucking out of the boys' bedroom; brother Michael comes running and, close behind, one-legged stepfather JRC comes clippity-hop on his crutch with the twelve-bore under the crutch-free arm. The lodger sidles round the door wearing his usual shifty leer, and flocks of white-pyjamaed servants materialise looking concerned. They are concerned not for the safety of the small sobbing boy but for the snake. Cobras are sacred animals; its death could bring down a mountain of bad luck on the household.

Ma throws open the door to the bathroom and marches in. The small boy hangs back trembling. JRC stuffs two cartridges into the twelve-bore and hops *clip-clack* past into the room, gun a-cock. The ayah clucks, the white pyjamaed servants chatter and strain forward. No cobra. It is gone, off to join the crows in the shade by the dunghill, where its mate lives and where it will not be disturbed by small boys coming to use the thunderbox in the middle of the afternoon.

I am the small boy. I was four at the time. I can picture the scene in all its intensity today but I have to admit that I cannot really remember it. I have heard the Cobra in the Bath story so many times that each part of the story is rich with detail but, try as I can, I cannot conjure up the real memory.

That is my Indian childhood: a collection of vivid mental snapshots, shot with heat, colour, light, tumult and the smell of spice. Which snapshots are real and which only seem real because of my mother's story-telling abilities is hard to say. The memories jostle and jumble for mind-room in no particular order, and the things I cannot remember, like the cobra in the bath, seem as real as the things like the duck shoot, the car rolling over and the crow that stole my cake, which I know I can remember.

2

India

We left India – Ma, my father, brother Michael and I – in 1946 to return to the chill world of post-war England. Grey the only colour there. No light or heat. I was two; Michael was just five. My parents' marriage was all but over by then; they were returning to England with the prospect of divorce, but we travelled back as a family. In 1946 there were no berths on ships returning to England for civilians travelling by themselves.

The story of how I was born I have heard so many times that I can picture it in the finest detail. It was December 1943. My father, a lieutenant commander at that time in the Royal Indian Navy, was commanding a destroyer whose home port was Vizagapatam, a naval base halfway down the right-hand side of India. The year 1943 saw Henry Morland RIN, or Bunny as he was universally known, pacing the bridge of his destroyer as he quartered the Bay of Bengal in search of marauding Hun or Jap. Why my father was called Bunny I never thought to ask. In retrospect it seems a strange name for an athletic six-foot naval officer. After my parents divorced, hungry for detail of my father's war, I asked Ma if he had destroyed anything in his destroyer.

'Yes,' she said, 'a submarine.'

'Good for Daddy. Did he get a medal?'

To a small boy in the 1940s, medals were important.

'No.'

'Why not?'

'It was an English submarine.'

'Oh no. What happened?'

'Well,' said Ma, 'no one ever really found out. His boat dropped some depth charges on a submarine, and not long after bits and pieces came floating up. When they reported this back to Vizag, they were told that no one knew anything about German or Japanese submarines in the area but an English one had gone missing.'

'Oh. Poor Daddy. What did they do to him?'

'Nothing. They never proved anything, and as it was the middle of the war they didn't see much point in making a fuss. Everyone was far too worried that they were going to wake up to find hordes of Japs raping their womenfolk and bayoneting the ayah. Old Buns was never much good as an active sailor. Much better on land. What he enjoyed was gallivanting around at cocktail parties in Bombay being aide-de-camp to an admiral and looking glamorous in his white uniform. He was frightfully good at that. It came as a nasty shock to him when the war broke out and he had to go and do something.'

Whether the alleged sinking was before or after my birth I do not know. My father was home, presumably on leave, at the time of my birth. The family album shows a photograph of him at the christening in the glamorous white uniform and standing on the Doric-columned steps of the Raj church in Vizag. The dozen or so people in the christening party have cheery smiles on their faces, none more so than my mother. This is peculiar as she has always insisted that she was extremely ill both while carrying me and at the time of my birth. She was suffering, she said, from various tropical diseases, none of which were susceptible to diagnosis by Vizag's only European doctor, Hamish, who had delivered me a few days before the christening.

Everyone in the picture looks happy but brother Michael, then almost three. He, also wearing a white uniform, is lurking in front of the smiling godparents. It looks as if he is hiding something behind his back, possibly concealing a murder weapon for use against his newly arrived younger brother as soon as the ayah's attention could be distracted.

I was born at home. Ma had had Michael almost three years earlier in Karachi Hospital. 'I wasn't going through that nonsense all over again. You've never seen such a place. And in any case Vizag didn't have a proper hospital.' Ma had great confidence in Hamish as a doctor despite his inability to diagnose her illnesses. That was lucky as otherwise the nearest European doctor was in Madras, some 400 miles away. There were no European midwives in Vizag either; they had been sent off to be nurses in military hospitals. The thought of having an Indian doctor to assist at the birth did not appeal to my mother. 'I wasn't going to have some Indian makee-learn poking around in my bits and pieces thank you very much. Anyhow, it wasn't necessary because Hamish was one of the best doctors I came across in India, and we had him sitting on our doorstep in Vizag. Well, he was a jolly good doctor until he had had a couple. He did like his drink.'

He was not quite on the doorstep. He lived the other side of Vizag. When my mother finally went into labour, on the evening of 18 December, a servant was dispatched to find Dr Hamish. He returned an hour later. No doctor. Things were becoming more urgent by now. 'Buns was flapping around being completely useless so I sent him off to find Hamish. Hours went by. Finally just as you were about to pop out, Buns and Hamish appeared together. I'm sure they had stopped off for a couple on the way. They arrived at about exactly the same time as you. Anyhow, Hamish took charge, got you cleaned up and Buns took care of the drinks. God knows what we were drinking. Indian whisky probably. We had quite a party. Hamish must have stayed all night. We were all completely pie-eyed in the morning.'

Ma maintained that I spent the first year of my life grubbing around naked on Vizag beach. Because I never wore any clothes I am reputed to have grown fur all over my body by the time we left Vizag halfway through 1944. The photographs of this period in the album do not bear this out. In most, it is true, I am naked and grubbing around on the beach, but in some I am wearing what must have been my favourite, and possibly only, article of clothing, a pair of white dungarees decorated with pictures of Scottie dogs. There is no evidence of fur. The only exceptional thing about me was that I was almost globular. I must have needed chocks to prevent me rolling down the beach. This may have been caused by my diet. My mother's undiagnosed tropical diseases meant that she was unable to breastfeed me. The shops of Vizag, five years into the war, lacked any kind of artificial milk or other items of what Westerners consider appropriate baby food. Consequently I was brought up, said Ma, on ground-up chicken food from the bazaar. Judging by my size and girth aged one, it made a fine diet.

Later in 1944 we moved from Vizag to Madras, as a result of my father being posted there by the navy. My parents quickly made friends in wartime Madras. One, Daphne Economou, wrote an evocative memoir of growing up called *Saturday's Child*. She remembers this story from war-time Madras.

Apart from the military men, couples and families arrived from the north, and Madras became a hub of social activity. There were the Morlands, Bunny and Susan, with their two red-headed little boys, Michael and Miles. They were a sensational couple to look at and were labelled 'great fun', a phrase that echoed the false gaiety of that precarious time. Everybody knew it was now or never, the foxtrot was all the rage and the song was 'Anything Goes'. Nobody I have ever known looked as elegant in a morning coat and grey top hat as Bunny, but it was Susan with her delightful exuberance who made all the difference.

The arrival of Susan became one of the Madras legends. Bunny had come ahead and Susan wired that she was setting out from somewhere up north with the two boys, two bearers, two wolfhounds and fifteen trunks. At the appointed day and hour, Bunny went to the station to meet his family. The train arrived, but there was no sign of Susan, the boys, the bearers, the wolfhounds or the trunks. Bunny was in a frenzy of anxiety and began to receive condolences, like a bereaved widower.

There had been a series of dacoit [bandit] episodes on trains, with lurid tales of cut throats and slaughtered children. Wires were sent to every stationmaster along the line, but no one had seen the Morland family, until a few days later, when they all arrived totally unscathed. The story according to Susan was that there was this young officer travelling down to Madras on the same train to join his regiment. 'Bound to be killed, poor chap. So why not give him a last happy fling . . .?' They had all got off at some nameless station and spent a couple of blissful days and nights, boys, bearers, wolfhounds, trunks and all . . .

That was Susan. She could have had any one of the husbands she wanted, including my father, but she never broke up a marriage. She had something called 'panache'.

I have often wondered what the state of my parents' marriage was when we left Vizag. I never heard my father's side of the story; the little pieces of evidence all come from my mother, and she was, for her, unusually vague. It was in Madras that Ma met Johnny Caldwell, the one-legged Scotsman with the shotgun, the man who was later to be her second husband. JRC, for Johnny was universally known in the family by his initials, was in India working for J & P Coats, the Paisley textile firm whose thread was sold in every corner of the British empire. JRC, perhaps because of his dour, God-fearing, Lowland Scots background, was the very opposite of dour and God-fearing. He sang, he flirted, he played the piano, he told long jokes of wonderful complexity, and – despite the wooden crutch, an ever-present necessity as he had lost his left leg to a bone disease when he was three – he danced, shot and played tennis, quite an accomplishment for a man with a crutch tucked Long-John-Silver-style into his left armpit.

He was an inspired mechanic, and his particular love was to drive fast cars at high speed, again an achievement for a man with only one foot to share between three pedals. He had spent time in South Africa as a young man and claimed to have held the Cape Town to Durban road record. He was a master of the clutchless gear-change, a manoeuvre that required perfect timing, but from time to time the clutch was essential, and JRC would dive beneath the dashboard while changing down at 60 mph and depress the clutch pedal with his left hand while changing gear with his right. The steering wheel would be directed meanwhile by his right, surviving, thigh.

JRC must have been a welcome butterfly in the starched and sharply creased white-drill world of wartime colonial India. Thanks to his one leg, he was one European in Madras

who was not going to be sent off to be killed in Burma. Taddy Dyson, the daughter of one of Ma's best friends in Madras, remembers him as a frequent and entertaining visitor to the Dyson household, where it is probable that he met Ma, this despite the efforts of Dr Dyson to ban Ma from his household on the grounds that she was 'the most dangerous woman in India'.

By 1946 my father had left the navy, and the most dangerous woman in India was back in England, their marriage ended.

3

Welcome to England

Immediately after our return Ma, all but penniless, found a job as a barmaid in a small pub in Bungay in Suffolk. This did not last long. The pub let out rooms and was a clandestine trysting place for homosexuals in the days when homosexuality, far from being a cause for celebration, got you five years' hard labour. It was not the principle of homosexuality that worried Ma, who was a broad-minded woman, but the fact that one of her duties was to make the beds. 'You wouldn't believe the disgusting mess the sheets were in after a night of bugger-boys playing around with each other. I simply couldn't stomach it.'

Ma left her job and with some financial help from her father bought a tiny cottage in Tollesbury, a little village above the marshes on the Blackwater estuary in Essex. Bunny, now living by himself in London, would come down for weekends in between job-hunting. For a time he had a job as a travelling salesman for Heinz. Ma was living on ten pounds a week from her father.

Our house in Tollesbury was called Broadgate, though its gate was the only broad thing about it, the house itself being scarcely wider than a caravan. It was the middle of a terrace of three. It had two bedrooms upstairs and a living room and kitchen downstairs. The bath was in the kitchen with a wooden platform that folded down on top of it to form the kitchen counter.

Tollesbury was an oyster village. It sat on a channel on the south side of the Blackwater estuary in Essex. The River Blackwater was where the prized Colchester oysters came from. Tollesbury harbour itself was a network of small creeks winding their way between salt marshes. On big tides the Tollesbury creeks were all but joined in a sheet of grey-green water which overflowed the banks and submerged the scrubby sea heather. At low tide the water drained away to leave behind a thick clinging ooze of shiny black mud. To put a boot in the mud was to lose it; your foot came out but the boot remained behind.

Lennox Leavett, neighbour, oyster man and part-time poacher, became a family friend. One evening he came into our tiny kitchen and pulled a newly shot hare from somewhere inside his coat; this was eagerly received by Ma in those meat-scarce days of rationing. He asked if Michael and I would like to go out on the oyster boats next morning. I did not sleep at all that night I was so excited. Next morning at five Michael and I bicycled down the long hill from the village in the cold pre-dawn dark to catch the tide. Lennox was standing on the hard beside a small wooden dinghy with the other four crewmen. Beyond, I could just see the dark shape of the oyster smack swinging to its mooring in the main channel.

'Come on, lads. Oysters ain't waiting.'

I was lifted into the dinghy as Lennox pushed it down the slip, while the other crew members climbed on board, not easy to do with thigh-length waders, even though they were rolled down to the knees. We wobbled in the over-loaded dinghy, the crew sitting on the thwarts, Michael and I perched on knees and water slopping over the sides while Lennox stood in the stern sculling us forward with a single oar lodged in the U-shaped rowlock cut in the sternboard.

Helped by a hand above and a push below, I flopped over the side rail on to the deck of the smack and caught the sharp scent of seaweed, shellfish, caulking tar and hempen rope. Someone ducked into the doghouse, lit a small lantern and set to priming the donkey engine. After a cough or two, the diesel kicked into life with the same *boogh, boogh, boogh* sound that still wakes you in Mediterranean fishing ports from Ibiza to Ios as the fishing fleet puts out to sea.

With the coming of first light, the mooring rope was cast over the side and the first of many mugs of strong tea, sweet with condensed milk, was passed around. The engine was revved and the smack slipped from its mooring to butt its way down Woodrolfe Creek and towards the chan-nel between Tollesbury and Mersea, while the crew busied themselves with preparing the webs of blocks, tackles, trawls, hoists, chains and nets. When the channel was reached the boat headed briefly into the wind to allow the big red main-sail to be hoisted and jib and foresail to be broken out. This done, the sheets were freed and the boat began to heel and gather speed as its great trapezoid mainsail, suspended on a gaff the size of a telephone pole, filled with the morning breeze. The engine was cut, leaving a silence broken only by the slop of water and the scrawling of gulls and terns. Half an hour later the oyster beds were reached, the sail dipped and the trawls cast over the side.

I waited, enthralled by the ship's busy-ness, careful not to get in the way of the straining tackle. When the nets finally came up, cascading water and bulging with sea life, I watched in wonder. Not all the haul was oysters. Trapped with them was a harvest of seaweed, the green-brown kind with poppable air bladders, and a wriggling mass of sea creatures. The net was opened to spill its cargo on the deck and the crew set to sorting. Oysters were thrown into different buckets according to size and type, care being taken not to mix the flat aristocratic 'natives', the true Colchesters, with the coarser 'ports', or Portuguese, easily distinguished by their deep ribbed shells. As the buckets filled they were taken down to the hold below. Fish the crew sorted without even looking at them. They kept Dover sole, and the rest, mainly flounder and plaice, went over the side.

My wonder, as I watched and strained to keep my balance against the rolling of the boat, was tinged with fear. I did not mind the fish; they were harmless. What I did mind were crabs and starfish. One bit, the other stung. The men sensed my fear. From time to time one looked up from sorting the catch and tossed me a crab or a starfish.

''Ere, Mike, catch this.'

In the hustle of the morning both Michael and I were Mike. We looked much the same with our freckles and red hair cut straight across the forehead, Michael but a bigger version of me. I giggled, trying not to show my fear as I flailed at the squiggling missiles, hoping to bat them away over the side before they bit or stung me.

On our left in Tollesbury lived Mrs Wombwell, an old widow who was forever tap-tapping around to the kitchen door with her walking stick to shout at Ma, 'Mrs Morland, I've just seen your boys throwing things at my cat, stealing my greengages, squashing my marrows . . .' Her complaints were well grounded. On the other side lived the Shakespeares. Mr Shakespeare was a fisherman, and Ma asked Mrs Shakespeare, the Tollesbury gossip, to keep watch on Michael and me when she went up to London.

Mrs Shakespeare had regarded us with puzzlement ever since the time when Ma was in London, and she had received a telephone call from someone who needed to speak to Ma urgently. When we told her she needed to ask directory enquiries for someone called Deare, as Ma usually went to see her mother – no longer Lady Hogg now that my grandfather was dead, but Mrs Deare, new wife to Nigel Deare, a retired naval commander with whom she had been carrying on an affair for years – Mrs Shakespeare snorted.

'No, dear, he can't be called dear. That's just what you've heard your Mum call him. I'm not calling up the operator and asking for a dear. They'd think I was barmy. Now, think hard, boys. What's his real name?'

Contact was never made that day.

Ma's mother, the new Mrs Deare, was universally known as Sammy, a name that was as inappropriate for her as Bunny was for my father. Pictures of her as a young woman show a helmet-coiffed willowy girl of cat-like grace. Someone had decided that this sinuous creature looked exactly like Sammy the Snake, a figure in one of the earliest cartoon strips. The name stuck. Sammy she remained for ever after, although in the family she came to be known as Jersey Gran after she and Nigel moved to the island in the early 1950s.

It was thanks to her that our first stay in Tollesbury was a short one. We arrived in 1946, and by 1947 we were on the boat back to India. My parents' divorce had come through in 1946. Ma had not asked for alimony, but the divorce settlement required Bunny to pay her maintenance for Michael and me and to provide for our education. But no money was ever forthcoming to supplement Ma's ten pounds a week from her father. Later Bunny married Alice, who was a rich woman, but she never gave him a penny to contribute to his children's upbringing.

Not long after the divorce Ma was summoned by her father to London and told that as a result of cancer he would be dead in three months; he had decided to leave all of his money to Sammy for her life, the wife who had been consistently unfaithful to him, and the weekly ten pounds would stop.

'I never understood it,' Ma told me. 'Pa was a poppet. He was a kind and gentle man. I had never got on with my mother, but Pa and I had been close. Mama treated him appallingly. I think she probably started being unfaithful to him on their honeymoon. She certainly never looked back after that. I just didn't understand it when Papa told me that he was going to give her everything. I was thunderstruck. There I was with two boys to support and not a penny coming in. I couldn't even get a job with you two to look after. I think in a queer sort of way Pops felt guilty because he thought he hadn't been a proper husband.'

I do not remember meeting my grandfather. He died that same year. Later I learned a little of his story from Ma. As the youngest of the three Hogg brothers he had been sent out to India to earn his living several years before the First World War, while his elder brother Douglas stayed at home and became a barrister, a trade well suited to the cantankerous Ulster Hogg spirit. That elder brother later went on to become lord chancellor, like his son Quintin, Mrs Thatcher's colleague for so many years and the first Viscount Hailsham.[*] Meanwhile my grandfather, Malcolm, joined the Bombay trading firm of Forbes Forbes Campbell.

In 1914 when war was declared everyone of my grandfather's background in India was expected to join up. He, then aged thirty-one, was a prime candidate to enlist. But, as Ma told the story, someone had to stay behind in Bombay to take care of Forbes Forbes Campbell. The partners drew straws; he drew the short one and stayed in Bombay to look after the business for the duration of the war while his partners, the winners, went off to fight the Hun and to be machine-gunned in the Flanders mud.

He stayed on in India after the war. So few of his generation and background were left there that he rose quickly, becoming Sir Malcolm Hogg in 1920 at the age of thirty-seven and a member of the Viceroy's Council, which ruled India. In 1925 he returned to England. Most of his contemporaries from Eton and Oxford had been killed. The few who had

---

[*] The story goes that when Stanley Baldwin plucked Douglas Hogg from obscurity and made him a cabinet member Lord Salisbury is reputed to have written to a fellow Tory grandee, 'No idea where he found the fellow but Baldwin has discovered this frightfully clever lawyer called Pigg and put him in the Cabinet.'

survived had shared an experience of which he knew nothing. For ever afterwards he felt an outsider.

If I had been asked as a five-year-old what I wanted to do for the rest of my life the answer would have been easy: take the boat out to India and back. We always travelled on ships of the Anchor Line from Liverpool to Bombay; it was the cheapest way. They had two liners which plied the route, the *Cilicia* and the *Circassia*. No sooner had we settled in Tollesbury than we were on the *Circassia*, bound from Liverpool for the Bombay we had left a year ago. Ma was going out to marry JRC.

There was nothing very big or impressive about the *Circassia* – it was about the size of a middling cross-Channel ferry – but to me it was the grandest boat that had ever put to sea. Though our cabin was on a lower deck, we were on the outside of the boat. That meant we had a porthole. The lower decks were cheaper, but for Michael and me being lower down was more fun because when storms came and a sea got up the cabin stewards would go around all the cabins and close the portholes, screwing them tight shut with the two big bronze butterfly nuts that stuck out above them like ears. In rough weather when the boat rolled the porthole was completely submerged in greeny-white foam.

We ran into a huge storm two days out from Liverpool as we crossed the Bay of Biscay. Chairs, tables, pianos and other movables were bolted down to stop them sliding across the floor; cutlery and crockery were put in special racks to prevent them flying off across the dining room. The bars and lounges emptied as passengers crept to their cabins gaunt with seasickness. On deck a scattering of people sat huddled on the sheltered side of the boat, faces white and jaws clenched, hoping the fresh air would ward off queasiness.

Few things are better than not feeling seasick when the rest of the world is on its knees and retching. The worse everyone else feels, the better you do. Michael and I were unaffected as the boat rolled and crashed from wave peak to wave trough. To us this was better than the fairground. We scuttled about the near-deserted boat, screaming, jumping on the furniture, sliding across the floor with the boat's roll, nudging ashtrays and glasses so that they flew across the room on the next lurch, opening doors to allow the wind and spray to howl in and then dodging through to stand outside on the boat deck, hanging on to the rail as the boat rolled down till it seemed the deck itself would be submerged, and then with a shudder halted its downward swoop and picked itself up to roll the other way while we wrapped our arms around the rail for support.

The trip to Bombay took about four weeks, with the *Circassia* chugging along at an unhurried fourteen knots around Spain, through the Straits of Gibraltar, across the Mediterranean, along the Suez Canal, down the Red Sea to Aden – our only stop apart from the canal – and then across the Indian Ocean to Bombay. I did four trips to or from Bombay between the ages of three and six: 'home' to England for the first time in 1946, out in 1947, back in 1949 and out in 1950 to change boats for the onward journey to Basra on the Persian Gulf. In my mind the journeys have merged into one happy odyssey. I was fascinated then by sea travel, as I have been ever since.

4

Dakota to Tehran

In 1950 Ma and I set off for Persia.

Michael, by now aged eight, had been left behind in England to start his career at Stubbington, the ferociously tough naval prep school near Lee-on-Solent to which my father had been sent from India some thirty years earlier. We had gone down in an unprecedented family outing – Ma, I, the Gran (now Mrs Nigel Deare) and Nigel himself – with Michael to begin his years at boarding school.

There is a photograph of the five of us standing outside the Stubbington pub where Michael was to eat his last lunch before being handed over to Mr Foster, the headmaster. Ma has a brave, fixed smile on her face; this was no day for tears. Nigel, sleekly draped in the pinstriped double-breasted suit that he might well have been born in, stands slightly apart with a roguish grin on his face. The Gran, hair coiffed in a tight helmet, three strands of pearls, a floaty couture dress, long cigarette nonchalantly in hand, stands with an expression of total distaste for everything that is going on. She has a slight list to starboard and is leaning against Nigel as if needing support for the proceedings. Michael stands in front wearing grey shorts, sandals and a white shirt with rolled-up sleeves. His body is limp; his arms hang lifeless by his sides, and his face is devoid of expression. Only one person looks happy. I stand half-hidden behind Michael, one hand in my pocket, fighting unsuccessfully to control a smirk of pure joy on my face.

Shortly after Michael had been left at Stubbington, Ma and I travelled out to Bombay, there to connect with a boat to take us to the Persian Gulf, where JRC was to meet us. JRC was already in Tehran, having been sent by J & P Coats to penetrate the Persian market with stout British thread.

The ship we boarded in Bombay for the last leg of our trip was the *African Lightning*, a rust-streaked cargo vessel with room for a handful of passengers. Why the *African Lightning* was making its living so far from Africa I did not know. By 1950 it tramped doggedly backwards and forwards between Bombay and Basra, calling at anywhere along the way where there were goods to offload or a cargo to be taken on.

It had not been our intention to visit Basra, the main port of Iraq; the plan had been for JRC to meet us in Khorramshahr, the last stop before Basra, and take us on to Tehran. We arrived in Khorramshahr ready to disembark, but found no one-legged Scotsman on the quay to welcome us. Our luggage was put back in the hold and we re-embarked for Basra. I did not mind. JRC, my stepfather now, was to me a friendly uncle figure, but he had not become like a father. It did strike me as odd that Ma and I had just travelled six weeks and 6,000 miles to join JRC in a new and alien country and he was nowhere to be seen. If she was worried she gave no indication of it. I do not remember ever seeing Ma look worried.

The *African Lightning* spent a few days in Basra unloading and taking on fresh cargo. In the absence of JRC we were allowed to live on board while this took place. I had a wonderful time. I sat on top of a pyramid of crates on the foredeck watching the coming and going of the vessels that populated the docks: hundreds of lateen-rigged dhows, each one packed to the gunwales with passengers standing shoulder to shoulder, some dragging goats on strings behind them or holding chickens; rowing boats like water beetles; rafts of palm trees bound together with little huts on them; tugs pulling strings of barges loaded with coal, timber, oil drums and unidentifiable lumber; coastal tramp steamers streaked with

oil and rust, many with precarious lists to port or starboard;
and big ocean-going cargo ships bound for Bombay, Aden or
Mombasa, with their decks dominated by huge derricks for
swinging cargoes into the hold.

The big cargo boats were the ones I liked most because
rising high at each stern was a four- or five-storey castle,
which contained the crew's quarters, and then, on top of
that, was the bridge, on to whose open wings officers dressed
in smart white or blue uniforms would from time to time
emerge and stroll around in a lordly manner, before leaning over and shouting commands to the Lascars on the deck
below. I longed to live in one of those crew castles, to walk on
the wings of the bridge in a white uniform shouting orders at
Lascars, and to travel the world on a cargo boat. As it was I sat
on the foredeck with my box of coloured crayons and filled
my exercise book with drawings of these ocean travellers.

Ma was happy to leave me so well occupied. Every day
she would go to the radio room, where the second officer
sat dot-dot-dashing on something that looked like a stapler,
to see if a telegram had been received. But none ever was.
Eventually the time came for the *African Lightning* to return
to Bombay so we gathered up our luggage and said goodbye
to the boat and its officers. Then we were down the gangway
and into the pull and push of the Basra crowd. Our trunks
followed us on porters' heads and into the customs hall,
where we had to stand at a desk and bicker with a sweating customs man whose stomach was so large it strained
against his uniform as if trying to find a way out of it. What
he wanted to know was where the white woman's husband
was and what she thought she was going to do in Basra. Ma's
answers did not satisfy him. Occasionally he would point at

me as if I were something Ma had brought along as a decoy and shake his head wearily.

Finally, the purser was called from the *African Lightning*.

'Oh 'ello, Susan. Spot o' trouble with the customs wallah, eh? Don't worry, let me have a word with the chappie. We've known each other for a long time, haven't we, Ibrahim old sport?'

The purser gave Ibrahim a playful poke in the folds of his enormous stomach. The two of them then went into the customs office and closed the door behind them. I could not hear what they were saying, but Ma and I could see everything that was going on since the office was half glazed to allow the customs men to sip tea and inspect the crowd without getting out of their chairs. Ibrahim was shouting at the purser. From my short experience I had noted that Arabs shouted the whole time; I was later to learn that, unlike the softly spoken Persians, this was their normal way of communicating and nothing to be alarmed about. While shouting, Ibrahim shook both hands rhythmically up and down in front of him as if he were trying to shake some small rodent to death. This culminated in a violent gesture in the direction of Ma and me as if he were trying to fling the now dead animal at us.

The purser put a restraining hand on one of Ibrahim's windmilling forearms and beckoned him with his index finger to come closer. Ibrahim leaned towards the purser, who whispered something in his ear. The purser then jerked his head towards us, acting as if we were unable to see the two of them. Ibrahim backed away, mouth open and eyebrows raised in a gesture of mock surprise, before breaking into laughter so powerful that he had to support himself on a desk. He paused for a moment and looked up at the

purser with an air of 'Tell me it's not true,' while the purser
nodded his head vigorously as if to say, 'Yes, really,' at which
Ibrahim slapped the purser on the back and bowed him out
of the room.

'Don't worry, Susan old girl. Don't think you and young
Miles here will have any more problems. Small misunderstanding. I've cleared it up. It's going to cost you five dinars
for a temporary visa, and Bob's your uncle.'

'What on earth were you boys getting up to in there?'
asked Ma. 'What were you telling that chap?'

'Don't you worry, Sooze. I know these chappies. Sometimes
you have to tell 'em a bit of a story to help 'em understand.
It's all tickety-boo now. You want to give me those five
dinars? I'll take care of it for you. Don't suppose you've got
any dinars. Five quid will do just as well, even better.'

Ma searched around in her handbag and counted five
green pound notes into the purser's hand. 'Well, I hope you
weren't telling him anything that will get us into trouble.
We're only going to be here a day or two till my husband
comes to pick us up.'

'Course. That's just what I told him.' The purser beckoned
to Ibrahim, who waddled over to us with a big smile on his
face, gave Ma what appeared to me an overly familiar wink,
pocketed the five pounds, and then bent down to chub my
cheek with his greasy fingers.

'Hello, boy. You and madame coming Basra now?' At which
he released a burst of laughter smelling worse than Bombay
harbour directly into my face.

Ma's passport, on which I was also entered, was taken;
the customs man stamped it, looked closely at the page, spat

vigorously on the inkpad and stamped it again, after which he handed it back to Ma with an exaggerated bow.

'Here, madame. You good now.'

Our destination was the Basra Airport Hotel. I was delighted to be marooned in Basra if that meant staying at an airport hotel. I had not at that time travelled in an aeroplane but I found the mere thought of planes even more intoxicating – if such a thing were possible – than boats. The hotel was part of the airport building, a three-storey whitewashed construction of modest size with a covered balcony on the third floor, which constituted the control tower.

I knew that planes on their way out to India had to make six or seven refuelling stops. Basra was more or less on a straight line between London and Bombay. The consequence was that every three or four hours during the day a huge four-propellered beast in the colours of KLM, Pan Am, Air France or BOAC lumbered up almost to the hotel veranda to fill the air with noise and vibration before its giant piston engines coughed and spat to a stop.

I sat on the veranda drunk with excitement; with any luck JRC would not turn up for months. But after three happy days watching the DC-4s and Dakotas thundering across the apron, a cable arrived and we were in a car to Isfahan, two days' drive away. There in a hotel of arcades and columns, fountains and gardens, mosaics and tapestries was a joke-cracking one-legged Scotsman. Isfahan was filled with old buildings and nothing like as exciting as the Basra Airport Hotel. The three of us went sightseeing. We saw mosques, palaces, madrasas, maidans, polo fields and gardens. This was interesting for them but not much fun for me. By the end of the first day I was ready to leave. In fact I could not wait to leave because I had learned that we would be flying to Tehran.

Flying. In an aeroplane.

Two days later we boarded a shining silver Dakota of Iranian Airways. Dakotas, in common with most planes of that era, came to rest with their tails on the ground supported by a small wheel. It was only the mighty intercontinental planes at Basra Airport that had nose wheels and sat level to the ground; the rest rested on their tails. This meant that the body of the plane was at a distinct angle, sloping up towards the nose.

I ran out from the airport building to the plane ahead of Ma and JRC, and scurried up the three or four steps to the door at the rear of the plane. Inside all was cool and ordered, the seats covered in crisp khaki cotton. JRC hopped up the stairs after me, and we sat across the aisle from each other with Ma in the seat in front. Soon, like an old smoker clearing his throat, the engines coughed into life, and the plane began to tremble. We taxied to the end of the runway and sat there with the two engines revving for what seemed like an unnecessarily long time.

Then we were away, thrumming down the runway, the twin engines in full song, every rivet in the plane vibrating in sympathy; we gathered speed, the tail lifted, the plane's fuselage came up level, the engines came to a crescendo and we were airborne. Floating.

I looked out of the window in wonder at Isfahan, with its great squares lying between the mosques and the minarets, all so tiny as they fell away below us. The plane banked and circled, JRC shouting above the engine noise that we were circling to gain enough altitude to fly over the pass in the mountains that formed the gateway to the north and Tehran. As we circled, the plane was thrown and bumped about on the rising air currents like a dhow caught in a steamer's wake. Each circle brought us face to face with the mountain flank, so close that we could see every bush and goat track. It did not occur to me to be frightened; this was too exciting for that.

Finally the Dakota had enough height to dodge its way through the pass and set course for Tehran. As the mountains fell away I found myself looking down on a dry and barren nothing which stretched to every horizon, but it was not long before another great range of mountains loomed up out of the flatness ahead of the plane. On its slopes were buildings that stretched into the haze from east to west.

Moving to Tehran seemed like coming home. It did not feel foreign. England had seemed foreign. It had seemed a mean place after India – the people with their grey, pinched, faces, not like the English people in India, who were healthy and tanned. It was not only the people that were grey in England. The weather was grey, the streets were grey, the rain was grey, the net curtains on the long lines of identical houses were grey, and the choking fog when we had been in London was the greyest thing of all. Nothing was grey in Tehran. Iran was like India. The sun shone hot in a never-ending sky; the earth was baked brown and red; the bazaars were full of noise and smell and colour; the people were paler than the Indians but they were certainly not white and pinch-faced like the English in England.

The first thing I noticed in Tehran was that it had a different noise to India. In India cars had been a rarity, and the streets had been full of rickshaws, cows and bicycles. In Tehran everyone seemed to have a car, and what cars they were. In place of the staid black upright Austins and Morrises of India and England, the Tehranis had American cars. I had seen few American cars before. The streets of Tehran gleamed with new-model streamlined chromed cruisers unlike anything I had seen before: Oldsmobiles, De Sotos, Packards, Pontiacs, Mercurys, Buicks, Studebakers, Hudsons, Kaisers, not to mention Chevrolets, Cadillacs, Lincolns and Fords. I fell instantly in love with these creatures and before long could distinguish a Buick from an Oldsmobile half a mile away, or the difference between the 1950 and the 1951 Chevrolet. The English cars on the streets, and there were a number – Wolseleys, Rileys, Vauxhalls, Standards and the occasional majestic Humber Super Snipe in addition to the more common Morrises and Austins – seemed boring in comparison, black, upright and angular alongside the airstreamed, whitewalled, multicoloured American cruisers.

JRC had been peegeeing in Tehran. Today, when people arrive to work in a new city, they stay in a hotel paid for by their employer. Not in the British empire and its associated parts sixty years ago. You peegeed. PG stood for paying guest. It was assumed you would always have a connection, maybe at one or two removes, with someone who would be happy to take you in for an indefinite period in return for a small amount. We joined JRC peegeeing for a few weeks, but then came the great day when we moved far up the hill towards the mountains and into our very own house.

5

Mahmoudieh and the Great Kanat Disaster

Our very own house was actually a stable. The horses had, it was true, moved out by the time Ma first took me to see it. Petrossian, our driver, drove us up the long slope from Tehran through the villages of Shemran and Gulhek towards the purple-grey Elburz Mountains, and on to Mahmoud-ieh. Mahmoudieh was not even a village. It was an area of open scrub, hills and stony pasture dotted with walnut and mulberry trees at the foot of the mountains. South and east of Mahmoudieh were villages, towns, metalled roads, buses and Tehran. North and west of Mahmoudieh was nothing but mountains topped by the mighty volcanic form of Demav-end to the north, and flat, open land running to the horizon to the west. Mahmoudieh itself was a country estate belong-ing to a member of the Shah's family. In the middle of the estate was a palace, a thing of pillars and porticoes set in acres of fragrant well-watered garden. To the west and separated from it by a mud-brick wall, was a compound of perhaps four acres, the stable compound.

This was to be our home. The stables themselves consisted of a small L-shaped one-storey building which had once contained four stalls for horses in the long part of the L and a tack room in the short bit. The furthest of the stalls became our sitting room, with a view through its far window into the garden; next to this was a bedroom for Ma and JRC; then came my bedroom, which I would have to share with Michael when he came out for the summer holidays, and finally up a few steps to the dining room. A bathroom had been carved out of one corner of the dining room. The tack room became the kitchen. There was no passage within the block so the only way to get from the dining room or bathroom to the sitting room was to walk through both bedrooms. Or you could go outside. All the rooms, having been stables, had doors on to the huge expanse of courtyard in which horses had once been paraded and dressed. Going outside was fine for eight months of the year but out of the question between November and February, when the snow came and the wind shrieked down from the Elburz.

Opposite the stable block stood a lean-to structure. The further bit of this was the garage. The nearer part, adjoining the gateway, consisted of the two small rooms which made up the servants' quarters. The servants were Ali, clothed always in baggy black trousers, white shirt and little black cap set on the back of his head, and Maryam, his kind and patient wife. Maryam needed to be kind and patient because Ali was for six days of the week a man of gentleness, humour and occasional efficiency; on the seventh day Ali got drunk. This was achieved by picking the lock on JRC's drinks cupboard and taking a bottle of his best Persian vodka.

After draining this, Ali was no longer gentle and humorous. The first act of Ali's vodka days consisted of him standing in the courtyard roaring at the sky and stumbling around like a drunken gunfighter in a western. The second act involved the declamation of Persian poetry; I assumed that these were poems of love and passion because they were accompanied by Ali rolling his eyes, ripping open his white shirt and beating his chest. Then followed speech-making; the Persians are great orators and Ali, after half a bottle of vodka, stood ready to measure himself against the finest of them. The speeches, which I assumed to be political in nature, were delivered to the dogs, who sat silently at his feet and listened with interest, moving only when they were in danger of being stumbled over. The final stage, after the roaring and the poetry and the speeches, was the weeping and the clasping of the head.

The mounting noise of these various stages brought about an end to Ali's vodka days. On his lucky ones Maryam would appear and gently lead him off, while his wails and sobs built to a crescendo of misery, to their quarters. On his unlucky days Ma would burst from the kitchen, shaking some dangerous-looking piece of kitchen equipment in her hand. 'Pull yourself together, Ali. Go straight to your room. I'll talk to you later. If I catch you like this again there will be trouble. Off with you unless you want a good kick up the backside.'

A good kick up the backside was Ma's universal remedy, although I never saw her administer one.

'Yes, madame. Going, madame. Sorry, madame.'

Ali and Maryam became my friends. Ma and JRC had a busy social life. They were out in Tehran most nights, and I would be left by myself in the stables with Ali and Maryam across the courtyard. I was terrified of the dark. I would lie awake in bed rigid with fear praying for Ma and JRC to come home. I am cursed with a vivid imagination, which had no difficulty in peopling the room and what lay outside it with an army of Persian night terrors. Sometimes the fear was too powerful. At half past nine, two hours after I had been put to bed, I would grab my torch from the bedside, put on my slippers and bolt across the open courtyard to bang on Ali and Maryam's door.

'Ah, Mr Miles, please come in,' said Ali as if my coming to call was the most natural and welcome event. Maryam was clearing up their supper things in the background.

'Oh Ali, what time will my mother be back?'

'Mr Miles, it is still early and they have gone into Tehran. Madame said that they were going to a big party at the French embassy. They will not be back until later. Is there anything you need?'

'Thank you, Ali. Well, no, not really. But I couldn't just stay and talk with you and Maryam for a bit, could I?'

'Of course. That would be a pleasure. Would you like a little *chai*?'

I wish I could remember what we talked about. The night-time bolts across the courtyard became increasingly frequent. I worried that Ali and Maryam might get bored talking with me so I came up with an idea. 'Ali, would you and Maryam like to play cards?'

The Persians invented the playing card.

'Yes, Mister Miles, if that is your pleasure. What would you like to play?'

My favourites at that time, games which Michael and I used to play when he was home for the holidays, were beggar-my-neighbour, two-handed whist and Pelmanism.

Neither two-handed whist nor Pelmanism was good for three people so Ali, Maryam and I sat around playing beggar-my-neighbour till the sleep finally closed my eyes, and Maryam or Ali gently carried me back across the courtyard. Ali taught me a Persian card game. I cannot remember the rules but I recall it involved banging a card down on the table and shouting. An excellent game.

My night-time trips across the courtyard were curtailed by Ma and JRC coming home early one night and catching me running back across the courtyard as they parked the car.

'Mileso, what on earth are you doing?'

'Nothing, Ma. I just went to ask Ali something.'

'But it's almost midnight. You should have been asleep hours ago. What did you want to ask him?'

'If he knew when you were coming home.'

'Well, we're back. Now you run along to bed.'

Something in my manner must have made Ma curious.

'Ali, how long has Miles been in your quarters?'

'Oh not long time, madame.'

Maryam had appeared in the background looking uneasy. Ma had a good nose for a cover-up.

'Now, come on. What was going on?'

'O madame. We were playing cards.'

'What?'

'Please, madame, bugger-neighbour.'

'No, Ali, no. Not what card game, but what was Miles doing playing cards with you in the middle of the night?'

'Ma, it was my idea. I was frightened by myself in the house and I came over to get some company.'

'I've never heard anything so silly. Now off you go to bed.'

The next day I was sat down after breakfast.

'Now, Mileso, you mustn't go disturbing the servants. Of course if there's an emergency you know they are there, but otherwise you must leave them in peace. Poor Ali and Maryam don't want to spend half their night playing beggar-my-neighbour with you. They work jolly hard and they want to go to bed. And you should be asleep.'

'But, Ma, they enjoy it. Ali said he liked playing cards with me.'

When the stables were separated from the estate and converted into a house, they had been left with a generous amount of garden. Trellises, walkways and pergolas heavy with grapes led from the house through paths of plums, peaches and cherries. Irrigated beds produced strawberries and melons. The strawberries were already ripe when we moved in. I loved picking them. I used to get down on my hands and knees and search under the leaves for the hidden red berries. Up some steps from the strawberry bed was a more formal garden with roses and a lawn surrounding a huge swimming pool.

Beyond the pool the garden sloped gently up towards the mountains. A wall of slender birch trees stood between the formal garden and the wild, overgrown land beyond, a place of mystery and danger. In the depths of the wild garden, surrounded by brambles and wild roses, was the Kanat, the deep well connecting to the underwater irrigation canals.

I was forbidden to visit the Kanat. This meant that as soon as I saw the cloud of dust that followed Ma's Chevrolet disappear down the road to Tehran, I scampered up the steps, past the pool and through the birches to the wilderness. The

Persians love gardens. Gardens need water, particularly in the terrible heat of a Persian summer. To provide this a system of interconnecting underground streams and canals had been built. These channels ran for hundreds of miles; they linked up with other channels; they split into two and three and formed whole tributary systems. JRC, who was fascinated by the workings of the Kanat system, said it was ten times bigger than the London Underground and worked much better.

I never fell down the Kanat but we did have the great Kanat disaster. Amanda the Poozle, our Alsatian dog, had a litter. Ma loved animals, dogs in particular, and the Poozle above all dogs. The Persians, in common with most Muslims, do not love dogs. They regard them as unclean. It was difficult therefore when Amanda had her litter to find good homes for the puppies. Most of the Europeans in Tehran already had enough dogs, or would soon be moving on and did not want to be encumbered with one; few Persians were considered suitable owners by Ma.

The litter was born in the night. I went to visit them first thing the next morning. I had never seen anything as lovable as the seven puppies, wet from Amanda's constant licking. I asked Ma how many we were going to keep and where the rest were going and when they would be going. She said that we would just be keeping one and pointed to the largest of the litter, which was slightly redder than the others, and that the rest were all going to be taken good care of. The one we were going to keep would be called Brutus.

After spending most of the morning playing with the puppies I went off to my room for my regular after-lunch rest, looking forward to playing with them again later on. Ma met me on the way to the puppies when I got up.

'I've got bad news,' she said. 'The puppies all walked into the pool by mistake and drowned. Only Brutus was saved.'

I was appalled. How were those tiny puppies, who could only crawl a few inches with difficulty, able to take themselves as a pack out into the courtyard, up six brick steps and hurl themselves as one into the pool? When I was able to speak I stuttered out, 'But, but, how did puppies get to the pool?'

'They just did. I can't think how they got there.'

'Oh . . . but how did they . . . ?'

'Mileso, go and find Brutus and see how he is. He must be feeling lonely. You'll have to take special care of him.'

Brutus was the cause of the Kanat disaster. As he grew up he proved to be a particularly energetic dog who was forever scrabbling around the garden doing skid turns in pursuit of crows, rats, mice and squirrels. I never saw him catch anything, but his optimism was as wide as his energy. One afternoon we were sitting in the garden drinking lemonade by the pool. It was hot, and Michael, seeming to me immeasurably grown up, was home for his first summer holidays from Stubbington. It was unusually quiet. Amanda lay in the shade panting.

'Boys, where's Brutus?'

'Haven't seen him.'

'Well I hope he hasn't started straying off into the bundu. Go and take a shufti and see if you can find him.'

So we did. He was nowhere to be found in the house. He was not in the courtyard. We looked in the dusty dirt road beyond the gates and saw no Brutus there. Michael and I quartered the strawberry beds and the melon patch; we trotted up and down chanting, 'Brooo-tuss, Brooo-tuss . . .'

'Ma, we can't find him anywhere.'

'Have you looked in the wild garden. Sometimes he chases things in there.'

Michael and I rocketed off past the birches to the wild garden. We heard a noise. It was not a bark; it was more like a mew. It was coming from the Kanat. We scurried through the bushes and stepped gingerly to the edge. We peered down. It was too dark to see anything thirty feet or more down at the bottom of the hole.

'Brutus, Brutus,' we called together.

We heard a whining and a scrabbling from the bottom.

'Oh poor Brutus. He sounds hurt. We must get him out.'

We rushed off to report the news to Ma.

'Ma, Ma, Brutus is down the Kanat. He's hurt.'

Ma hurried back with us to inspect the situation.

'There's nothing we can do. We must get the Kanat man. You two stay here and keep Brutus company. I'll go with Ali to Gulhek to find the Kanat man.' Ma strode off to the garage, calling for Ali.

An hour later we ran over to the courtyard when we heard the car coming back.

'He's still alive, he's still alive. We can hear him.'

Ma and Ali got out of the front of the car. A villainous-looking man in faded battledress slid out of the back. He bore a broad-bladed pickaxe in his right hand and had a coiled rope looped over his left shoulder. He and Ali were in hot discussion.

'This way,' commanded Ma.

The Kanat man continued to argue while Ali tugged him along by the sleeve of his battledress.

'Is it going to be all right?'

'How's he going to go down the Kanat?'

'How will he bring Brutus up?

'Shh. Quiet. He doesn't want to do it at all,' said Ma. 'He's not keen on going down after a dog. I've had to promise him a lot of *floos*.'

'Hurry, hurry,' Michael and I said together. 'Listen to poor Brutus.'

We could still hear the whining and the scrabbling from the bottom of the Kanat but much feebler now than an hour ago. The Kanat man and Ali continued to argue. Voices were raised and arms were waved.

Ali took Ma off to one side for a hurried conference. 'Very well, Ali. But not a rial more.'

'Very good, madame.'

The news of the renegotiated fee was reported back to the Kanat man, who gave a roar of approval and hugged Ali.

'Come on, come on, get on with it,' said Ma. 'I'm obviously giving him far too much. Tell him to get a move on, Ali.'

'Yes madame. He going fast now.'

The Kanat man gave a string of instructions to Ali, who stood there nodding vigorously while looking nervously at Ma. He then tied one end of his rope around a nearby tree, keeping the other end looped around his left shoulder. He returned to the mouth of the Kanat, looked down and spat once on each hand and once down the Kanat. Then, like a spider disappearing into a hole, he hopped over the edge and disappeared. We crowded round to watch the rescue. He was walking down, feet planted against one wall, shoulders just free of the other, while he paid out loop after loop of rope in a kind of jerking motion. He was about fifteen feet below us, almost out of sight in the gloom of the Kanat, when there was an ominous rumbling, crumbling noise. This was followed by a great Persian oath from the Kanat, the rope jerking tight and then going loose and the noise of earth falling accompanied by the solid crump of body hitting ground. A thick cloud of dust wafted out of the mouth of the Kanat. A few more clods of earth fell and then there was silence for a short moment followed by a great wail of pain from the bottom. This was a human, not a canine cry. The noise from Brutus had stopped.

'O madame, O madame. He fall. Lose rope. Kanat break.'

'Yes, Ali. I can see that. Shout down and find out if he's all right. You might have to go down and fish him out.'

'Yes, madame. No, madame. I shout. No fish.'

The wailing from the bottom of the Kanat got worse. Ali edged as far as he judged safe towards the mouth and shouted down. Terrible groans and a few gasping words came back.

'O madame. He hurt. He fall when Kanat break.'

Ma went and peered down the Kanat.

'Ask him if he's got Brutus.'

More shouting down the well.

'O madame. Kanat man arm very bad. Arm broken maybe.'

'Yes, yes, Ali. I don't give a damn about his arm. What about Brutus?'

Ali shouted some more down the Kanat. Louder groans and angrier noises echoed back from its depths.

'Yes, Ali? Can we get the dog up?'

'No, madame. Kanat man fall on dog. Dog dead.'

6

A Persian Education

The grounds of Mahmoudieh offered unlimited opportunities for adventure, exploration or just messing around and getting dirty. Beyond the walls were mountains, hills and wilderness which stretched from Demavend to the setting sun. The gates from our courtyard opened to the west, from which a bumpy dirt road led up the hill to where it joined another even bumpier road, which ran parallel to the Elburz Mountains. The junction itself was marked by an old mulberry tree the size of an oak. In the late summer the earth around the junction was stained purply-red with blotched mulberries.

This road led to our local village, Gulhek, a mile and a half away. It had a main street which was a permanent tangle of hooting, jostling cars, buses swaying under cargoes of pyjama-clad passengers, most of whom seemed to be hanging on to the buses outside or sitting on the roof, and enormous growling trucks, buckling under their loads of logs or bales of cotton tied down by the flimsiest of frayed ropes. Animals were everywhere. The side of the road was given over to donkeys.

Our front drive, Mahmoudieh

Poor thin creatures with enormous loads contained in carpet bags slung across their backs trotted along while their drivers followed at a shuffling jog, rhythmically tapping the donkeys' bony hindquarters with sticks. Once, as we were driving through this jumble of activity, Ma saw a donkey limping along on three good legs and one bad under a load of impossible size. Its driver was shouting oaths and beating it.

'Stop the car!' said Ma to Petrossian.

'Not here, madame, too much traffic.'

'Stop right now! I want to get out,' said Ma, her voice rising. It was rare for Ma to raise her voice. The times she did almost always involved animals. She leaped from the car. I followed her nervously. She strode up to the donkey-beater and caught the stick in his hand as it came back to give the donkey another blow.

'Stop that this instant! What do you think you are doing, you horrible man?'

The startled drover turned round to be confronted by a red-haired English woman shouting unintelligible words at him in a strange language. I looked on aghast. A sudden calm came over the street. Business ceased. People crowded out from the entrance to the bazaar to form a tight circle round Ma and the donkey man, who were trapped like two boxers in a ring of people. I stood behind Ma certain that we would soon be engulfed and trampled by the crowd.

'I won't have it, do you hear? How dare you beat that poor beast like that? It's half starved. Can't you see it's practically dead? You should be ashamed of yourself.'

The man stood there with his stick by his side, mouth agape, eyes darting to the crowd and then back to his persecutor. His donkey had meanwhile set off at a limping trot and was making for the bazaar. I could hear a low but rising muttering coming from the crowd.

'Ma, Ma,' I said in an uncertain voice, tugging at her skirt, 'let's go. Please.'

'Quiet, Mileso. Here, give me that,' Ma said to the donkey man.

She snatched the stick from his hand and brought it down with a great *whap* on his right shoulder. She then took it in both hands and snapped it over her knee. A great 'Aiiii-eeee' came from the man.

There was a momentary silence broken only by the drover's cry and then the crowd erupted in a riot of laughter. They rocked back and forth and tugged at each other's clothes and pointed while they passed the tale of the white woman with red hair beating the donkey man to the latecomers hurrying up to see what the commotion was about.

'Come on, Mileso.'

Ma grabbed my hand and marched us brusquely back to the Chevrolet and Petrossian. The crowd parted before her.

It was shortly after our move to Mahmoudieh that I was put into the American school. Ma took me to the school, where I was introduced to the headmistress, who informed me that I would be joining First Grade. I had no idea what First Grade was but it sounded rather advanced. Ma left me, and I was taken along by the headmistress to a group of three or four classrooms separate from the main school building. She knocked on the door of one and opened it.

'This is Miles. He's English. He's going to be joining First Grade.'

I had not up to then got to know any Americans. I knew they were different: they were aggressive and pushy and spoke English in a strange way and said things like 'Hi' or 'You can say that again.' My shyness at being left with these threatening people in a school where I knew no one rendered me close to dumb. The classroom had within it fifteen or so boys and girls and was presided over by a smiling blonde lady. She came out from behind the teacher's desk and took me by the hand.

'Well, greetings, young man. Welcome to First Grade. I'm Mrs Johnson. And what did you say your name was?'

I stood transfixed beside the desk with my eyes lowered.

'Erms.'

'I'm sorry. I didn't catch that. Now, what was your name? A little louder, please.'

'M-m . . . Miles.'

'Class, this is Miles. He's going to be joining our little group in First Grade. Mind you–all make him feel at home. Say hello to Miles.'

'Hello, Miles,' the First Grade chorused, though the welcome of the words was offset by sniggers and nudges. I was sure they were laughing at my accent.

The children sat in rows on low benches drawn up to low tables. I was placed at the end of one of these rows beside Billy, who was instructed by Mrs Johnson to move over to make room. He did this reluctantly and then turned and muttered something I could not catch to the boy sitting the other side of him. They both giggled. I sat blushing with my eyes firmly fixed on the table in front of me.

'Now, First Graders, we're real pleased to have a new guy with us so I want you to make Miles feel welcome. Before we go to break in a few minutes, I'd like to tell a little story. Now, when we walk along we have to be very mindful of what is waiting just round the corner, don't we?'

'Yes, Mrs Johnson,' chorused the class including me, although, unlike them, I did not have the vaguest idea as to what was waiting just round the corner.

'That's right, class. We know why we have to be careful. Now, Miles, what is it that is waiting just round the corner that we have to be so careful of?'

Despite my joining in and saying yes, this was one question to which I did not know the answer. The other children were straining forward with their hands up.

'Yes, Miles? And what do we find just round the corner?'

What was usually round the corner? It all depended. It could be anything. But I knew one thing you were certain of finding in the northern suburbs of Tehran.

'Er, mmm, a tree, miss?'

The class howled. They shrieked. They clapped the tables in front of them and turned to their neighbours and repeated in an exaggerated English accent, 'Ay treeee, miss.'

'Quiet, class,' said Mrs Johnson. 'No, Miles, there may be a tree round the corner but that is not what we have to be so careful of. Class, what is it that is waiting round the corner that we have to watch out for?'

'Trouble, Mrs Johnson.' The First Grade spoke with one voice. 'Trouble.'

'That's right, class. Miles, it's trouble. When we go outside and we walk along we must always be on our guard because we know that trouble is lurking right round the corner, and if we are not on our guard it will catch us.'

This seemed a puzzling attitude. Half the fun of living in Tehran was finding out what was lurking around the corner.

First Grade was not a success. I had already learned multiplication and division while First Grade was engaged in cutting up bits of coloured paper. I was taken out of the American school and enrolled ultimately in the British school. This was a much more comfortable and familiar place. To start with its sixteen pupils wore the right clothes.

Language was not the only reason I felt different at the American school; I dressed differently. Or rather they did. The boys, and indeed many of the girls, wore jeans or long khaki trousers. In my world six-year-old boys did not wear long trousers. Even my nine-year-old brother Michael was not yet in long trousers although he had informed me that he expected to be so next term. At Stubbington, he told me, you wore short trousers until you were five feet tall. Indeed, most of the grown-ups I knew did not wear long trousers any more than they had to; at the first opportunity all the English adults I knew shed their long trousers and got into shorts.

The American children wore jeans on their bottom halves. These were far too hot for Tehran, and I was glad I did not have to wear denim. And what they wore on top was even odder. Most of them did not wear shirts but turned up to school in vests with round necks and funny short sleeves. These vests – or so I learned from Billy, who after his initial hostility became a temporary friend although the friendship may have been based more on mutual curiosity than a feeling of genuine liking – were called tea shirts. I never found the courage to ask Billy what their vests had to do with tea. The answer was likely to be obvious and I did not like the thought of being on the receiving end of Billy's 'Aw gee, Miles, whaddya mean why is this a tea shirt? Don't you know anything?'

It was not that the Americans could not afford to dress properly. I noticed that the ones we got to know in Persia had far more money than we did. What I found really bizarre about these tea shirts were their colours. All my underwear was white and my outer garments were grey, blue or khaki. I certainly had nothing in yellow or red. But the tea shirts came in all kinds of bright colours, the jazzy effect often compounded by patterns. I had not previously come across white people wearing bright colours. For people of my age to go to school wearing long denim trousers with a brightly coloured vest on top was to me far more outlandish than the fact that most Persian men walked around the street wearing pyjamas. At least the pyjamas were in sensible colours or discreet stripes.

However, before going to the British school it was decided I should learn French. I was duly enrolled in the Tehran lycée, a forbidding brick building in a leafy part of central Tehran.

When Ma and I arrived, hundreds of children were running around the playground shouting at each other in a language more foreign than Farsi. We were directed to the headmistress, with whom Ma exchanged words in the unintelligible language and I was led off to the appropriate class for my age.

This was even worse than the American school. Here I understood nothing. I sat mute at the back of the class. There was one teacher for about thirty children, most of them Iranians whose French was only a little better than mine, so it was easy to avoid attention. The next day and the day after that Petrossian dropped me off, and I went to sit silent and miserable at the back of the class. To my relief school ended each day at 1 p.m.

On the fourth day I went in through the big main gate, hovered around for a few minutes until I was sure Petrossian had gone, and then slipped out again and sauntered off to spend the next four hours wandering around by myself, dipping in and out of shops and sitting on benches reading Captain Marvel or *Popular Mechanics* with its detailed reviews of the latest American cars. The places I liked best were stationery shops with their fountain pens, geometry instruments, cloth-bound ledgers, blotting paper, different coloured inks, notebooks of every size, quires of stationery and above all the intoxicating smell of crisp white paper. I don't know what the owners made of an English seven-year-old mooching aimlessly around their shops for an hour and a half but no one ever bothered me.

I would return to the lycée just before one o'clock and stand by the gate waiting for Petrossian.

'Good day, Mr Miles?'

'Yes, thank you, Petrossian.'

After a few days of this I came up with another scheme. 'Tomorrow is a school holiday,' I announced to Ma.

'Oh really? Why?'

'I'm not sure. I couldn't understand what they said but one of the Iranian boys who speaks some English told me. It's a special saint's day.' This worked well so I tried the same trick a few days later. 'Ma, we've got another holiday tomorrow. It's Republic Day, I was told.'

'Are you sure, Mileso? They seem to be having an awful lot of hols.'

'Yes, really.'

Later that day Ma took me with her on a shopping trip. We met an Iranian woman who Ma knew.

'Oh, hello, Susan,' she said. 'What's Miles doing here? Why isn't he at school? He must be ill. Poor boy. How are you feeling, Miles?'

'No, he's perfectly OK,' said Ma. 'It's a holiday at the lycée today.'

'No, no, Susan. You are mistaken. My Hamid is at the lycée. There is no holiday today.'

Half an hour later I was back at the school in the headmistress's study, dragged there by a very irate Ma. My unexplained absences had been logged and were exposed. I had nowhere to hide.

I received a talking-to of record length and was confined to home as a punishment. But I was taken out of the lycée and placed in the British embassy school where I could speak English and wear normal clothes.

7

Trouble on Ferdozeh Boulevard

After Mahmoudieh we moved to a little house in an alley off Ferdozeh Boulevard in the middle of Tehran. Most of the big embassies had compounds in that part of the city, none bigger than the British compound, which occupied a site of some fifteen acres less than half a mile away from our little house. This was the main embassy, occupied for all but the hot summer, months when the ambassador and his imperial retinue moved up the hill to the summer site in Gulhek. We often went to the embassy compound; it was a good place for me to be left to play by the swimming pool watched over by other mothers and nannies. At the entrance were two massive iron gates topped with spikes and curlicues and guarded by silk-turbanned Sikh havildars. Inside was a whole town in miniature centred around the crenellated Edwardian villa that was the ambassador's palace.

The reason we moved from Mahmoudieh to central Tehran was that Ma had got a job. She had become manager of the Tehran Club, the meeting place for Tehran's European and American community. The back entrance to the Tehran

Club was opposite our little house across the alley, so when I was not at school I could mooch around in the house with the servants but always run across the road to the club if I needed anything. I had orders not to stray by myself further than the newspaper shop fifty yards away at the end of the alley. To this I would commute as often as my pocket money would allow to trade Captain Marvel comics. I was not allowed beyond there unaccompanied. Ma, however, was too busy to enforce this law; one day she was trying to talk the French embassy into releasing their chef to oversee a French night at the club, the next wondering where she could source hot dogs for the 4th of July party.

The Tehran Club had a cosmopolitan membership. About half were English and American but the rest were French, Italians, Armenians, Greeks, Scandinavians and other colonials – Australians, South Africans, Canadians. The club was for expatriates so it had no Iranian members, although elegant and cosmopolitan Persians were frequent and welcome guests in the bar and the dining rooms. I do not remember any Germans and there were certainly no Russians. Nor were there Arabs or Turks. I soon discovered that the Iranians look down on both races. We had a lot of Iranian friends and nothing amused them more than a Turkish joke. These jokes would be long and complicated and would usually involve donkeys – animals with which the Turks had a great affinity if our Iranian friends were to be believed. The Arabs they regarded as being so inferior as to be not worth even joking about.

Tehran in the early 1950s, with the Soviet Caspian border no more than a few hours' drive away, had an atmosphere of wartime frivolity and let's do it today. From listening to the gossip at our own lunch table I gathered that it was a place where people came and went with bewildering speed, stopping sometimes only long enough to have an affair with someone else's wife. However, in 1952, towards the end of our time in Iran, the political situation was balanced on the edge of anarchy.

Everyone talked in nervous voices of Muhammad Mossadegh. This man was a mystery to me. I looked at pictures of him in the magazines and newspapers that lay around the Tehran Club. Most important men on the front pages of the newspapers in 1952 wore formal suits, some even with wing collars. Mossadegh, who had just become prime minister of Iran, was often photographed in pyjamas lying on his bed, frequently weeping. This was the man everyone in the Tehran Club was frightened of. The word most often used to describe him was dangerous. Although I could not follow all the politics, I had heard constant talk of how worrying the situation was. This seemed strange as the Iranians we knew remained as urbane, charming and polite as they had ever been. I had heard that Westerners were at some risk if they were in the wrong place at the wrong time; one or two had been killed as a result of finding themselves unwittingly at the centre of a disturbance.

I loved wandering around Tehran and paid no attention to the newspaper-shop boundary. This almost cost me my life. One of my favourite excursions was to walk down Ferdozeh Boulevard past the British embassy and then turn right into a busy shopping street, where I would window-shop and search for cut-price comics. After an hour or so I would buy a strawberry ice-cream cone and wander back to the house. This was a pleasant and regular beat.

One day I was returning from such an outing, ice cream in hand. As I rounded the corner and walked back up Ferdozeh Boulevard, I could make out in the distance a deep rumbling sound such as I had never heard before. I remember that noise today with exactness but did not know how to describe it until I heard my first avalanche. The noise of rush and tumult was the same. The noise grew and then suddenly, tumbling into Ferdozeh Square, some half a mile away, and erupting out of it and directly towards me down the boulevard, came the Tehran mob.

They filled the boulevard from side to side. The front rank waved clubs and knives, a few pistols; some had flags and banners with slogans. At their head was a dark bearded man brandishing what looked like a chair leg. The noise changed. As they got nearer the roar defined itself as high-pitched chanting.

The mob, in full career, was no more than four or five hundred yards from where I stood, motionless with terror, ice cream dripping down my hand. Where they were going, I did not know. Probably to sack the House of Assembly. One thing I did know: a seven-year-old English boy caught in their path would be swept underfoot and left a smudge on the road in their wake. Flight was impossible; I was too far from the crossroads to turn back and hide in the side road. Ahead of me, perhaps twenty yards away, were the great iron gates of the British embassy. The silk-turbaned Sikh sentries were stepping back from their posts outside the gates to safety within. The mob by now seemed almost upon me although the rioters must have been still 200 yards away. The noise seemed to get shriller and their speed to increase as they roared closer.

I dropped my ice cream and bolted for the embassy, as did a number of other passers-by. The gates were a scant body's width open when I reached them, the Sikhs trying to pull them closed, those on the outside trying to shove them open far enough to get in. A mighty red-sashed Sikh stood in the opening pushing bodies out. If I had been bigger I would be dead today. Luckily I was small enough to wriggle at knee-height under the shoving bodies in the gateway and pop out the other side. As I did the gates clanged shut and the bolt was thrown across.

Seconds later the mob howled past. The gates shook; rocks and sticks were hurled over their top by passing rioters, but the British embassy was impregnable.* For what seemed like minutes the tumult roared and thundered past the gates and then, as suddenly as it came, the noise retreated into the distance, the howl became a mutter and then silence.

I stood in the entrance of the embassy compound behind the bolted gates. I was not crying – the shock was too great for that – but every muscle of my body shook. A giant Sikh standing by my side patted my head. Twenty minutes later they opened the gates. The Sikh patted me once more and gave me a friendly push; I scurried out of the embassy, up the boulevard, across the road into the alley, past Captain Marvel and home. Four hours later I was still trembling.

* Or so it was until 29 November 2011, when a government-inspired group of students stormed the embassy and sacked it. The same day they also invaded the summer Gulhek site, where I used to go to school.

8

Midnight in Meshed

The road to Meshed lay across a dry and stony desert. It was going to be a long dusty two days' drive from Tehran. JRC announced that we would have to leave before dawn and, if we were lucky and did not find that the road had been washed away by a sudden storm or blocked by a lorry colliding with a bus, we might arrive in time for supper on the second day. We were going to stay with the Macleods. Mr Macleod, whom we had got to know in India, was the British consul in Meshed.

It was a hot, hot day when we set off. We had all the car windows open with the little quarter-lights in the front windows turned backwards to catch the air and create a breeze in the car. This worked well until we needed to overtake another vehicle, a process which involved a long and complicated manoeuvre. Virtually the only other vehicles on the road were the creaking lorries that spluttered and groaned their way along the Persian trade routes. They were always loaded to twice their carrying capacity with unwieldy

burdens that had often slipped to one side and threatened to
fall off at every bend in the road. The road itself was set up on
an embankment for most of the way to allow it to traverse the
dried-up wadis that cut across it at frequent intervals. It began
to lose its tarmac surface about twenty miles from Tehran and
soon petered out into a track of ruts, dirt and stones.

Every twenty minutes or so we saw a huge smudge of dust
more than a mile away, which got thicker and thicker as we
caught up with the truck stirring it up. When we were about
200 yards behind, the order was given to close windows to
keep out the dust that was beginning to billow into the car.
Before the overtaking manoeuvre began, Petrossian pulled
out to the far side of the road to see if he could spot a plume
of dust signalling a truck coming in the opposite direction, as
once we got close enough to begin overtaking, the dust was
so thick we were driving blind. Once Petrossian had checked
for oncoming traffic he changed down and accelerated into
the thick brown dust-fog. All the time the horn was sounded
non-stop, sometimes in a continuous blare, sometimes sharp
hoots, and from time to time Petrossian hammered out an
Armenian tune. The truck always made a point of driving in
the middle of the road. There was never any question of it
hugging the side to give us a little extra space on the narrow
raised surface to squeeze past. During most of the time we
were overtaking the truck driver also sounded his horn, his
deeper *purmp-purmp* sounding in counterpoint to Petrossian's
parp-parp.

Once Petrossian had pulled out and committed to overtake, there was a tense silence in the car. The heat rose quickly
with the windows and air vents closed. Each of us apart from

Petrossian rocked backwards and forwards making giddy-up noises to urge the car to greater speed. Meanwhile the dust got thicker and thicker until all we could see were the pounding truck tyres no more than inches from our windows as we ground past. And then at last the air cleared as we breasted the truck's bow wave of dust; we were past and out blinking into the sunlight and winding the windows down as fast as we could, grateful for the stream of cool fresh air that blew in from the quarter-lights.

As evening fell on the second day we saw the minarets of Meshed ahead of us. We joined the slow procession of carts, donkeys, camels, buses and trucks pushing its way through the Tehran Gate in the great mud walls that surrounded the city and into a crowded tree-lined boulevard down the middle of which ran a wide stream. White-robed pilgrims were everywhere. The consulate was set in wide grounds behind a high stone wall. The gates through which we drove were almost as big as those at the entrance to the Tehran embassy, and like them were guarded by giant silk-turbaned Sikh soldiers, who peered into the car and then, seeing we were European, stood back and saluted smartly as we drove in. The main consulate building reminded me of the house we had had in Bandra, north of Bombay, except that it was bigger and grander. The garden had sweeping cedar trees, a beautifully trimmed lawn and rose beds, a little piece of Wiltshire in the middle of the holiest city in Iran.

We were glad to have a quick supper followed by an early bed after the long drive, as the next day was to be a busy one. JRC, Ma and Petrossian had been talking about the famous mosque of Meshed in the car. It was the holiest place in all Iran because the Imam Reza was buried there. Shi'ites came from all over the Muslim world to make a pilgrimage to his shrine. Non-believers were not allowed into any of the mosques in Iran at that time, and this one, because of the special holiness created by the presence of the Imam's tomb, was particularly forbidden to those who were not Muslims.

Even in peaceful times it would have been a brave Christian who attempted to set foot in the mosque. At times like this, when tempers were frayed and tension between Iran and the West was in the air, only the most foolhardy would have contemplated trying to get inside, as discovery would cause a riot in which lives would almost certainly have been lost, the intruder's first among them. Against this background, Ma with her striking red hair and blue eyes had expressly come to Meshed to get into the mosque.

The Macleods had reluctantly arranged for Yasmin, a Persian lady who had lived in the West, to be her guide. At ten o'clock the next morning Yasmin arrived with a little suit-case containing Ma's mosque-visiting clothes. Ma went off to her bedroom with Yasmin, who had herself arrived at the consulate wearing smart Western clothes. Half an hour later two black-chadored figures glided out from the bedroom. Nothing could be seen of them apart from one pair of hazel-brown eyes and one pair of light blue eyes. But then Ma scrunched up the face bit of the chador from inside and the light blue eyes disappeared.

We all then got into the car, JRC and I squeezed into the back with Ma. It was not deemed safe for a car with Europeans in it to drive too close to the mosque. The huge square in front of it was choked with pilgrims making their way to pay their respects at the Imam's tomb, and there were few other cars. As we edged our way forward through the crowd, with Petrossian giving discreet little beeps on his horn rather than the full-blooded toots he used in Tehran, we were the subject of hostile stares from the pilgrims who were forced to make way for us, and when they looked inside the car and saw Europeans with chador-clad Muslim women there was angry and threatening-sounding muttering.

'I think it's time for you girls to walk,' said JRC. 'These laddies don't look any too friendly. Time for us to leave you to it.'

'Bye, Ma. Good luck,' I called as Ma and Yasmin climbed out of the car and were swallowed up in an instant in the pushing throng.

'Right, Petrossian. Let's get out of here,' said JRC briskly.

Petrossian reversed gingerly out of the crowd, turned the car as soon as he was able and sped back to the consulate, where I mooched around the garden while JRC put his leg up on the veranda rail and fidgeted with old copies of *Country Life*, not something I had ever seen him read before. Neither of us felt much like talking. Petrossian had agreed a rendezvous with the mosque-goers an hour and a half after we had dropped them off. It was thought inadvisable for us to accompany him in view of the mood of the crowd. If there had been any trouble with Ma at the mosque, two more Europeans arriving in a large American car would only make it worse.

Petrossian set off. I mooched some more. JRC ordered a gin and tonic and concentrated furiously on his *Country Life*. Twenty minutes passed. Then half an hour. Finally, just as we

were giving up hope and about to ask Mr Macleod and the
Sikhs to organise a rescue mission, we heard a car sweep up
behind the consulate. I ran around, JRC hopping alongside
on his crutch.

A solitary Muslim lady in a chador emerged from the back
of the car. JRC and I stopped simultaneously. Where was Ma?
Was she all right?

'Hi, Mileso, hi, Johnny,' said the chador.

'Oh, Ma. Are you OK? Where's Yasmin?'

'We dropped her off on the way back. Don't be so silly.
I'm fine.'

Later, over lunch, Ma told us of the visit.

'I had a great old time. Yasmin had told me that all I had to
do was to follow her and do the same as her. I did exactly what
she did. Of course, the bits the women are allowed in were
so dark and crowded that you could hardly move and you
couldn't see that much. The men had a much better view.

'But we did go and see Reza in his shrine. I must say, I've
been in some pretty niffy places but I've never been anywhere
quite so smelly as that. Literally hundreds of barefoot sweating Persians milling around in a room about the size of the
black hole of Calcutta. And then when we got up close to the
shrine there was so much pushing and shoving that you could
hardly breathe. I had to kiss the brass bits on the outside of
the shrine, and if you peered hard you could just see something wrapped up on the inside. Funny little dried-up chap
he must have been.'

'Did you have any dangerous bits?'

'Not really, because all I needed to do was follow Yasmin
and copy her as she bowed and scraped, though there was one

moment when I got separated from Yasmin and of course all those Persian women look exactly the same in their chadors and I found myself following the wrong woman, who turned round and gave me a very funny look. I just screwed up my chador so she couldn't see in through the eye hole and then luckily felt a tug on my sleeve from Yasmin. But that was the only time. Otherwise there was nothing to worry about.'

'Well I'm jolly glad you're back,' I said.

That night the Macleods took JRC and Ma out to dinner with the French consul in Meshed. I was given an early supper and tucked up in bed. I had been put in a great echoing bedroom with two enormous beds; it had a high ceiling and two large uncurtained windows through which I could see the shapes of the tall trees in the garden silhouetted against a moonlit sky. When Ma came to say goodnight we went through our usual dialogue.

'What time will you be back?'

'Don't worry, Mileso. I don't expect we'll be late. It's been a long day.'

'Yes, I know, I know. But what time will you be back? Will it be after ten?'

'Oh, I don't know. We may be a bit later than that. I can't say exactly.'

'By eleven?'

'Yes, I suppose so.'

'Promise?'

'Well, I'll do my best. Now tush and go to sleep. See you in the morning.'

One of the things I remember most strongly about Iran was being frightened of the dark. I spent hours each night lying in bed, rigid with fear, until I finally fell into an exhausted sleep in the small hours.

My nights were peopled with faceless burglars adept at slipping into houses through the barest crack of open window, crazed Iranians skilled at climbing walls like lizards out to avenge themselves on the *farangi*, people with swords and cutlasses, members of sinister oriental cults bent on ritual murder, bat-men who flitted from tree branch to tree branch before effortlessly appearing in your bedroom, people who lurked just out of sight at the bottom of your bed when they were not hiding in the cupboard, and of course a legion of venomous snakes, scorpions, deadly spiders and poisonous biting millipedes, which writhed, clung and slithered under your bed, on the back of the chair and across the floor on the way to the bathroom.

Now here I was, alone in Meshed in a huge curtainless bedroom in a strange house. There were some servants but they were out of sight and out of earshot in their distant quarters. I could hear an irregular scratching noise in the hall outside. Then silence. Then there was a bang, like a door or a shutter closing. Then silence again. Through the tall barred windows I could see shapes in the trees. There were dark man-sized creatures among the waving leaves of one of the trees. I could see their black wavy shapes outlined against the streaky grey night sky. One of the creatures appeared to have wings. I thought about turning the light on, but then the creatures would be able to see me. I looked at the luminous hands of my watch. Half past nine. An hour and a half till Ma got back. I was lying on my back so I could see out of the window. I did not dare turn on my side away from the window in case the figures in the trees moved closer. They had changed shape. There was a third one, bigger and more threatening than the first two, in another, larger tree. Down the hall the scratching noise had started again. From the streets of Meshed I could hear the distant barking of the pye-dogs, the raucous night-time music of every Persian town.

Ten thirty. Ma would be home in half an hour.

Now there was a crouching shape in the corner of my room, next to the tall wooden cupboard standing against the far wall. I inched my hand over as quietly as I could to the bedside table and felt for my torch. I flicked it on and shone it quickly at the shape. The shape disappeared. The danger-ous crouching shape was only a shadow cast by the moon on the towel stand. I put the torch back and looked out of the window once more. The shapes were still there among the windblown leaves. I had to concentrate to see them, but then one and then the others would come into focus.

At half past eleven Ma was still not back. I decided to go and look for her. I turned on my torch, shone it around the room to make sure that there was nothing lurking anywhere and looked under the bed for my slippers. These were solid rubber-soled Stubbington slippers handed down to me by Michael, who had outgrown them. I put them on along with my green tartan dressing gown and crept to the door. It made a creaking noise as I opened it. Outside the passage was dark. I switched on the light and made my way carefully along it to the top of the stairs, switching on the landing light as I went. I tiptoed down the stairs into the echoing front hall. Fortunately a light had been left on there. I made my way to the front door and reached up to the huge brass knob. The door was not locked. It took both hands to open the door, but then I stepped out into the driveway, which was illuminated by a single light, and walked towards the gate.

There were voices coming from the gatehouse. As I approached it one of the Sikh guards emerged and looked at me in astonishment. He called out something in Punjabi and the other guard appeared. They both stared at me in silence. Then the first one found his voice.

'Hah. Hello, master. What you want, please?'

'Excuse me, do you know where my mother and Mr Macleod are? They said they'd be back by eleven and it's past that now and they're not back and I have to go and find them.'

'Hah? Sahib not here. Go to house, please.'

'But where did they go? They went in the car.'

I made driving motions with my hands and pointed down the road beyond the gate.

'Please, not know. You go back.'

Furious Punjabi ensued between the guards.

'Well, I've got to go and find them.'

With this I walked through the gates and out into the streets of Meshed, leaving the Sikhs gazing after me and shaking their heads.

The street outside was barely lit and empty of people. Bits of rubbish blew in the wind. Two hundred yards away was a junction. I padded towards it in my slippers while the wind tugged at my dressing gown. I was nervous but not as frightened as I had been lying in the consulate bedroom looking out at the shadows. When I got to the junction I looked both ways. To the right the street was narrower and ran between tall buildings, but I could see lighted houses at the end of it. I walked that way. As I started off I heard the noise I dreaded. Until now the feral pye-dogs which inhabit every Persian town had been a distant chorus, but suddenly I heard a snarl behind me and turned to see a yellowish dog baring its teeth at me. It had come out of the rubbish-filled alleyway I had just passed. Another joined it. The two of them snapped at each other and then one made a lunge towards me. I was too terrified to turn and run, and anyway some instinct told me that if I did they would be on me in an instant.

'Go away! Go away!' I screamed, backing away. More dogs appeared. There were six or seven snarling, growling, snapping curs. They all looked rabid with their froth-flecked teeth.

'Help! Go away!'

Perhaps they understood Persian.

'*Imshi! Imshi!* Please go away.' I could feel my voice rising.

The street was empty. Each lunge brought one of the dogs closer. It was only the fact that they were distracted by fighting with each other that had kept them away this long. I saw a mud brick in the street. I picked it up and hurled it at the lead dog. It yelped and backed off.

The headlights of a car came around the corner. The dogs scattered as it drove towards them. I jumped up on the pavement to get out of the way. The car skidded to a stop. Ma jumped out of the front seat before it even came to a halt. Mr Macleod was driving. JRC and one of the Sikhs were sitting in the back. They all leaped out of the car after Ma.

'Mileso, are you all right? What are you doing?'

'Oh Ma. I was so frightened. The dogs.'

'Silly chap. Where did you think you were going? You're all right now. Come here.'

She gave me a big hug and shepherded me back to the car. JRC swung his crutch at the nearest dog.

'Bugger off before I throw my crutch at you,' he shouted in his most fearsome voice. Then, turning to me, 'You all right, Mileso, old boy? You gave us quite a scare when we got back. Don't know what a wee lad like you is doing out in the streets of Meshed at this time of night. You'll frighten the mullahs.'

'Mileso darling, what did you think you were up to?'

'Well, you said you'd be back by eleven o'clock, and I was worried when you weren't there. I thought I'd come and find you.'

'You should have been asleep. Was something keeping you awake?'

'Well, not really. I just couldn't sleep.'

9

I Set Fire to Rustumobad

From the first time I met him I could see that Franco was different to the other people we saw. First of all, he dressed in a different way. In Tehran he always wore a suit. So did most of Ma's English and American friends, but Franco's suits sat on him differently. Theirs bagged and hung; Franco's draped naturally around his tall frame. His whole manner was different. He seemed to be both more casual and more formal with his high domed forehead and his serious-looking face, which all of a sudden would break into a grin like a thirteen-year-old's, and his laugh, which was both catching and conspiratorial.

I do not remember the first time I met Franco. He was not around at the time of our first Christmas in Mahmoudieh, but by the time we moved to the house in Tehran he seemed always to be there. It was not just Franco's dress and manner that were different; he was the first person who treated me as if I were a grown-up. JRC was away most of the time, either travelling on business to exciting-sounding places like Beirut, Baghdad, Damascus and Amman or, I had realised from a chance remark of Ma's, in Tehran but not living at home. That seemed perfectly natural. My friends' mothers and fathers lived together and did everything together; JRC and Ma on the other hand, though always on cheery, chatty terms, were living increasingly separate lives after our first few months in Tehran.

Franco was, Ma told me, the Italian ambassador. I knew all about ambassadors as Tehran at that time was full of ambassadors and other diplomats. It was not long before Ma and I moved in with Franco. Moving in with Franco meant moving to Rustumobad. Rustumobad was about ten miles from Tehran. The road there soon petered out into dirt, as did almost all roads out of Tehran apart from the main road to the Caspian, and bumped its way through orchards and fields surrounded by irrigation ditches with sturdy wooden sluices to a small village on the side of a hill.

This was Rustumobad. It had one main street with a few dark alleys leading off it. A huddle of little shops on the downhill, south, side of the road sold food, groceries, ironware and paraffin. Most of the north side consisted of a long baked-mud wall more than twice as high as a grown-up, so high you could not guess what happened behind it. Set into this wall, which was the depth of a building, were various enterprises with doors leading on to the street. There was a hammam, where, Franco said, the men of the village went to sit in the warmth and to gossip. Beyond the hammam was the *chaikhana*, the tea house, where the men of the village went to go on gossiping after they had been to the hammam, out of doors in the summer and indoors during the icy Tehran winters. And beyond the hammam and the *chaikhana*, standing by itself, not part of the great mud wall, was a small mosque with a stunted little minaret, where, according to Franco, the men of the village would go to gossip before they went to the hammam and the *chaikhana*, or even after they had been to the hammam and the *chaikhana*.

'Who does the work if the men are gossiping the whole time?' I asked.

'The women.'

In the middle of the wall, between the hammam and the *chaikhana*, were two great wooden doors with intricate carvings on them and complicated metal fixings. Nothing gave any clue as to what was behind.

We parked in the dusty street in front of the doorway. Franco banged hard on the doors, and soon there was the noise of bolts being withdrawn, and a wicket gate set into one of the mighty doors creaked open. I stepped in over its sill and gasped. Before me was a seemingly unending garden. Every surface was covered with exotic plants, flowering bushes, creepers hanging in long tendrils, tall trees. In the middle of this was a square ornamental pool.

Stairs led up from the garden to the most amazing house I had ever seen. Even in India I did not remember anything like this. There I had seen forts and castles and maharajahs' palaces that had been bigger and grander, but this was not one of those. This was a private house, a house where I was going to live.

Franco, Ma and I had been driven up there by Ben, Franco's driver, who like Petrossian was an Armenian. Ma had said that Franco was going to be moving in as soon as it was ready, but when we reached the house and I had recovered from my initial amazement I could see that there was one major drawback to Rustumobad. It was a ruin. Bits of wooden scaffolding were holding up walls and pillars everywhere. It must have been many years since anyone had last lived there.

Rustumobad

For what seemed like months the place was buzzing with workmen, all wearing the same baggy black trousers and baggy white shirts; a few of the craftsmen wore embroidered waistcoats on top of the baggy shirts, and everyone had a hat, for most a tight-fitting cap although one or two had mini-fezzes. The people working in the house usually wore caps, and the people in the garden had the fezzes.

On most days Ma and I would be up there by ourselves with the workmen while Franco went about his diplomatic duties. In the late afternoon Franco would arrive to inspect the work that had taken place that day. He was like a little boy opening a Christmas present. I trotted along behind pretending interest but was bored by the works taking place.

Sometimes Franco would turn to me and seek an opinion. 'Miles, old chap,' he would say with a smile and an exaggerated

English accent, 'what do you think of the way they have done this? The tiles, are they too bumpy here, not smooth enough? Or do you think it is better to leave a few bumps? We don't want this to end up looking like a new house, do we?'

'Mmm, yes, I think you're right, Franco. I agree.'

'Thank you, Miles. I'm glad you do.'

Usually I had no idea what Franco was talking about. Why would anyone in their right mind want to have uneven tiles? But I was skilled at working out what it was adults wanted to hear and agreeing with them, even though many of their opinions seemed unaccountable. It was also nice to be asked my opinion just like a grown-up.

While the work was going on, Franco and Ma had made expeditions to different parts of Iran. They went to Yezd, Persepolis, Shiraz and other places I had never heard of, and wherever they went they came back with the car filled with junk. At least that is what it looked like to me, although they behaved as if this stuff were the most precious treasure in the world: pieces of old pottery, wood and glass, some of it still covered with dried mud. 'Miles, my friend, look at this. What do you think this is?'

'Well, I don't really know, Franco. I, er . . . It looks like a dirty old pot.'

'Exactly, it is a dirty old pot, but do you know why I bought it? This pot was made more than 2,000 years ago, before Christ was born.'

'Gosh.' It was difficult to think of what to say to this piece of news.

'But,' continued Franco, 'it's not just a dirty old pot. You remember the story of Aladdin?'

'Mmm.'

'And what did Aladdin have that he used to rub?'

'I know. A lamp. And when he rubbed it a genie flew out.'

'Well, go and get Aldo and ask him if he will bring me a little oil and a piece of wick from the paraffin stove.'

Aldo was Franco's cook, butler and general looker-after. I ran off to the kitchen to fetch Aldo, who was having a quiet nap. Aldo's duties were light, and he spent most of the day sleeping. I woke him up and explained what was needed. Aldo spoke excellent Farsi but no English. My request elicited an offer of ice cream or pannetone. I ran off to get Franco, and the problem was solved by a burst of Italian from Franco and puzzled head-nodding from Aldo. We followed Aldo back to the kitchen. Franco carefully poured oil into the pot from a bottle Aldo handed him, dipped one end of the wick in the oil and then laid that end along the groove on the top of the lamp's spout while putting the other end in the oil.

'Aldo, a match.'

He put the pot down on the kitchen table and handed the matches to me.

'Now, Miles, light a match and touch the end of the wick with it. Let's see what the dirty old pot can do.'

I did as I was told and watched as the black smoke from the end of the wick turned into a small yellow flame.

'*Ecco*. Aladdin's lamp.'

Then one day Rustumobad was finished.

When Michael arrived for the summer holidays, I set about showing him around my new territory. At the Tehran end of the garden beyond where the servants hung the washing to dry was a jungly bit. Michael and I made a tunnel into the middle of the bushes, where there was a clearing the size of a small tent completely covered and enclosed by the leaves. The tunnel was too small for a grown-up to crawl along so we were safe from interruption in there. We collected furniture for our secret camp. An upturned wooden orange crate made a good table and we had logs for chairs. From time to time we sneaked food from the kitchen and scurried off down the tunnel to have a camp feast. None of the adults knew about the camp; they were probably just pleased that we seemed to be so peacefully occupied most of the time. One day, Paul, a boy of my age with whose mother I would often be left for a couple of days when Ma and Franco went off on one of their trips, came up to spend the day at Rustumobad. His mother dropped him off in the morning.

'What are you boys going to get up to?' Ma asked.

'Oh, we'll just muck about,' Michael said.

The three of us headed off to the Tehran end of the garden. We checked to make sure no one was looking and, Michael leading, ducked into the tunnel on our hands and knees. I was delighted to see how impressed Paul was.

'This is amazing. We haven't got anything like this at home. Bet you spend all day here,' said Paul.

'It's jolly good, isn't it? Here, would you like some cake?' Michael asked. We had stolen a large piece of iced sponge from Aldo's larder.

'Wouldn't it be fantastic if you could cook in here,' said Paul. 'You could make toast and things like that.'

'I know,' I said. 'I've got a really good idea.'

'Fat chance of your having a good idea,' said Michael. 'What is it?'

'Well, I know what we could use to cook over. Franco's got this old pot, but it's really a lamp and you can light it and it'll go on burning.'

'What? You sure?' asked Michael.

'Yes, really. You just wait here. I'll show you.'

I hurried back to the house and checked carefully to see if there was anyone around. The coast was clear. Five minutes later I crawled into the camp holding the lamp and a bottle of oil which I had selected from one of several in the empty kitchen. Aldo must have gone to do the shopping. I had brought some bread to toast on the lamp. All this was in a bag I had found in the kitchen.

'What have you got in there?' asked Michael. 'Let's have a look.'

'You'll see,' I said. 'You go on playing cards and I'll tell you when it's ready.'

I put the bag on the ground and carefully took the lamp out, got the oil, and carefully poured enough into the lamp to half-fill it. The oil poured easily and quickly. It seemed thinner than the oil Aldo had used when he had filled the lamp and it smelled a bit different.

Michael and Paul had stopped playing cards and were watching what I was doing.

Finally, feeling very grown up, I got the wick out and dipped one end in the oil, making sure it got good and soaked. I laid this carefully in the grooved spout just as I had seen Franco do and submerged the other end.

'There, now watch this.'

I carefully lit a match. Tongue between teeth I leaned forward and touched the end of the wick with it.

FFFFFWHHHHOOOOOOOOOOOOOSSSSSSSSHHH HHHHHH!

A giant gout of flame shot up so high that it ignited the branches that made the roof of the camp. I must have kicked the lamp as I threw myself back away from the leaping fire as the liquid spilled and flamed all over the camp. Smoke and fire were everywhere.

'Quick. Christ! You idiot. You silly bastard. Out! Get out, quick!' It was Michael's urgent voice.

The heat was searing and the flames were moving fast to fill the entire space. We crawled out as fast as we could along the tunnel.

'You bloody fool,' said Michael. 'You know what you must have put in your famous lamp?'

'Um.'

'Petrol, you idiot.'

What to do now was the question. No one had yet appeared. If we could hide in some other part of the grounds, we could then reappear in a few minutes when the fire had been discovered and ask what was going on. That way no one would suspect us.

Our plan was thwarted by the arrival of Muhammad, Franco's head gardener, followed by Aldo. Aldo was running. I had never seen him do anything but shuffle before. They were both shouting at us, Muhammad in Farsi, Aldo in Italian. Then other people came rushing from different parts of the garden. Daud, Muhammad's five-year-old son, with whom I sometimes played, was sent to open the gates on to the street to allow more people in to help. Aldo stood a safe distance from the fire shouting in Italian and otherwise doing nothing. Meanwhile Muhammad sent some people for buckets, arranged hosepipes, detailed others to get spades and told them to shovel earth on to outlying bits of the fire while he set up a human chain between the ornamental pool and the blaze along which buckets raced hand to hand.

The three of us stood open-mouthed watching the flames, interrupted only by occasional snorts of 'Bloody idiot' from Michael.

We escaped lightly for creating the Great Fire. Fortunately for me, Franco did not believe in people being beaten. Michael was full of tales about the daily floggings that were handed out at Stubbington, and I knew that some of my friends in Tehran got belted by their fathers from time to time, but Franco considered English boarding schools barbaric. Franco liked to treat everyone as if they were a grown-up; I never once saw him angry. He preferred to give you a talking-to.

As a result of the fire I received my longest talking-to yet about the stupidity and irresponsibility of what I had done. Michael got an even longer talking-to.

We were the only foreigners in Rustumobad. One day Ma took me aside after breakfast. 'Now, listen carefully, Mileso, this is something serious.'

'Yes, Ma.'

'You've probably heard us talking about all the trouble that's going on with the government and how unpopular foreigners are.'

'Yes, I know. It's Mossadegh, isn't it?'

Mossadegh did not like the Shah and was thought by everyone who came to the house to be too friendly with the Russians. Mossadegh, I heard, was also very good at 'getting the bazaar out'. I asked Franco what this meant.

He gave one of his conspiratorial smiles and said, 'It's not the bazaar he gets out, it's the people who work there – the bazaaris, the big merchants, the people who really count in

Iran. If they don't like the government, then it's all over for them. That's why Mossadegh is so clever. He's very good at getting the bazaaris on his side, and that's why the Shah is in a difficult position. The bazaaris have had enough of him.'

I had of course experienced the bazaaris first hand not long ago, when I had been so nearly killed in the riot which stormed past the British embassy in Tehran. After the Shah, the British were the people Mossadegh was most angry at, because we, it seemed, had all the oil in Iran. And after the British came other foreigners – the Americans, the French and the Italians. The result, Ma told me, was that Tehran was not as safe a place for Europeans as it had been when we first moved there. Every week there were stories of Europeans being attacked by mobs and sometimes even killed.

The puzzling thing was that life seemed to go on exactly as it had before. The parties and the picnics continued. Everyone seemed to be in a good mood the whole time, and I noticed lots of new people arriving. On the days when we were in the city I would often be left to amuse myself in the Tehran Club, which Ma was still helping to run on a part-time basis. A year ago the reading room had seldom had more than a couple of people in it; these days it was packed with people, few of whom looked familiar, all talking excitedly. And despite the danger I had been told of, we seemed to go into Tehran and drive about much as we had done before. I asked Ma why this was safe.

'Well, most days it is. Everything's just as it was before. Then Mossadegh will be up to his tricks and want to stir things up and get the bazaar out. Those are the days when we have to be careful and you don't want to show your face in public.'

'But Ma, how do you know the days when he's going to get the bazaar out?'

'Oh, everyone knows that. The servants tell us days before. We always have lots of warning, and anyone who doesn't listen to their servants is looking for trouble.'

Then one day Franco, Ma and I were being driven back to Rustumobad and the main road on the way out of Tehran was blocked. There were people everywhere, spilling out on to the road, jostling and shouting. They were all moving in one direction but they were not running like the people I had seen in the demonstration outside the British embassy.

'What's going on?' I asked. 'Has Mossadegh got the bazaar out? Are we going to be all right.'

Franco spoke urgently to Ben in Farsi and then turned to me.

'No, it's not a riot. It's nothing to worry about as long as we keep our heads down and don't get out. It's Ashura. It's a religious thing. I'd forgotten it had started. I'll tell you about it when we get home. The next few days are going to be a good time to stay out of sight.'

When we got back to the house and the gates were closed behind us, Franco explained: 'Ashura is a special time of the year for Iranians. It's really just something the Iranians do. Muslims in other parts of the world aren't very interested in it. It all started 1,000 years ago with this man called Hussein. He was the son of Ali, who was married to Fatima, the daughter of Muhammad himself. So Hussein was Muhammad's grandson. There was a big battle and Hussein got killed. And – it gets a bit complicated here – the Iranians think that Hussein was a very holy man and most of the other Muslims don't.

So every year, to commemorate the death of Hussein, the Iranians go into mourning, and they take to the streets and beat themselves.'

'What, they beat themselves? No. They can't do that. Why do they do that?'

'I mean it. You'll see. Look. The further away from Tehran and into the country you get, the more seriously they take all this. It's a very big thing here in Rustumobad. That's why you must not, under any circumstances, go outside the gates while this is going on. They get very strange while this is happening.

'Come and see for yourself what they're like. Aldo says they are going to be having a procession through the village later this afternoon. We can go down to the bottom of the garden and have a look. But we must be careful. We don't want them to know we're watching. That could be dangerous.'

When the time came, Ma and I went down to the bottom of the garden while Franco went off to find a ladder. Franco put the ladder up against the back wall of the hammam, and the three of us climbed up on to its roof. At the front of the hammam roof, on the street side, was a low crumbling mud parapet.

'There,' said Franco. 'We'll crawl up behind the parapet and we can crouch behind it so no one can see us. It's got enough cracks and holes in it. We can see what's going on through those. But Miles, please, for God's sake, keep your head down and don't do anything to draw attention to yourself.'

We crept up to the wall. It seemed to me that Franco was making a bit of a fuss because what could happen to us up here, where we seemed to be completely safe? I peered down to the street below, usually empty apart from a couple of goats and a pye-dog at this time of day. But today it was packed with figures in black chadors. All the women in the village, who usually spent most of their time indoors, were standing in the street making a kind of keening noise. I could not see any men.

'Franco, Franco,' I whispered as loudly as I dared, 'where are all the men?'

'Shhh. Be quiet. Watch. It may be a little time yet. Just wait.'

Minutes passed. I was getting restless and wanted to stand up.

'Is anything going to happen? Are they coming?'

'Shh. Listen.'

The women's keening had risen in tone, but there was another noise coming from the Tehran end of the road. It sounded like shouting, but it was not like anything I had ever heard before. It sounded like 'Ya-ya-ya.' Then I saw them. Almost jogging up the hill came a long stream of men. They were naked apart from white cotton loincloths – no shoes, nothing on their heads, their chests and backs completely bare. At first I could not see what they were doing; they seemed to be shouting and chanting and waving their arms in the air. Most of them were holding things.

As they got closer I could see that many of them had whips. These looked like the cat-o'-nine-tails that I had seen in pirate books, short handles with lots of whippy strands attached to them. They were chanting, 'Ya-ya-ya,' and bringing the whips down on their backs. Others were holding knives or pieces of glass, which they were using to cut themselves. They were clawing at their chests with them, and the blood was running down to their legs.

There were children in the procession, some younger than me, naked to the waist and cutting themselves. And grandfathers, men in their eighties, were stumbling along, chanting, 'Ya-ya-ya,' in strange mad voices while slashing themselves till the blood ran.

'Franco, what are they saying?'

Franco bent towards me, careful not to show himself above the parapet.

'"Ya Hussein, ya Ali." They go on chanting it over and over again. Shhh now. Watch.'

The procession was going right past us. The nearest men were no more than six feet away from us. I crouched as low as I could and peered through a crack in the mud parapet. Their eyes were wide open and looked like glass. Everyone stared straight ahead with trance-like glazed eyes. I felt that they were so distant that we could have stood up and shouted and they would not have noticed us. 'Ma, Franco, look. It's Muhammad. It's Muhammad.'

There, naked but for his loincloth, eyes of glass, flecks of foam on his face, terrible cuts in his chest from which blood was coursing down, the whip rising and falling, *thwickthwick*, on his back and his arms, 'Ya Hussein, ya Ali,' was Muhammad, our gardener, the one who had so coolly arranged things on the day of the fire.

And next to Muhammad was Daud, his son. Daud was like me, a shy boy, but I considered him my friend. He even spoke a little English. He and I had had several rather formal conversations with him saying politely, 'You like Rustumobad?' and me replying, 'Oh yes. Rustumobad very good. I like.'

Daud was a year or so younger than I. He was moving with a jerky sort of jiggy step like someone doing a strange dance. His lips had froth on them as he shouted, 'Ya Hussein, ya Ali.'

A few days later I saw Daud in the garden. It was as if Ashura had never happened. Muhammad and another man were calmly clearing a blocked drain near the gatehouse when the little door set in the main doors opened and Daud stepped over the lintel to come in. He was carrying what looked like a small wooden tool, which he handed to his father, who thanked him and continued with his work.

Daud was wearing the loose-fitting robe that all the boys wore. It covered his body down to his ankles so I could not see the state of his chest. I wondered how his mother had treated his wounds and whether she had put dressings on them. I had a picture of his chest covered with a hundred pieces of crossed sticking plaster.

Daud saw me looking at him and gave me a little smile.

'*Salaam alekhoum*, Master Miles.'

'*Alekhoum salaam*, Daud.'

'You are good?'

'Yes, thank you, Daud. How about you? You good?'

'Yes. I good.'

'Good.'

I longed to ask him if I could have a peek. I wondered if he knew I had seen him. But before I could think of how to ask him to show me, he gave me a shy little wave and scampered off through the still-open door into the street.

10

Cars and Boats and Trains and Planes

I was upset that Franco had got the 1951 Chevrolet with the normal boot on it rather than the racy-looking one whose back ran in a straight line from the roof to the bumper. I never knew what this style was called. I called it slideback and I thought it was the smartest thing I had ever seen on a car. It was a feature of several of the new models; Oldsmobile, Buick and Ford all had models available with it. Franco did not share my passion for cars, nor did he appear to have my knowledge, gleaned from hours of hard study of *Popular Mechanics* or from looking at the new car advertisements in magazines which grown-ups left lying around such as the *New Yorker* or *Time*.

The reason I liked the *New Yorker* was the advertisements. There were four types of advertisement I liked. First there were the ones for cars. The cars looked sleek and elegant; they whispered their glamour at you from the page. Everything shone, while their lines, particularly those of the 1951 models, were smooth and streamlined. They also looked enormous.

I did not have to look at too many *New Yorkers* before I realised that there was a trick involved here.

Every advertisement featured the new De Soto or Packard or Pontiac parked, gleaming, starbursts of light reflecting from its chrome trim, on a raked gravel drive in front of a white, porticoed, suburban house. Round the car stood a group of people, rapturous smiles on their faces, silent as the Magi in admiration. They were either a married couple with two children or four adults, two men and two women, with the men looking knowledgeably at the outside while the women gazed open-mouthed at the roominess of the well-appointed interior. But something was funny about the people in *New Yorker* advertisements. They were tiny. Even the men stood hardly taller than the door handles. I knew from looking at real people standing next to 1951 cars that a grown-up could look over the roof of a car without standing on tiptoe. The people in the advertisements could hardly see into the back seat. Of course the effect of these shrunken people was to make the cars look enormous.

These were my favourites. Then came the ocean liner advertisements. Ships the size of skyscrapers sliced through the water and across double-page spreads of the *New Yorker*: the majestic *Queen Mary*, the world's largest ship, with her three funnels, and her sister ship the *Queen Elizabeth* with just two; the liners of the Union Castle Line, the *Durban Castle*, the *Edinburgh Castle*, plying their trade from London to Cape Town and back; the mighty P&O ships, which I had gazed on in envy so often in ports on the way out to India and back, where they dwarfed our humble ships of the Anchor Line (no advertisements for the Anchor Line in the

New Yorker); the elegant ocean greyhounds of the French Line, whose advertisements showed candlelit dining rooms and chandeliered ballrooms; and all the other continental lines, the Holland America, the Norwegian Line, even Spanish and Italian companies. I had done my share of ocean travelling on the *Cilicia* and the *Circassia*, but they had no chandeliered ballrooms, no slim, elegant men in double-breasted suits talking to high-heeled women with cigarette holders over a cocktail at the bar. Travelling on these *New Yorker* ships was something to dream about.

Next came the airlines. New airliners were being introduced in 1951: the mighty DC-6 to replace the DC-4. The biggest, and only, plane I had been in was the Dakota, or DC-3, which had brought us from Isfahan to Tehran. That had been the most exciting trip of my life, but the Dakota, with its little tail-wheel sitting on the ground, was tiny compared with its distant descendant the DC-6, which in the pages of the *New Yorker* was so big it seemed to tower over airport buildings. But the DC-6 did not have the skies of the *New Yorker* to itself. Even bigger, more powerful and the most beautiful piece of machinery in the world was the new Lockheed Constellation. Surely it was impossible for aviation to advance beyond this. Instead of the straight, masculine lines of the DC-6, everything about the Constellation was smooth and flowing, almost feminine, with the top of its graceful fuselage flowing back from the cockpit in a long curve, for all the world like a horse's neck.

The mighty Pan American World Airways, in its light blue livery, was the champion of the DC-6; against it was the bright modern red of TWA and its fleet of super-sleek

Constellations. They were not the only planes that caught my eye in the pages of the *New Yorker*. Pan Am had the most exciting of all planes, the giant Stratocruiser, which it operated on the Atlantic route and down to glamorous places in South America like Buenos Aires and Rio de Janeiro. These were so big that they had an upstairs and a downstairs. They had beds where you were tucked in for the night; they had dining rooms on the lower deck where you sat at tables laid with white linen while elegant stewardesses in crisp uniforms poured you champagne. I yearned to fly on a Stratocruiser, to be tucked up in bed at 14,000 feet, as the mighty Pratt & Whitney engines throbbed on through the Atlantic night.

American airlines were the most modern and the most exciting, but I had a special affection for BOAC, the great British Overseas Airways Corporation, which connected Tehran with London and brought Michael out for the summer holidays. BOAC did not yet have DC-6s or Constellations but it did have its own unique plane. The Argonaut, I knew from my reading, had the body of a DC-4, the predecessor and smaller version of the DC-6. But it also had something special. It did not have the normal Pratt & Whitney engines, but Rolls-Royce Merlins, which were the best in the world. Rolls-Royce Merlins had powered the Spitfires that won the Battle of Britain.

The fourth thing that I dreamed about were trains. The *New Yorker* advertisements were for long-distance American routes. They had romantic names: the Super Chief, the Santa Fe, the Cannonball, the Zephyr. I knew that some trains had sleeping and dining cars. I remembered overnight trips on Indian trains, but the cabins on those had been equipped as if you were going on a camping trip and everything was green or khaki. I did not remember corridors between carriages. If you wanted to go to the dining car you would have to wait till the train stopped, sometimes between stations, get off and walk a few carriages, and then, when you had finished your lunch, you would have to wait until the train stopped again before you went back to your compartment.

American trains were not like that. They were peopled with the same impossibly glamorous beings who went on TWA Constellations and parked 1951 Buicks on their gravel driveways. Everything in a sleeping compartment on the Super Chief was aluminium and streamlined, and the colours were the colours of the future, reds, blues, yellows, not the army colours of Indian Railways. Black attendants in resplendent uniforms with funny caps brought you cocktails while your bed was being made up, or you sat eating long meals at restaurant-style tables with little shaded lights on them while the prairies thundered past your window. Best of all was the observation car. American trains, or at least the ones in the *New Yorker*, had special carriages with domed glass roofs, where you could sit sipping a drink as the train glided past mountains, lakes and trees turning improbable shades of gold and red.

II

On the Argonaut

It was April 1952, and our time in Iran was at an end, as was my freedom. I was eight. It was time to join Michael at Stubbington. The three of us, Ma, Michael and I, made our way to Tehran Airport. I was excited at the thought of the long flight to England, which would be on one of the famous BOAC Argonauts.

Three days after the Argonaut landed at Heathrow, then a small collection of temporary shacks just off the A4, I was at Stubbington for the summer term. Ma drove Michael and me down to the school, said a quick goodbye and left, with both of us fighting back tears but determined not to show them. Eleven years of boarding school had begun. The only pools of light in the darkness of those years were the holidays. I would start counting the days to freedom from the day term began.

For our family 1952 was a watershed year. Ma and Franco had parted; she and JRC were once more living together. I asked her what had happened.

'Oh well, we drove back from Tehran together in Franco's car, all the way to Italy. It was an amazing trip, particularly when we were going through Yugoslavia. What a beautiful country.'

'And?'

'Well, Franco had to go off to be ambassador in Tokyo. That was a big job.'

'But. You and he?'

'Mileso. It was one of those things. I've got you two to look after. Franco and I had very different ideas on how you should be brought up.'

'Why? Franco and I always got on so well. He used to treat me like a grown-up. I'm sure he liked me.'

'Yes, I know he did. He was very fond of you. But he didn't believe in English boarding schools and I'm not sure he wanted to take on two children that weren't his. Let's leave it at that, shall we?'

JRC had to leave Tehran shortly after we flew to England. The temporary overthrow of the Shah and the establishment of the Mossadegh regime had made Tehran unsuitable for the regional headquarters of a British business. At first he relocated to Beirut, and it was there that Michael and I went for my first Christmas holiday from Stubbington.

My Beirut memories are less vivid than the Iran ones but I well remember our journey there. The BOAC plane to Beirut was delayed by twenty-four hours because of fog in London. In the pre-jet era flying to Beirut required a refuelling stop in Rome and another in Athens and took fourteen hours compared with the five non-stop hours it takes today. Our plane was further delayed in Rome by a technical fault, which was going to keep us on the ground for five or six hours.

BOAC rounded up the Beirut passengers in the transit lounge, apologised for the delay and announced that they would take us on a bus tour of Rome. It is difficult today to conceive of a time when airlines as a matter of routine would take delayed passengers off on sightseeing tours to pass away the wait. We saw the Pantheon and St Peter's, and stopped at the Colosseum to eat the packed lunch which BOAC had provided. The lunch included Chianti in a tradi-tional-style half-bottle half-encased in straw. I didn't like wine, but Ma and JRC did so I stuffed it into the pocket of my Stubbington Burberry raincoat to give to them when we arrived. Eight hours later, after a stop in Athens, we landed in Beirut at 10 p.m. I was nervous that I would be apprehended for smuggling in the Chianti. I asked Michael whether I should declare it.

'Don't be so wet,' he said. 'They'll never find it as long as you don't look suspicious.'

I sauntered out of the plane as unsuspiciously as I could. I had my Burberry open so the outline of the bottle in my pocket would not be apparent. As a result I knocked the pocket of my nonchalantly flapping raincoat against the plane door. Despite the straw protection around the bottom of the bottle, it shattered. I could feel liquid running down my leg. My trousers soon had a spreading stain, and red liquid was leaving a trail on the floor behind me. It looked as if I were the victim of a botched murder attempt.

The customs were bound to see. Would I be arrested for attempted smuggling? Was that as bad as real smuggling?

'Michael, I've broken the wine bottle in my pocket. What should I do?'

'Christ, you're an idiot. Just keep walking. Say nothing.'

Michael didn't have a wine bottle. He had drunk his Chianti at the Colosseum.

We got through customs and immigration without arrest and burst out into the arrivals hall to meet Ma and JRC. It was 10.30 p.m. They were not there. We searched everywhere. Not a sign of them. We were now alone with ten shillings in English money between us in an emptying airport in a Middle Eastern country where we had never been before and knew no one. I began to cry. Michael was made of sterner stuff. After three years of Stubbington tears were out of the question for him but he did look rattled.

Possibly because of the noise I was making we were approached by one of the BOAC ground staff. We explained our plight to her. No, we didn't have a telephone number. No, no address. We were going to be picked up, that was all we knew.

Miss BOAC disappeared, telling us not to move and that she would be back very soon. Ten minutes later we were in a car on our way to a hotel forty-five minutes away in central Beirut. I was still crying. We later discovered that our car passed that of Ma and JRC on their way out to the airport. They had been told by BOAC that our much-delayed plane was arriving an hour later. Michael and I, I still snivelling, were checked in and told by Miss BOAC, who had accompanied us from the airport, not to worry; our parents would be along soon to pick us up. As BOAC had no telephone number or address for them this seemed unlikely. I was going to spend the rest of my life as an orphan in Beirut.

An hour later Ma and JRC turned up. They had gone to the airport and been told that two un-met children, one of them bawling, had been sent off to a hotel in downtown Beirut.

The rest of the Christmas holiday was a celebration of freedom. It was so wonderful not to be at school, to eat good food, to go to bed at 9 p.m. not 6.30, to be able to get up when I wanted and do what I wanted without being trammelled by rules, rules and rules. We were peegeeing with some friends of JRC's in a house on the outskirts of Beirut. Our block was made up of neat modern houses which could have been in an American suburb, but around us was scrubby wasteland. The city had not yet expanded this far. It was not a good place for exploring or going for walks. Within half a mile of the house was a giant refugee camp, where Palestinians who had been squeezed out of what had become Israel were eking out a miserable existence in tents and shacks. If they saw anyone who appeared to be European or American they hurled stones and shouted insults.

Michael and I had fun exploring central Beirut with its tangle of alleys, shops and stalls; mosques and churches stood side by side. Unlike in Tehran, where many of the people we came into contact with spoke English, here few did. French was the universal language of commerce.

I had my ninth-birthday party in the St-Georges Hotel on the corniche. While not a big hotel it was the place to go. It was a fancy-dress party. I have a photograph of me with dozens of other children in fancy dress. As I knew no one in Beirut and Ma and JRC knew only a few adults it is a mystery who the other children were or where they had come from.

Michael was given an air rifle for Christmas. We spent hours on the flat roof of the house trying to shoot pigeons. Michael killed one when a lucky shot hit the bird in the eye. I shot none. Our next game was to shoot out the light bulbs in the street lamps. That stopped after a visit from the gendarmes. A couple of weeks later the holidays were over and we were once more at the airport for the flight back to London and Stubbington. There had been two big thrills over the Christmas holidays.

On Christmas Eve we, and the rest of Beirut, hurried down to the beach near the airport. Four hundred yards offshore the *Champollion*, a French luxury liner that plied the Marseille to Beirut route, had struck a reef, broached and been pushed over on its side by a midwinter storm of a suddenness and violence that one sees only in the Mediterranean. It was lying at a forty-five-degree angle in surf so powerful that when the waves broke over the liner the whole boat was submerged in green and white foam. The Lebanese army, fire service and police force had set up encampments on the beach. It was too rough to get a rescue boat out to the ship. I could see what remained of a wrecked lifeboat, which had been swept on to the beach. A few passengers had tried to swim ashore. They were the first dead bodies I ever saw. They were covered in black oil from the ship's tanks.

At lunchtime a cry went up from the watchers on shore as the *Champollion* split in two. More bodies fell into the sea to be washed up later. The Lebanese air force had planes circling overhead dropping orange rubber dinghies. Most missed, but no one was foolish enough to use any of the ones that landed on the boat to get ashore. That would have been suicide. We watched till teatime. On the beach there was a party atmosphere. People had brought folding chairs, picnics and bottles of wine. Vendors patrolled up and down with Lebanese pastries. Men with binoculars gave authoritative commentaries.

We went home and returned again on Christmas morning. The storm had subsided, and although the sea was still rough the wind had gone down, so that the liner was no longer submerged in surf. At 10 a.m. a speedboat driven – so said the crowd on the beach – by a dashing Beirut playboy got close enough to the listing ship to take off some passengers. This was announced by the men with binoculars, JRC now one of them, and a great cheer went up. Soon a procession of fishing and pleasure boats was nosing its way up to the *Champollion* to take off survivors. The fun was over. We went home to eat our Christmas lunch.

Of the 230 passengers, 38 were killed and about 100 injured. No one ever seemed to quite know what had happened. There was talk that the storm had been so strong that it had over-powered the liner's engines and forced it on to the reef. The story taken up by the newspapers was that the captain, who was known to be what Ma referred to as a plucky drinker, had mistaken the bright new airport lights for the harbour beacon and had attempted to dock the *Champollion* at the airport.

The other thrill came at Beirut Airport. After we had been checked in Michael and I went into the departure lounge, which overlooked the apron where the aircraft parked. As we entered the lounge we noticed an intense whining sound unlike anything I had heard before. Usually the planes on the apron would make coughing and growling noises as their great piston-fired engines roared into life. The sound we could hear was quite unlike that; it was a high-pitched but immensely powerful-sounding whine. There, in front of us and scarcely more than 200 feet from the airport window, was the most beautiful piece of machinery I had ever seen, the de Havilland Comet. I knew all about the Comet from my magazines. It was the world's first jet passenger aircraft. It went into service in the colours of BOAC in 1952, a moment of pride for Britain. At that time the first American passenger jet, the Boeing 707, was merely a doodle on a drawing board.

I had never heard a jet engine before. I was electrified by its unique sound, somewhere between a scream and a roar. The Comet was taxiing gently into a parking place on the apron, its long silver fuselage gleaming in the airport lights. Next to the DC-6s and Super-Constellations with their huge clunky piston engines, it looked like an eel among alligators.

At first sight the Comet appeared to have no engines at all. When you looked more closely you saw that there were two elegant oval openings a third of the way along the wings on either side. The de Havilland Ghost engines were actually embedded in the wings. I watched transfixed, admiring the aircraft's elegant lines, the smart dark-blue BOAC livery, the upright tail and the large square windows, so much bigger than the windows in the Qantas Super-Constellation standing next to it, which was to take us to London.

How I longed to go in the Comet. Although I was to do a lot of travelling in the next few years back and forth to the Middle East for the holidays, I never did. I may have been lucky. Two years later, in January 1954, one blew up over Elba twenty minutes after leaving Rome Ciampino Airport. Six weeks after that another Comet blew up over the Mediterranean near Naples. The Comet was grounded worldwide, never to fly again. Eventually the navy dredged up the wreckage of both aircraft, which was painstakingly jigsawed together at Farnborough. Meanwhile several other aircraft were pressure-tested to destruction in water tanks. The pressure testing showed that after about 1,000 flights a hitherto unknown phenomenon, metal fatigue, resulted in a fatal weakness appearing at the corners of the big square windows; the window would rupture, and the plane would go through explosive depressurisation, as a result of which it would literally disintegrate in mid-air.

De Havilland were unlucky. Whoever developed the first passenger jet would almost certainly have had the metal fatigue problem. It was four years before jets next began flying passengers. De Havilland's improved Comet 4, with a stronger skin, was in a race with Boeing's 707 to be the first to offer transatlantic service in the autumn of 1958. Some British pride was salvaged when the Comet 4 beat the 707 into service by three weeks, but the triumph was a temporary one. The Comet was considered an unlucky aeroplane and did not sell well; the Boeing 707 became the world's best-selling plane in the 1960s. But I still remember that moment of magic at Beirut Airport in January 1953 when I first saw the eel among the alligators.

That was our only holiday in Beirut. Flying was expensive, and during our next holiday Michael and I were billeted with Mr Williams, the French master at Stubbington. He and his wife took in boys as paying guests during the holidays. We used to tell stories about the part Mr Williams had played in the French resistance; some said he had been dropped into occupied France. Many of the boys at Stubbington had parents dotted about bits of the British empire who could not afford to fly them out for the holidays. Most had uncles and aunts they went to stay with. Michael and I had our father and Alice, but we did not stay with them for the holidays. I was relieved. Offered a choice between Mr Williams, a kindly man who had probably never been nearer to France than Brighton, and my stepmother, Mr Williams was the better choice.

In Ma's words, 'Alice used to treat the boys like the servants' children.' That was how I felt when I visited them.

Baghdad Days

When we next went home for the holidays it was not to Beirut but to the one city in the Middle East that was going to be permanently safe for Westerners. The one country on which we could depend was Iraq. The Baghdad Pact was the keystone of the alliance between the West and Iraq. Feisal II, Iraq's boy-king, guided by his uncle Abdul-Illah, the regent, had been educated at Harrow and knew better than to argue with Britain and America, his sponsors in the turbulent Middle East, a region which the USSR was doing its best to subvert. Baghdad was the West's bulwark against communism.

JRC relocated his business to Baghdad, and in 1953 Michael and I flew out there for the eight-week summer holidays. As always, Ma and JRC had found someone to peegee with. In this case it was Tom Walters.

Tom had learned to fly before the war, much of which he had spent in different parts of Africa flying for the RAF. When the war ended he was looking for something interesting to do and signed up with BOAC, which had just been given a contract by the Iraqi government to set up and manage its new airline, Iraqi Airways. Tom went out to Baghdad as part of the BOAC team; he had responsibility for the flying side of the airline. He needed to find and train Iraqis to fly modern planes and to work with the financial staff, also provided by BOAC. The airline had been set up as a subsidiary of Iraqi Railways.

Tom had a big airy house on the road to the airport in the Railway Compound, a mini-village in which senior airline and railway staff, many of them expatriates, lived; the village was centred on the Railway Club with its tennis courts, croquet lawn and swimming pool. Although Iraq was not part of the British empire, the expatriates behaved as if it were. The club could have been in any one of a hundred towns in India in the days of the Raj. Tom's house was set in a large garden of palm trees, eucalyptus, bougainvillea and roses; it could have been in Poona.

The house was presided over by Ibrahim, a cheerful Sunni who had been Tom's chief factotum ever since he had arrived in Iraq. He had learned his English from the RAF during the war, as a result of which he spoke a colourful form of the language. The people in the bazaar who, he assured Ma, were constantly overcharging him, were 'them bloodies'. If he liked something he would say it was wizard. Best of all, to this day every time the sun comes out from behind a cloud, I say, 'The sun he come,' and I think of Ibrahim's smiling face.

When Ma and JRC moved in with Tom, his wife Bea had just left to return to Rhodesia, where she had been born. I never met Bea, but according to Ma, 'The poor woman was barking mad. They never really found out what it was.

A combination of schizophrenia and depression, they said. I mean you never knew where you were with her. One minute she'd be absolutely charming and getting you a drink and the next she'd be screaming blue murder. Poor Tom didn't know which way to look. She certainly was not capable of living a normal life and she was having a terrible effect on poor Penny.' Penny was their daughter. She was almost exactly my age, a lovely gentle girl, who often ended up on the receiving end of Michael's and my rough boarding-school manners.

When Michael and I arrived for the summer holidays Bea was no longer there; she was in Cape Town. Coming out to Baghdad for eight weeks away from the mean pettiness of boarding school was a dream. Baghdad was very different from Tehran. Tehran was a city of tree-lined boulevards, belle époque houses set in stately gardens, long vistas over the trees to the Elburz Mountains and the mighty Demavend, a city of majesty and ambition. Baghdad was a collection of mud huts on the Tigris. Baghdad had no grand vistas and tree-lined boulevards, but even I was aware of its history as the centre of one of the great Islamic empires, and that gave it character if not majesty.

Michael and I were delighted with the new set-up. JRC and Tom, united by a love of engines and all things mechanical, had become firm friends. They had clubbed together to buy a 1929 Rolls-Royce 20/25. The car had been in Baghdad since before the war and was in terrible condition. JRC and Tom lovingly rebuilt it. I have never been mechanical, but Tom was a brilliant teacher, perhaps why he was such a success with his Iraqi pilots. He drew diagrams to show Michael and me how the gearbox and the suspension worked. Some of the parts to rebuild the car were flown out from England but the majority were made locally to meticulous drawings done by Tom. Although Tom had a Chevrolet and JRC an Oldsmobile for office use, the Rolls-Royce was the car we used for expeditions.

It was the perfect desert car. The Chevrolet had a ground clearance of seven or eight inches, the Rolls of sixteen. It had a saloon body into which you could fit almost unlimited amounts of people and cargo. We had two dogs, a German shepherd and an English setter. Every day we would load them into the car and head out into the desert to give them a run. The heat in Baghdad in the summer is unimaginable, so we did our dog walking in the early morning, just after sunrise, or in the cool of the evening. Although the heat was immense it was an utterly dry, desert heat and less oppressive than the sweaty mugginess of Bombay.

The desert where we walked the dogs was not a flat stretch of Empty-Quarter-style sand and dunes. The Mesopotamian Arabs had learned the art of irrigation from the Persians, and although parts of the land surrounding Baghdad were dry and barren most was irrigated by a complicated system of sluiced channels feeding off canals themselves fed from the Tigris. Every few miles were groves of date-bearing palm trees. Alfalfa, cereals and cotton were grown. Sometimes after a flash storm the whole character of the desert changed, and where before had been sand as far as you could see were now shallow lakes alive with birds. There was a surprising amount of water thanks to the irrigation networks; small reed-bound lakes were common even in the driest of the summer.

Tom had two shotguns with which he taught Michael and me to shoot. One was a grown-up twelve bore and the other an elegant Holland & Holland twenty-eight bore, a lighter gun more suitable for me. We shot in the date groves. We parked the Rolls and then walked behind the English setter. She quartered the ground ahead of us, tail wagging furiously, until on an instant she froze as she scented a partridge. She stood utterly still, tail straight out behind her, one front knee raised pointing at where she scented the bird. This gave us time to catch up. When we were close enough she darted in and put the bird up. On a good day we shot three or four partridge and a few pigeons. We might stop by one of the lakes on the way back and see if we could get a duck or a snipe. Once we shot a coot. It tasted disgusting. We never shot another.

Shooting was fun but better was driving. Baghdad is where I learned to drive. Tom gave Michael and me patient lessons in how to drive the Rolls. The gear changes were difficult because, unlike a modern car, it had no synchromesh to control the speed of the cogs in the gearbox when you changed gear. Consequently you had to move the lever into neutral, wait for a carefully judged moment, and then flip the throttle for just the right amount of revs to allow you to slip it into a new gear without a terrible grinding noise coming from the gearbox.

Initially I drove with Tom by my side. I had to sit on top of two cushions so I could see over the dashboard. People a few feet away couldn't see me so it appeared that the Rolls was careering along with no one behind the wheel. After a while Tom judged Michael and me to be competent drivers. We took it in turns to drive the Rolls around the desert paths and tracks while the others walked the dogs and potted partridges. Driving the giant car along dusty rutted roads and between date groves was a thrill. We soon learned tricks. Michael showed me how to do handbrake turns. He found a patch of muddy ground where a salt lick had almost dried up, wound the Rolls up to its top speed of 45 mph, then jerked the wheel and yanked on the handbrake at the same time to lock the rear wheels. The huge car went into a majestic spin. What the workers in the date groves made of the sight of a grey Rolls-Royce, more suited to a coronation procession than a desert track, pirouetting in a Mesopotamian mudpatch I do not know.

Michael and I were each allowed a twenty-minute turn with the Rolls when we went out dog walking. You can go a long way in that time and certainly well out of sight of dog walkers. Once I was bouncing along a road built on an embankment with a drop on either side into a ditch, when I swerved to avoid a rut and the car went over the edge. The Rolls was now in a ditch in the middle of an empty desert. I got out to have a look. I climbed back in again, restarted the engine and gunned it. The wheels spun and spat mud everywhere; the car juddered and sank deeper into the ditch. There was a smell of burning clutch.

Then, out of the empty desert, people began to appear – farm workers, date pickers, sluice men – to be greeted by a not-quite-five-foot-tall English boy in short trousers. They seemed to think this was a huge joke. I knew no Arabic, but they could see what needed to be done. By sheer manpower they levered the car out of the ditch and back on to the road. I thanked them warmly and offered them some money. They were horrified and refused even to look at it. Then I had an idea. I dug around in the back of the car and got out my cartridge belt. I distributed cartridges as a thank you. Smiles everywhere. The twenty-eight-bore cartridges would not have fitted whatever they used to shoot with, but Tom later told me that cartridges were used by the desert people as a form of currency. Size was of little importance.

JRC was often away on business for weeks at a time. One day shortly after Michael and I arrived in Baghdad for the Christmas holidays Ma came into the bathroom and perched herself on the edge of the bath. We boys usually took our bath together and often would end up fighting or accusing each other of peeing in the water. Ma looked serious.

'Boys, I've got something I want to tell you. It may come as a surprise.'

'I hope it's not too serious,' said Michael.

'Yes, me too,' echoed I.

'Well,' said Ma, 'JRC and I have decided to get divorced. It's all very friendly. And I'm going to marry Tom.'

Michael and I looked at each other and laughed. I was the first to speak.

'Ma, that's not really a surprise. We've been expecting this for some time. In fact we've talked about it and we're surprised you didn't do it sooner.'

Ma looked relieved. 'Oh good. I was worried it might come as a shock to you. JRC's been a jolly good stepfather to both of you and has helped me look after you, but we agreed it was time to move on. JRC's travelling at the moment but he'll be back tomorrow. He's agreed to be best man.'

And so he was. After the very friendly divorce came through, the wedding was performed at the British consulate followed by a small lunchtime reception back at the house in the Railway Compound. JRC, looking very dapper in his best suit, sported a red rose in his buttonhole, as did Tom. JRC made a gracious speech for which he had saved two of his best jokes and then proposed the happy couple's health.

After that first summer holiday in Baghdad Michael and I spent our summers in the relative cool of Jersey, where Ma and Tom had bought a little granite farmhouse. We loved Jersey. It was a paradise for a teenager as long as you liked doing things in the water. You could swim, surf, sail, snorkel or just sunbathe on the magnificent five-mile-long St Ouen's Beach, one of the best surfing beaches in Europe. Jersey was also home to lots of people of our age and had, unlike Baghdad, a good party life. Baghdad was still however somewhere special. I used to look forward with excitement to going there for the winter and Easter holidays.

Towards the end of the summer term of 1958, by which time I had left Stubbington and was in my second year at Radley, I was summoned urgently to my housemaster's study. Previously such a summons had always ended with him holding a cane and me bent over a chair. I searched my mind for what I might have done so I could manufacture a suitable excuse. I could not believe I was going to be flogged just two days before the end of term. I knocked on the door.

'Come.'

'You wanted to see me, sir?'

He rose to his feet, came over, patted me nervously on the back and waved me to a chair.

'Sit down, Morland, sit down. Would you like a cup of coffee?'

I quickly checked his desk and was relieved to see that for once there was no cane there. He was also trying to be friendly. This made me deeply uneasy. What was going on?

'No, thank you, sir.'

'Um, your parents, Morland. They're in Iraq, aren't they?'

'Yes, sir. Although my mother is in Jersey right now getting ready for the summer holidays.'

'Oh, good, good. And your stepfather? It is your stepfather, isn't it?'

'Yes, sir. He's in Baghdad. He runs the airline there. But he'll be coming to Jersey soon to join us for the holidays.'

'Ah. You see, I've just been listening to the news on the radio. There's been a revolution in Iraq.'

I shot forward in my chair. 'What? What do you mean?'

'Well, the news is unclear at the moment, but someone in the army called Kassem has taken control. Early reports say that the king and most of his family have been shot. I'm so sorry to have to tell you this, Morland. I'm glad your mother is not there, but I'm sure your stepfather will be all right.'

Later that day I was given the unprecedented privilege of being allowed to call Ma in Jersey. She sounded much calmer than my housemaster.

'Don't worry, Mileso. I've spoken to some people at BOAC who've been in touch by radio with their people there. There's a curfew and things aren't much fun, but Europeans are not being threatened and the new regime is keen to get things back on an even keel as soon as possible. I'm afraid there's a nasty witch-hunt going on for people close to the royal family including several people we know well, but apparently the embassies are telling Europeans to stay at home and not to fret.'

Two weeks later Tom was safely in Jersey.

'What was it like?' we asked.

'Pretty dreadful. The old life is finished. They came the second day and took both the shotguns. You're not allowed to drive anywhere outside Baghdad. Poor old Ibrahim came to work a week ago with a lapel button showing a picture of Kassem. I'd never seen Ibrahim looking embarrassed before. I asked him why he was wearing Kassem's picture.'

'Oh, sir,' Tom reported him as saying, 'we must all wear pictures of this Kassem to show that we love him. But how can a man love another man?'

Baghdad, for us, was finished. Tom went back there towards the end of the holidays to resume his job at Iraqi Airways.

The new government was keen for him to stay on and offered him almost twice the salary he had been receiving before. He declined politely and began packing up. He had to leave everything but his clothes behind. The other expatriates were in a similar position so there were few buyers for other belongings. Tom ended up giving away most of our household possessions to Iraqi friends and selling things for derisory prices to the foreigners who had decided to stay on. The Rolls went to an English oil man for a hundred dinars, a dinar being worth slightly more than a pound.

Although Tom was never threatened directly, he knew he was under surveillance. The revolutionaries had been brutal to the top people of the old regime. Some of our Iraqi friends had been tortured and killed. The king and nearly all his family were shot at the palace. Nuri es-Said, the long-standing prime minister and the pillar on which US and UK Middle East policy had rested for over twenty-five years, attempted to flee disguised in a woman's chador. His shoes gave him away. He was caught.

'They half-killed him and then dragged him through the streets of Baghdad behind a jeep to finish him off,' Tom said.

That was the end of my Middle East childhood.

PART II

THE DOOR CLOSES

13

Locked Up in Berkshire

The English boarding school system is brilliant. Few things have served their purpose better. In 1857 Britain suddenly found itself with an empire as a result of the Indian Mutiny, or First War of Indian Independence, depending on your viewpoint. Up to then the foreign possessions of Queen Victoria were either populated by more-or-less self-governing whites who had killed off, inebriated and enslaved the locals in places like Australia, New Zealand and Canada, or by non-whites whom the British had little desire to rule but every desire to trade with. Their exploitation and administration was entrusted to chartered companies of which the East India Company was the biggest and grandest. The chartered companies may have been grand but they and the people who worked for them had the morals of pickpockets.

Following the Indian Mutiny it was decided that the pickpockets should no longer be left in charge. The East India Company lost its mandate to rule India, which along with most of Britain's other foreign possessions was brought under

the direct rule of the Crown. Rule by swashbucklers, bucca-
neers and pickpockets was to be replaced by that of men of
probity brought up to serve the empire rather than themselves. The problem was where to find them.

When there was a demand for something, no one was
quicker and more adept than the Victorians at supplying it.
Just as factories had sprung up to produce textiles and metal
goods, they set up factories to produce people to go out and
govern the empire: Wellington, Marlborough, Cheltenham,
Bradfield, Clifton, Haileybury, Monkton Combe, Malvern, St
Edward's Oxford and Radley were all founded within a few
years of each other to meet this need. What Stephenson was
to the steam engine, Dr Arnold was to the English boarding
school. Thomas Arnold invented the Victorian public school.
He had become headmaster of an older school, Rugby, in
1828, and changed the model. It was this model that was
copied by the new foundations.

Wikipedia sums it up well.

*His force of character and religious zeal enabled him to turn
it into a model followed by the other public schools, exercis-
ing an unprecedented influence on the educational system of
the country. Though he introduced history, mathematics and
modern languages, he based his teaching on the classic languages.
'I assume it as the foundation of all my view of the case, that boys
at a public school never will learn to speak or pronounce French
well, under any circumstances,' so it would be enough if they
could 'learn it grammatically as a dead language'. Science was
not taught, since in Arnold's view 'it must either take the chief
place in the school curriculum, or it must be left out altogether'.*

He developed the Prefect system in which order was kept in the school by the top, sixth, form who were given powers over every part of the school. The novel, Tom Brown's Schooldays, *portrays a generation of boys 'who feared the Doctor with all our hearts, and very little besides in heaven or earth; who thought more of our sets in the School than of the Church of Christ, and put the traditions of Rugby and the public opinion of boys in our daily life above the laws of God'.*

What is missing from this description is the deification of team games. The older public schools had pursued sports like hare-coursing, bare-knuckle boxing and steeple-chasing. Those were not going to train empire builders. Organised team games lay at the heart of a Victorian public-school education: cricket, football, rowing and of course rugby – invented at Arnold's school – were the core sports.

The new schools trained you to be a district commissioner in some far-off part of Asia or Africa, a single white man surrounded by half a million darkies for whose administration, order and justice you had sole responsibility. You had to be self-reliant but not independent in mind or behaviour; your first loyalty was to the team, in this case Team Victoria; you could never show emotion in public; you had to be tough enough to shrug off primitive conditions; you could never ever rat on another member of the team; and you had to follow an arcane and arbitrary set of rules laid down by someone who had never been within 1,000 miles of where you were posted.

Women were unlikely to play much of a part in your life when you were at the age when you most fancied them;

fancying other chaps was fine as long as it was done in a manly way without nancying about. Above all you needed the self-confidence that came from knowing you were part of a superior race and that belonging to that race made you, a twenty-four-year-old Englishman, superior to every darkie in your domain, be he mahout or maharajah. The Spartans had had a similar system 2,500 years earlier.

The Stubbington Tug o' War

Radley and the other Victorian foundations were brilliant at turning out people who met these requirements, but by the time I went there in 1957, after five years of beatings and boredom at Stubbington, England was casting off its empire as quickly as it could. No one had told the public schools. They went on training people to go out and govern the darkies for years after there were no darkies left to govern. This training was not well suited to a late-twentieth-century life work- ing for, say, ICI or British Leyland, which may be why ICI and British Leyland went bust when they were exposed to competition from German, American and Japanese companies whose managers had not had the benefit of an English public-school education.

However, the older schools – Eton, Winchester, Westminster, Harrow – did admit the importance of things beyond getting your cricket colours. Poets and pianists and even aesthetes could flourish at these schools. George Orwell, the reluctant Etonian, wrote in *Burmese Days*, 'The chief virtue of the great public schools, with their traditions of High Anglicanism, cricket and Latin verses, is their atmosphere of literary scholarship and masters from whom one absorbs wisdom unawares.' Radley aped the High Anglicanism, the cricket and the Latin verses (we also put on a Greek play every year) but lacked the atmosphere of literary scholarship and, for the most part, lacked teachers from whom we might absorb wisdom unawares.

At Radley poets, pianists and aesthetes, although no one really knew what an aesthete was, were given a binning. A filthy metal dustbin was procured from under a sink and the victim pushed into it bum first, preferably wearing the suit he wore to matins on Sundays. Sour milk would be poured over him (sour milk was always available as every boy had a seldom-drunk third of a pint provided daily by the government until Mrs Thatcher stopped the practice), and then the bin would be rolled down a flight of stairs with the victim doubled up inside with only his head and feet sticking out. Injuries could and did result, following which the victim would stumble off to the infirmary to have his limbs bandaged and to explain how he had tripped and fallen down the stairs into a milk crate.

The poets and the pianists got the most bullying, but bullying was an equal-opportunity activity at Radley, certainly in E Social. Radley, which aped Eton in many ways – we wore academic gowns and were 'wet bobs' or 'dry bobs' according to whether we rowed or played cricket – did not refer to its houses as houses. They were called socials, and our housemasters were social tutors. Everyone got bullied in their first year. For your first two years you lived in Social Hall, a communal room where some twenty boys had their lockers and did their prep. After that you graduated to a tiny study, which you shared with one other boy.

Most of the serious bullying was done by second-year boys on first-year boys in Social Hall. In addition to binning – common to most socials – each social had its own specific methods of bullying dictated by its topography and equipment. In E Social, or Llewellyn-Jones's, each social also being known by its tutor's name, we had tabling, pushing a boy under the central table and assaulting him with billiard cues and broomsticks from all angles while he lay in a ball trying to protect his tenderer parts; piping, whereby boys would be made to hang from the burning-hot pipe that ran along the top of one side of Social Hall till their hands blistered; and a number of esoteric activities such as forcing a new boy to climb up the fire-escape ladder to the sub-tutor's study and peer in. Mr Goldsmith, the sub-tutor, would look up from doing the football pools, rush to the window as the boy scampered down and lean out. 'Boy, how dare you, you impertinent boy? Go and find Mr Llewellyn-Jones this instant and ask him to beat you.' 'Yes, sir.'

Apart from bullying, beating and buggery were the two other things that distinguished Victorian public schools. Many of my tougher companions got beaten frequently and shrugged it off as a minor irritation. I got beaten frequently and hated it – both the pain, which could be acute, and the humiliation, which was absolute, of being forced to remain bent over an armchair while someone methodically and deliberately hit you with a cane.

There were four types of beating. For minor offences you were caned by the head prefect of your house while the other house prefects looked on and laughed. For more serious offences committed in your social or which brought your social into disrepute, you were beaten by your social tutor. After the Reverend Llewellyn-Jones retired, David Goldsmith took over E Social. I have seldom disliked a man more. He was a small-minded sadist who would sit interviewing you for whatever sin you were alleged to have committed with two canes on his desk, a thick one, the Big Boy, and a more slender unnamed version.

I was once summoned after evening chapel to his study after a house rugby match in which Goldsmith's had played King's. I had been conscripted as a second-row forward in Goldsmith's under-fifteen XV.

'Morland.'

'Yes, sir.'

'You know why you're here, don't you?'

'No, sir.'

'Don't lie to me, boy.'

Goldsmith had both canes on his desk and was fondling the Big Boy with his right hand while he twisted the forelock of his cropped head with his left. He always twisted his forelock when he got excited.

'Do you remember what you shouted out on the rugger pitch today?'

I had no idea what he was talking about but a feeling of dread began to creep over me. This was not going to have a happy ending for anyone other than David Goldsmith.

'No, sir,' I said with perfect honesty.

'Bugger.'

'I beg your pardon, sir? What?'

'You shouted, "Bugger," after you lost the ball and caused a scrum.'

'No, sir, that can't have been me. I never use that kind of language.'

'Don't argue with me, boy, or I shall have to use the Big Boy on you.'

Goldsmith picked up the thick cane and twisted his forelock even more energetically.

'No, sir, really, sir. I'm sure it can't have been me. I mean there were a lot of people on the field, and everyone was shouting for the ball all the time. It must have been someone else.'

'It was you. It was you. Don't lie to me, boy. What would your parents say if they heard you use language like that? Huh?'

'Well actually, sir, they frequently use language like that themselves. I'm sure they wouldn't mind.'

'Ha! There! And you say you never use words like that, but yet your parents do the whole time.'

I had dug a trap for myself and fallen in.

'No, sir. Believe me, I'd remember if I'd sworn on the rugby pitch, and I'm absolutely sure I didn't.'

'You leave me no option,' said Goldsmith, leaning forward, eyes a-gleam. 'I am forced to use the Big Boy. You have brought this on yourself. Go and bend over that chair in the corner.'

The worst beating was from the Warden, as the head-master was called. It was called a 'flogging' and usually administered on a bare bum. This was for capital offences such as drinking, smoking, or being caught in flagrante with another boy.

For offences against school rather than house discipline you would be beaten by the senior prefect. That meant being summoned to Pups' Study, the common room where the pups, the school prefects, lounged around waited on by fags. Each gradation of beating, head of social, social tutor and then Pups' Study, was meant to be harder than the level below it, although Goldsmith took such pleasure in laying it on that any of his social would happily have chosen the worst Pups' Study could hand out over the Big Boy.

Despite the numerous canings I had in my Radley career I was only once summoned to Pups' Study. That was for an 'offence on the river', a serious matter at Radley, where rowing was next to godliness. In the winter term everyone played rugby, but in the Easter and summer terms the wet bobs were required to go out on the river for at least an hour every day. If you were hopeless at rowing, which I was, you went out by yourself in a little wooden clinker-built sculling boat called a fenny after a Major Fenwick, who had invented them.

One freezing March day when the river was in spate from melting snow I sculled all the way upstream to Sandford Lock, a distance of almost two miles. Just below the lock a fork of the river branched left into the weir stream. A bridge crossed this stream. I thought it would be fun to nose the boat into it and up closer to the thundering waterfall and white water of the weir itself. As I edged the boat past the central pier supporting the bridge the current swept the fenny sideways and trapped it against the pier with half sticking out one side and half the other. The weight of the rushing water held the boat firm. The fenny had gone over on to its side when it hit the pier, and I had been tipped into the water. It was icy cold, but I was so busy trying to save myself and the fenny that I hardly noticed the temperature. Luckily I'm a strong swimmer so I had no fear of drowning, but I knew that if I let go I would be swept away, and that if I returned to the boathouse without the fenny I would be in serious trouble.

I struggled for maybe twenty minutes to free the boat. This was made more awkward by the fact that the sculls were still in the rowlocks. I knew that if I freed them they would be lost downstream in the current. Suddenly there was a cracking noise; the boat broke in half and both bits shot off downstream. I was holding on to one and somehow managed to keep hold of that and kick myself over to the other half as we surfed down. I would not be able to keep hold of them for long. The water was raging; I was frozen to the core and exhausted after the battle to free the boat.

By hard kicking I managed to get the two boat halves to a standing depth on the Radley side of the river and dragged them ashore. What to do now? I knew that leaving the pieces there would get me in trouble so I grabbed hold of the riggers of both halves and began slowly wading back to the boathouse. No one could blame me for getting caught in such a strong current and being thrown against the bridge. At least I would be congratulated for getting the pieces back. It was not beyond the skill of the school boatyard to put the boat back together.

An hour or more later, as it was getting dark, I reached the boathouse. My teeth were chattering so hard I felt they could be heard in Abingdon and I was all but dead on my feet. I found Ron, the only boatman still on duty, and explained what had happened. He was not pleased. He asked my name but did not seem worried about the state I was in. We put on our rowing clothes every day at the school itself and then biked 'in change' the three miles or so down to the boathouse. Ron did not offer me a towel or ask if I'd like to get warm. I left him with the pieces of fenny and climbed on to my bike for three ice-cold uphill miles back to Radley.

That evening as I left chapel I was accosted by Donald Legget, the captain of boats and a pup. I was told to present myself at Pups' Study that evening after supper. I knocked on the door.

'Enter.'

I did. The senior prefect and the seven other pups were standing in a semicircle. Legget spoke. 'Morland, you have been reported for returning Boat Club equipment in a different state to the way you took it out in.'

'Yes, Legget. I'm very sorry. The current caught me unawares by Sandford Lock, and there was nothing I could do. It was too strong for me. I tried to save the boat but I couldn't free it in that current. But I did manage to salvage the two pieces and bring them back for repair. I had to wade for two miles pulling them.'

'That's as maybe,' said the senior prefect. 'School equipment has been damaged thanks to your thoughtlessness, and you must now take your punishment. I'm going to give you eight strokes. Bend over that armchair.'

I don't know when beating stopped at Radley. Probably about the time that they realised that they were meant to be preparing pupils for the twentieth, not the nineteenth, century. The old clichés 'It never did me any harm' or 'The little bleeders are the better for it' did not resonate with me.

The dons, as the masters at Radley were called, were a rum lot. None rummer than Cecil Gilbert. Cecil had been an outstanding cricketer and won his blue keeping wicket for Oxford. After Oxford he had gone to teach at Bradfield, where he coached the cricket first XI and soon became a housemaster. Bradfield, like Radley, was a place where housemasters were allowed to beat misbehaving boys. One day screams were heard from Cecil's study. Some boys broke in, thinking someone might be in trouble, and indeed someone was. Cecil was beating one of the younger members of his house and had lost control of himself. Stroke after stroke was slashing down on the small boy, who was trying to defend himself against the onslaught. The boys pulled Cecil off and took away his cane.

After this Bradfield asked Cecil to leave but no other action was taken. He was promptly snapped up by Radley to teach as head cricket coach. He was told that he would never be a housemaster or put in a position where he could beat boys. He was given a small eighteenth-century half-timbered house in the grounds of the school known as The Cottage, where he lived by himself.

Two or three evenings a week he would ask the boys he favoured to dinner at The Cottage, usually by themselves. As a wet bob I was not one of his favourites, but he did ask me to dinner once. I must have been fifteen or sixteen at the time.

Cecil greeted me: 'Hello, Morland. Do come in. May I give you a glass of beer or maybe a sherry?'

Alcohol was forbidden at Radley, and to be found drinking resulted in a certain trip to the warden and possible expulsion, but a blind eye was turned to supper with Cecil.

'And how is that charming bwother of yours – Michael? Such an outstanding boy, a vewy fine cwicketer. In the navy now, I believe?' Cecil had never mastered his 'r's.

Michael, a brilliant cricketer, had been a special favourite of Cecil and a frequent diner at The Cottage.

'Yes, sir.'

Dinner was mushrooms on toast, followed by steak and then ice cream with chocolate sauce, all this cooked by Cecil, who had after years of eating his own cooking become bigger round the middle than he was up and down. He had centrally parted black hair which glistened with Jermyn Street brilliantine. He looked like Humpty Dumpty. Between courses he waddled into the tiny kitchen next door, still talking over his shoulder. Cecil made idle conversation about school events until the steak was on the table. Then he leaned over, placed one pudgy hand on my thigh and fixed me with his beady black eyes.

'You're in Goldsmith's, yes?'

'Yes, sir.'

'I hear that Mr Goldsmith likes beating the boys in his house.'

'Well, I couldn't really say, sir.'

'Oh, weally? And how many times have you been beaten?'

'Gosh, sir, I really don't know. Far too many.'

'Oh, weally?'

Cecil kneaded my thigh. He was starting to pant.

'Huh–huh, and when were you last beaten?'

'Well, sir, about two weeks ago.'

'Oh weally? And how many stwokes did you take?'

'Six, sir.'

None of this was coming as a surprise. When I had told friends that I was going for dinner in The Cottage I had been warned what to expect.

'Only six? Have you ever had eight?'

'I'm afraid so, yes, sir.'

'Ah, ah, and were they eight vewy hard stwokes?'

'Yes, sir, I thought so. Very hard. It was a Pups' Study beating.'

'Oh weally? You must have been a vewy, vewy bad boy. Vewy hard was it? Eight stwokes. Well . . .'

Sweat, or it could have been melting brilliantine, was now coursing down Cecil's panting face.

'Morland?'

'Yes, sir?'

'How many do you think you could take fwom me?'

'Sorry, sir. How many what?'

'Huh–huh, silly boy. How many stwokes of course? How many stwokes do you think you could take fwom me?'

'Oh gosh, sir, I really wouldn't like to think.'

'Shall we have a little game then? A contest?'

'Sir, it is getting late. I think I should be going.'

'No, no. Stay. Let's have a beating contest. I have some canes. They're behind the piano. You choose one, I choose one. Then you bend over and I give you a good stwoke and then I bend over and you give me a good stwoke, and we see who can take the most stwokes.'

'Sir, sir, I'm sure I couldn't take many from you but I must be going.'

Others who stayed longer than I told of Cecil chasing them around the table, cane in hand, trying to catch them a good stwoke. He was so fat that he was easy to evade.

In addition to teaching and being head cricket coach, Cecil was head of the Old Radleian Society. He was also the careers master. So when he was not chasing fifteen-year-olds around his table waving a cane over his head and asking them how many they thought they could take from him, he was thought by the school to be the man best placed to give you advice on what you should do with the rest of your life.

As for buggery, it was difficult to know how much of this went on. If you lock 600 males up together in their most hormonal years for nine months of the year without sight of a girl things are bound to happen. From time to time at Stubbington I would go off with four or five other boys to the loos or to hideouts in the bushes, and we would pull our pants down and inspect each other, but few of us had reached puberty by then and the inspections were driven more by curiosity than anything overtly sexual.

When I went to Radley and reached puberty I started to fancy other boys both older and younger than me. This didn't stop me fancying girls in the holidays, and offered the choice I would have taken the girls over the boys. However, my term-time desires went unsatisfied. No one ever propositioned me and I never quite knew how to proposition other boys. Everyone else appeared to be at it like hamsters. Two or three times a term rings of boys would be caught in flagrante. They would be flogged by the warden, their parents told, and life went on. Whenever one of these groups was uncovered I asked myself, 'Why did no one ask me to join in? I would have been up for it.' But they never did.

But the problem was not the bullying, the beating or the buggery; it was what an English boarding-school education did to your mind. Before I went off to Stubbington I had been hungry to learn. I didn't mind what. My mind soaked it all up. Books, poetry, encyclopedias, dictionaries, long multiplication: I loved it all. Even at Stubbington energy and the habit of learning carried me through the first year or so. I was exposed to the excitement of Latin for the first time. For years I had yearned to learn Latin. But somewhere, probably in my second or third year there, learning stopped being fun. The teachers taught in a routine and unimaginative way. We were there to learn what we needed to get us into public school, the brighter of us with a scholarship. The idea that learning might be fun or involve feeding our curiosity would have been treated with incomprehension.

I wouldn't have minded the absurd rules, the bullying, the discomfort and the disgusting food if my mind had been fed, if there had been something of Orwell's atmosphere of literary scholarship, if there had been teachers from whom I could have acquired wisdom unawares. But lessons which at the age of eight I had relished had become drudgery and boredom by the age of ten. That went on for the whole of my school career. I did not recapture the joy of learning until after I left university.

A couple of years ago I saw the Alan Bennett play *The History Boys*, about a group of sixth-formers at a northern grammar school and their form master, who despised the prescribed syllabus and encouraged the boys to explore every byway and cranny of learning into which their curiosity led them. As a result they loved learning; they revelled in it. I watched with envy. If only Radley had been like that. There the worship of team games and the dreariness of the teaching may have been appropriate for turning out district commissioners, but it also turned us into philistines. England is the only European country where being called an intellectual is an insult.

Today, I am told, the public schools have changed into caring, nurturing institutions that devote themselves to preparing their pupils to lead relevant lives in twenty-first-century England. My first reaction to that is they would say that, wouldn't they? But I sometimes meet friends' children who have been at Radley, Wellington or Marlborough, and most have good things to say about the experience. Beating went years ago, as did fagging. Bullying, they say, has gone too, and as for buggery, most schools are now co-educational, although Radley is one of the few that is still single-sex. As for literary scholarship and wisdom unawares . . .

A strange thing happened during my last two years at school. Radley is one of the great rowing schools of England, and in

1961 Ronnie Howard arrived as the new head rowing coach. Ronnie was a remarkable man who had been president of the Oxford University Boat Club and put together a crew which won the Boat Race in 1959 by an easy margin despite the fact that a number of American squad members staged a mutiny during training. English rowing at that time was done the way it had always been; new training methods were viewed with suspicion. Ronnie wanted none of this. He had seen Karl Adam's German Ratzeburg club win every gold medal available, leaving English crews far in their wake. Ratzeburg had adopted interval training, a method introduced to rowing from long-distance running. Their crews were, as a direct result, superhumanly fit.

When Ronnie arrived at Radley my rowing career was a miserable thing. When I was not being beaten for offences on the river I was sneaking off to play tennis, which I loved. I even got selected for the school tennis team and played at Schools' Wimbledon. However, tennis, not being a team game, was sneered at, and to play it as your main sport you needed to be a dry bob. I asked Mr Goldsmith if I could change.

'Sir, I'm no good at rowing. Could I please have your permission to change to a dry bob so I'll be able to have the time to play tennis seriously?'

'Nonsense, boy. Just because you're not good at something doesn't mean you should stop doing it. You certainly can't change. You must stick to it.'

That was the only thing Mr Goldsmith did for me that had a happy outcome.

I'm not sure how it happened, but in my second-last year Ronnie Howard spotted some well-hidden kernel of rowing talent in me. I was given a trial for one of the top eights, and a year after being beaten for trashing a fenny I found myself rowing number six in the Radley 1st VIII at Henley Royal Regatta. The 1st VIII were the greatest of all the Radley sporting gods, and overnight I found myself transmuted from heckling on the sidelines of school life as a bolshie intellectual to being a rowing deity. The following year, 1961–2, even more remarkably, I found myself Captain of Boats.

I had never excelled at a sport before. I was a reasonable tennis player and my large size and thuggishness had resulted in my being put in the second row of the scrum for the Radley 1st XV, but rowing in an eight coached by Ronnie Howard was in a different universe.

Ronnie had imported the Ratzeburg method wholesale. Interval training involved rowing 500 metres flat out, then coasting for 500 metres before doing another 500 flat out and so on. Sometimes the intervals would be 500 metres and sometimes 1,000. The idea behind interval training is that because you row shorter distances you can do it absolutely flat out, then recover your breath before doing another interval at 100 per cent. It is brutal. The traditional method, whereby you do long stretches of rowing or running without a break, means that for most of the time your body operates below maximum because you are tired. The proof that interval training worked could be seen in every gold-medal-winning distance runner in the 1960s and in the all-conquering German crews.

As the training went on we knew we were becoming fitter than any Radley crew had ever been before. In a boat, when things are going well, eight supremely fit athletes drop their oars simultaneously into the water at the moment of the catch and in a fraction of a second transfer their energy and strength to a drive with the legs, a spring with the back and a pull with the arms, eight people in absolute unison. After a time, in a good eight you can do this with your eyes closed; you just follow the rhythm and eight oars will cleave the water at exactly the same time. You feel as if the boat is sitting up out of the water and flying. The boat is singing, oarsmen say. There are times too, when the wind blows from ahead, the water is choppy, you are tired and the rhythm has gone, when rowing turns from magic to ill-tempered drudgery. But the moments of magic are unique. They are moments when you glory in your own physicality.

Before Henley the 1st VIII traditionally entered one or two preparatory regattas. At Wallingford, as a special test, Ronnie entered us for both of the two top events, the Grand and the Senior Eights. We would be rowing against adult crews from some of the top rowing clubs and from Oxford and Cambridge colleges. We won both events with ease. For Henley we were entered for the Princess Elizabeth Cup, the schools' championship. A week before the regatta there was despondency at Radley when the draw was announced. We had been drawn in the very first round against Shrewsbury, another great rowing school, which had won the event the previous year. This year's crew was unbeaten and reputed to be even faster than its predecessor. They were hot favourites to win the event.

Henley racing is two abreast. You start at Temple Island, a mile and a half downstream, and race for 2,112 metres to finish in front of the Stewards' Enclosure, where the grandees sit in their brightly coloured blazers. Times are taken at three points: the Barrier, after almost two minutes, Fawley, the half-way point, and at the Finish.

We rowed down to Temple Island for the start very conscious of the loud cries of 'Good luck, Radley' from the five hundred-odd Radley boys on the bank. The whole school always came over by train for the first day of Henley. When we got to the stake boat for the start we looked over at the Shrewsbury crew. We knew they were heavier than us but now they looked like giants. 'Are you ready? GO!' came from the umpire.

Shrewsbury shot off at astonishing speed, and after only twenty strokes as I looked across from my number-six seat, I was already opposite a fast-disappearing Shrewsbury rudder. They were streaking further away on every stroke. We, however, had settled into a good rhythm at about thirty-four strokes a minute, while Shrewsbury were rating almost forty, an unsustainable pace. We knew we were fitter, but would they get so far ahead we wouldn't be able to catch them over the second half? By now they were out of sight from my seat. When we passed the Barrier they were almost a length and a half ahead of us. Their time to the Barrier broke the schools' record by three seconds.

Iain Brooksby, our cox, who was later to cox Cambridge, kept us calm. 'Keep the rhythm. They're tiring. We're starting to move on them.'

And so we were. As we approached halfway I could see their rudder starting to appear in the corner of my eye. There is nothing more morale-sapping in rowing than being ahead in a two-boat race and then seeing the other boat starting to move up on you. Shrewsbury were exceptionally strong physically and knew that they only had to hold on to win. Normally over the Henley course crews will wind the rating up for their final sprint as they come to the enclosures for the last minute of the race, but as we came up to Fawley, only halfway along the course, Richard Syme, our wild Irish stroke, began our sprint. This verged on madness. By starting so early, there was a real risk that one of us might collapse.

We passed Fawley. Shrewsbury were still ahead but only by half a length. As we approached the enclosures there must have been a tumult of noise from the Radley contingent but none of us heard it. Our concentration was fixed utterly on the boat and keeping going, running on the reserves Ronnie had trained into us on those interminable afternoons doing intervals. Richard had by now taken the rating up to forty, a rate that is impossible to maintain for long, and we still had a minute to go.

Suddenly we were moving very fast on Shrewsbury. They had nothing left. We had broken them. I saw their rudder alongside me, and shortly after that their cox and then their stroke. It felt as if we were taking a yard on every stroke. As we stormed past the enclosures they dropped further behind. Nothing was going to stop us. We finished a length ahead. Our time for the course broke the record for the event by five seconds. It was many years before another school crew did it faster. Still, sometimes, when I am lying in bed today unable to sleep, I relive that race.

The rest of the Regatta was an anticlimax. I don't remember the other races in detail. We came up against some excellent school crews – Pangbourne, St Paul's, King's Canterbury – but after Shrewsbury we knew they were not going to challenge us and that the cup was ours.

My father, whom I seldom saw, had come to Henley with my stepmother Alice. Their plan was to watch the first day's racing and then return to Scotland, where they lived. My father, who worshipped sports, was so carried away by the excitement of our Wednesday victory over Shrewsbury that he decided to stay on to watch us on Thursday. Alice didn't stay. As it happened, my mother and Tom, my stepfather, were coming to watch that day.

As we put our boat away after the race I saw Ma and Tom standing in the crowd clapping. So was my father, who was on the other side of the boat as we carried it into the tent. When I came out my mother and father were standing about six feet apart, and it suddenly hit me that they hadn't recognised each other. I drew them together.

'Good heavens, Susan. I didn't know you were going to be here.'

'Well, Bunny, how nice to see you. Didn't Miles row well? This is Tom, my husband.'

And we all went off together for tea and scones.

14

Let Out in Oxford

Balliol was my chosen college at Oxford. Ma's father and brother had both been there, and although I knew little about it I had heard it was a place where brains and a contrary spirit were valued. It was also thought to have the highest proportion of Indians and Africans of any college. With my Indian background that appealed to me.

I sat for a scholarship in English to Balliol. At the beginning of December I caught the bus from Radley to Oxford for two days of written exams. Term had ended at Oxford and I was housed in an undergraduate's room. I breezed through the first day of exams, doing particularly well in the Shakespeare paper, or so I thought. I have always thought that *Henry IV Part 1* is Shakespeare's best play and was delighted that the exam questions allowed me to write at length about it.

That night I went out to the White Horse pub in Broad Street and sat drinking beer in one of its tiny rooms with photographs of boat crews and cricket teams on the walls. The pub was crowded with undergraduates who had stayed up after the end of term; they were laughing, joking and arguing. I was intoxicated by the atmosphere and pictured myself sitting there in a year's time as a Balliol scholar. I left to get back to Balliol in time for dinner in the college hall. On the way I bought a bottle of gin.

Next day's papers were likely to be easier. They were general English, and there would be a wide variety of questions about eighteenth- and nineteenth-century poets and writers. As you only had to choose three or four of the topics to write about and you had a wide choice, I was confident that there would be questions I could handle well. None the less I had brought exercise books full of notes and quotes with me, and I sat up till well after midnight, memorising quotes, taking a swig of gin mixed with a little tap water and revising some more. And then taking another swig of gin. At half past one or so I stumbled off to bed, feeling mellow and confident. The gin bottle had no more than a quarter left in it.

I had not drunk spirits since the summer holidays. Other people have described hangovers better than I could ever do. Mine, the next morning, was bad. On a scale of one to ten it must have been close to nine. Somehow I fumbled my way through six hours of exams. The questions were ones I could have well handled in a sober state, but my brain was in poor condition for framing responses. I swore never to drink gin again.

A week later I was home for the Christmas holidays. On 18 December, my birthday, a telegram from Oxford arrived. I tore open the envelope. There had been a mistake. 'We regret to inform you that we are unable to offer you a Scholarship at Balliol. Since you had not previously requested a place we have no vacancies left for the 1962/1963 year but would be pleased to offer you a place for the 1963/1964 year. The Senior Tutor, Balliol College.'

I checked the address. Yes, it was addressed to me. I literally could not believe it. I had been so confident and arrogant it had never occurred to me that I would not get a scholarship. Why I was so confident is difficult to say. I had spent much of my last year at Radley enjoying my new-found and unfamiliar status as captain of boats and school god. I was now head of house and even Mr Goldsmith was nice to me. But I did very little work. I coasted along confident that natural ability would get me through. The telegram told me that my natural ability fell well short of the Balliol scholarship level.

For the next few days I went about in a daze. I'm sure that anyone who knew me well at the time would say that the setback was good for me and helped to replant my feet on the ground, but I have seldom enjoyed things that are good for me. I cursed the gin bottle. If I had not been so stupid as to get myself epically drunk in the middle of the exams I would have been right now getting myself measured for a scholar's gown. It must have been the General English papers, written under a fog of gin, that had let me down.

In early January I was able to arrange to talk on the phone to the English tutor at Balliol who had marked the papers. I asked how mine had been and said how disappointed I was. 'Mr Morland, your papers were not bad, and if there had not been such an exceptionally promising group of scholarship candidates I am sure you would have been up for consideration. Your work, I'm afraid, was patchy. Your essays on general subjects were admirable, and the work you gave up for the General English papers was more than adequate. Your Shakespeare let you down. You seemed to skate over the subject.'

Once more I came down to earth with a heavy bump. So it was not the gin, it was me. The thing I thought I was best at had let me down. I had sailed through the General English papers while the clear and sober answers I had given to my best subject had been deemed inadequate. There were certainly lessons to be learned from the debacle, but I am still trying to work out what they were. I did, however, make one change in my habits as a result: I never drink gin.

At that time the Oxford colleges were divided into groups of three or four for entry purposes. You applied to a group and nominated your favoured college within it. If that one did not want you you could then take your exam papers off to one of the other colleges in the group. Balliol had said they would take me but not for another year and I didn't want to delay. In 1962 gap years were unheard of. It never occurred to me to go off to Thailand and spend a year getting stoned as a precursor to university. If I had thought of it I might well have done, although if I had people would have thought it very odd.

The other two possible colleges in the Balliol group were Lincoln and Wadham, about which I knew nothing, so I trotted off to seek the advice of Cecil, the careers master.

'Wadham??' he thundered. 'Oh dear me, no. No, no. No. I don't think we've ever sent a Wadley boy there. A most unsuitable college. Bowra, the warden, has a vewy unsavouwy weputation.'

This was Sir Maurice Bowra, the famous wit, intellectual and friend of Evelyn Waugh. Wadham, I later learned, had a reputation for being both left-wing and tolerant of homo-sexuality in an era when others were not. Cecil was a faithful Tory and, like so many queers – as they were then called – of his generation, intolerant of public displays of queerdom by others. Wadham, in his eyes, was doubly damned by its politics and sexuality.

'Lincoln, on the other hand, is an excellent place. One of the best of the smaller colleges. We have sent some of our best boys there, some fine cwicketers and even,' Cecil leaned forward and squeezed my knee, 'some oarsmen. Yes, I think you'd be vewy much at home there.'

Academic matters were of no interest to Cecil.

So I took my Balliol papers across the Broad and down the Turl to Lincoln, 200 yards away. Lincoln did not seem upset at playing second fiddle to Balliol and said they would be happy to offer me a place in the coming year and that they looked forward to seeing me in September. I accepted.

I had hated my ten years of boarding school not because of the bullying and the beatings but because of the loss of freedom and the way the teaching had squelched my love of learning. After school Oxford was literally unbelievable. People doing science or medicine or mathematics had busy week-long schedules which kept them bent over desks in classrooms and labs; people doing arts subjects, in my case law, had untrammelled freedom. Once a week you trotted off to see your tutor; he would suggest a subject to look at about which you might like to write an essay and hint

LET OUT IN OXFORD

at books you might consult in the course of doing research for the essay. A week later you returned and read out the essay. My tutor, Brian Simpson, was a remarkable man. He died in 2011; I cut his obituary out of the *Guardian*. It started: 'Brian Simpson, who has died aged 79, was one of the greatest academic lawyers of his generation in the fields of legal history, legal philosophy and – more recently – human rights. His commitment to excellence in scholarship combined with his gift for a good story to make him a superb teacher and raconteur.'

Intoxicated with the unaccustomed freedom of Oxford, I did not take work very seriously. I went to a few lectures but that soon petered out. The last lecture I attended was halfway through my first term. Ironically it was being given by the law tutor at Balliol in a hall which could have held 400 people. The subject was Roman law, which had attracted an audience of about thirty. The lecturer was bent with age and had long flowing white hair. He was also blind. He stood at the lectern reading out his lecture in a frail monotone voice as his hand travelled across his Braille notes. Outside it was a beautiful day and the pubs were open.

After ten minutes one of the audience quietly folded his notebook, rose to his feet and tiptoed out of the room. Then another. The boredom was absolute. I continued to take notes but a few minutes later I too got silently to my feet and crept out leaving the blind lecturer chanting away to an increasingly empty room like an Old Testament prophet.

I am not a regretter but I am sorry about the opportunities I missed at Oxford. If you were in residence at the university you were free to go to lectures given by anyone in any subject.

While I was an undergraduate some of the great figures of the literary and historical world were teaching at Oxford and lecturing regularly. I could have listened to A. J. P. Taylor or his arch-enemy Hugh Trevor-Roper lecturing about history. Robert Graves had succeeded W. H. Auden as Professor of Poetry and gave regular talks to anyone who cared to come and listen. From the older generation A. L. Rowse spoke on history and Lord David Cecil on English. Even the great polymath Isaiah Berlin gave lectures. These were scholars respected across the world who had the ability to hold and entertain an audience not just instruct them. Fascinating and learned people lectured on politics and architecture. What an opportunity. And one I chose utterly to ignore. Unlike Steve Jobs, who said in his famous Stanford commencement speech how fortunate he was to have dropped out of college but to have stuck around on campus. That meant that instead of going to classes that bored him in his required subjects he could drop into classes on any subject that fired his imagination.*

It was necessary to do some work in your first two terms as you had an exam at the end of your second term called Moderations. In law and most other arts subjects, if you failed your Mods, that was it. You were kicked out and not invited back. As far as I could see the law syllabus at Oxford was designed to be of no practical use at all. God forbid that you should want to use it for anything so mundane as to

* One of these was calligraphy, and it was this which gave him a lifelong interest in the subject. When he began making Apple computers it was his fascination with calligraphy that got him to include so many wonderful fonts, a feature later copied by Microsoft. If he had never dropped in to calligraphy classes we would probably today have 5 rather than 205 different fonts on computers.

practise law. Oxford saw itself as an academic institution, not
a vocational school. Somehow I passed my Law Mods, and
after that I and every other first-year arts student was faced
with no further exam until finals at the end of their university career.

Oxford was an easy place to make friends and an easy
place to have a good time; your second, exam-free, year was
a time for doing both. Mine passed in a blur of late nights,
11 a.m. breakfasts in the Covered Market, girlfriends who
never seemed to last very long, twenty-four-hour poker
sessions, pubs, sitting around in the Junior Common Room
arguing for the sake of arguing, afternoons in punts, more
pubs, and sessions of beer and shove-halfpenny in Deepers,
or Deep Hall, the college bar situated in a cellar under the
main dining hall.

Having spent so much time rowing at school and knowing what a time-hungry sport it was – you needed to spend
several hours a day six days a week training if you wanted
to be in a competitive crew – I was not sure how much I
wanted to get involved in rowing at Oxford. But without
thinking too hard about it, in my first term I found myself
rowing in the University Pairs competition and then I put
myself forward for Trial VIIIs. In the winter term trials were
held to select the squad of sixteen oarsmen who would make
up the Blue Boat, as the Oxford crew is called, and Isis, the
reserve crew.

I was selected for the squad, and in January, after Christmas
at home, I presented myself along with fifteen other oarsmen
and two coxes for training. The Oxford crew never trains on
the Isis, as the Thames is called where it flows through the

city, as it is too crooked and too crowded. Instead the squad got in a bus and went to Wallingford or Radley to train. The only problem when we turned up in early January 1963 was that the river had frozen over. Two weeks later people were driving cars on it. There were snowdrifts ten feet high. The winter of 1962/3 was the coldest winter since the Little Ice Age ended in 1740. For six weeks the temperature in Oxford did not go above freezing.

But rowing at Oxford and Cambridge is a serious matter. Ten feet of snow and a frozen river were not going to be allowed to interrupt Boat Race training. We climbed aboard the crew bus in the Broad and set off past mountainous snow-drifts for Henley, an hour's drive away. The river at Henley is wide and straight. It had not frozen over but it did have ice floes the size of ping-pong tables rocketing down on the current. Racing shells in 1963 were made from the thinnest of plywoods, not fibreglass or carbon fibre as they are today. A collision between a racing shell at full stretch and an ice floe would shatter the boat, thereby plunging eight oarsmen and a cox into the arctic water. But that was not going to stop us either. Copper sheaths were made for the bows of the two boats, and we took to the water bow-heavy but safe from being sliced to shreds by the ice. In 1963 health and safety were not a concern.

The cold was so severe that the spray kicked up by the oars froze as soon as it hit your hair. Likewise the oars themselves were soon coated in gleaming tubes of ice. Despite the cold we did not put on extra clothing; in those days rowing in track suit bottoms was considered effeminate. We rowed in shorts, a T-shirt and a dark blue cotton sweater. Gloves were thought a bit girlie. Fortunately rowing is a high-energy sport and our bodies, if not our extremities, warmed up quickly. After ten minutes a watcher from the bank through the blizzard would have seen the shimmering apparition of two copper-sheathed racing shells and sixteen oarsmen with glinting helmets of ice with bodies steaming like racehorses on the December gallops.

Six days a week we made the journey to Henley, and gradually the squad divided into the prospective Blue Boat to row against Cambridge, and Isis, the reserve. It was proving difficult to find the right combination for the Blue Boat. Everyone from Isis was tried at one time or another with the exception of me. Finally the crew was announced, and two weeks before the Boat Race the Blue Boat departed for Putney, where they would spend their time getting used to the Tideway and rowing the Boat Race course to Mortlake. I was disappointed that after ten weeks of training in arctic conditions I had not been selected or even tried in the Blue Boat.

Ten days before the Boat Race I was walking into Lincoln one afternoon when the hall porter stopped me. 'There's a Mr Graham Cooper looking for you, sir. I just sent him along to your room.' Graham had rowed for Oxford in 1960, when the Oxford crew had been selected to represent Britain at the Olympics, and again in 1961. While not one of the coaches in 1963, Graham did a number of things to support the crew. I met him on the way to my room and we went inside.

'Sit down,' he said. 'I've got some news for you. Do you know what this is?' He rummaged around in a grip he had brought with him and took out a dark blue flannel blazer with blue silk trimming.

'Yes, of course. That's a Blue Boat blazer.'

Graham got other things out of the bag: a blue-trimmed T-shirt, a dark blue sweater with crossed oars and OUBC in gothic script above them.

'They're yours.'

Graham rocked back in his chair, hooted with laughter then handed the kit to me. I was utterly bemused, wondering if this was a complicated practical joke.

'Here's what's happened,' he said. 'Toby hasn't been rowing well, and that's been slowing the boat down.'

Toby was Toby Tennant, an amiable and easy-going Scottish aristocrat who was president of the OUBC – the captain of the crew.

'He's spoken with the coaches, and they've agreed that he's going to stand down from the crew. You're going to replace him. I've got your kit here. I've squared it with your tutor so you can leave Oxford before the end of term. Pack whatever you need and let's go. I'll drive you up to Putney.'

We drove up to London with me in a daze. How strange that the only person who had not been tried in the Blue Boat should be parachuted in at the last moment. At that time there was a team of amateur coaches, all old Oxford blues. Most of the coaches in 1963 came from Eton, the most powerful rowing school, but Ronnie Howard, my old Radley coach, was also a member of the team. I knew that Ronnie had a good opinion of me as an oarsman following our win the previous summer at Henley and I could only think that he had vouched for me. Sean Morris, one of the linchpins of the 1962 Radley crew and the most determined man I have ever met, was already in the Blue Boat.

At 9 a.m. the next morning the Oxford crew took to the river at Putney with me replacing Toby in the number-four position. The boat was rowed in a more old-fashioned style compared to the one I had learned under Ronnie at Radley. In the modern way, as practised by the German crews and adopted by Ronnie, the body hardly moved, remaining upright throughout the stroke with all the work being done by the drive with the legs. The Eton style involved a long lie-back at the finish of the stroke. It took me a little time to get used to the old-fashioned way, but after half an hour or so the boat seemed to be moving well, and everyone else seemed to think the rhythm was better than it had been in recent days.

In the 1960s the Boat Race got far more publicity than it does today. The next morning the change in the Oxford crew was featured in all the major newspapers, and I found a large picture of me in Blue Boat kit staring out of the first sports page of the *Daily Telegraph* with the heading FRESHMAN TAKES OVER.

Ten days later we were up against Cambridge. They were heavy favourites to win, with Oxford's last-minute crew change seen as a sign of desperation. I was expecting to be very nervous on the day of the race and I was certainly nervous enough the night before, trying to sleep while knowing that in a few hours' time I would be on television in front of a giant audience.* Everyone expected us to lose, and I hoped that we would not disgrace ourselves.

---

* A few years ago I was helping to find a new sponsor for the Boat Race. This involved knowing what kind of audience it attracted on television. To my surprise it normally attracts about seven million viewers, more than the Derby or the women's final at Wimbledon. That is just in the UK. It is also broadcast all round the English-speaking world.

But once you get into the crew bus to go down to the boathouse, nerves evaporate and routine takes over. You change, carry the boat out, put it in the water, fetch your oars, and then one by one climb on to a little wooden platform to step into the boat, slip your oar into the rigger and wait for the command from the cox to start the easy paddle out to the start. All this is done on autopilot. You have done it many times before.

Toby, now our non-rowing captain, had won the toss and chosen the Surrey station. This gave Cambridge the advantage of the bend for the first four minutes of the race, and then, a minute after that, we would have the Hammersmith bend in our favour. Cambridge were known to be lightning-fast off the start. Their strategy would be to use the advantage of the first bend to get far enough ahead of us to move over and take our water. This would nullify our advantage around the long Hammersmith bend as they would then have us line astern of them. As the umpire raised his flag to signal he was about to start us, I glanced across at the Cambridge crew. They looked enormous and very confident. And there, looking particularly confident in the number-seven seat was Donald Legget, the man who had had me beaten at Radley.

The script unfolded along the expected lines. Cambridge shot off the start and soon I could see their rudder moving out of my sight line as they accelerated away from us. But we had one advantage: our stroke, Duncan Spencer, an iron-willed American who had broken a long string of Harvard victories when he had stroked the Yale crew. We knew how tough Duncan was and trusted him absolutely. He would not be panicked as Cambridge disappeared out of the sight of everyone but our cox. When I watched the race years later on a television replay I realised how far ahead Cambridge had got. They had clear water between us and them. Another six feet and they would have been able to move over safely into our water and leave us bucketing around in their wash.

We never gave them that six feet. As the river first straightened and then the Hammersmith bend began, Duncan shouted, 'C'mon, guys, let's go,' and wound the rating up. Everything came together and the boat began to sing. The rhythm was perfect. When a boat is singing you feel as if you have handed over control of your body to some outside power. You do not feel tired, you do not think about what you are doing; instinct and rhythm drive everything. As Duncan took the rating up we felt unstoppable. And then out of the corner of my left eye the Cambridge rudder came back into sight, and then their stroke man, followed quickly by Legget.

Chris Strong, our cox, was yelling, 'I've got stroke, give me seven. They're cracking. We've got them. I've got seven, give me six,' as he moved past each member of the Cambridge crew. Chris's yells encouraged us, but more importantly we knew they could also be heard by the Cambridge crew and how demoralising they would be.

A minute after Duncan had started our spurt, the Cambridge boat had gone from being a length and a bit ahead to being alongside us. Half a minute later we shot Hammersmith Bridge with Cambridge a third of a length behind. We had rowed right through them and they had no answer. Twelve minutes later we crossed the finishing line five lengths ahead.

In retrospect I should have got out of the boat after what seemed to me the miraculous victory of 1963 and spent the rest of my time at Oxford doing non-sporting things. I might even have gone to listen to Robert Graves giving a lecture. But spending five hours a day rowing or in a bus going to rowing for another year when I had already, six months into my Oxford career, been lucky enough to have been parachuted into a decisively victorious crew at the last moment, seemed like returning to a well which could offer me no sweeter water. And, as Ma would frequently tell me, 'Mileso, you never know when to stop.'

So, six months later, there I was in September 1963 presenting myself once more for Trial VIIIs. As a returning blue I now had an almost guaranteed place in the boat, and we were hot favourites to beat Cambridge. I was so confident I was thinking of rowing with a bottle of champagne under my seat, which I would pop open as we passed the finishing line victorious.

I do not need to tell you the result of the 1964 Boat Race. Cambridge shot away from us at the start, and this time there was no question of rowing them down. They continued to shoot away. At the finishing line they were six lengths ahead of us. Thank God I had not taken the champagne.

I cannot describe the awfulness of losing the Boat Race. If you were to ask Matthew Pinsent, who won four gold medals at consecutive Olympics, his most powerful rowing memory it would probably be the day his strongly favoured 1993 Oxford boat lost to a weaker Cambridge crew. In our case we did not just lose; we were humiliated. Cambridge were out of sight after two minutes, and we knew that we were not going to see them again, but we still had another fifteen minutes of heart-bursting rowing ahead of us. To say that losing the 1964 Boat Race left a sour taste would be an understatement. I could not walk away from rowing with that as my last experience.

Duncan Spencer and I were the only members of the 1963 and 1964 crews who returned for 1965. Sean Morris, my Radley companion who had been in the winning 1963 crew, had chosen not to row in the 1964 boat because he did not like the coaching methods. For 1965 I was elected president of the OUBC, with Sean as my deputy and co-conspirator.

Sean and I decided we would do away with many of the revered traditions that had served us badly in 1964 and take Oxford rowing into the modern world. We asked Ronnie Howard to be the chief coach; he would be using the methods that had been working so well in Germany for Karl Adam. Ronnie was going to do half of the twelve-week final training period, and for the second half we enraged the Oxford rowing establishment by not asking an Oxford blue but inviting Sam Mackenzie to coach.

Sam Mackenzie was a giant Australian who had won the Diamond Challenge Sculls at Henley six times. Sam did his best to annoy the Henley old guard. He would stop in the middle of a race, adjust his clothing, wave at the crowd in the Henley Stewards' Enclosure, the holy of holies of British rowing, wait till his competitor had caught up and overtaken him and then set off again and demolish him; sometimes he swept past the enclosures wearing a bowler hat. We liked Sam's aggressive nature.

We had good material to pick from. Some of Duncan's Harvard-beating Yale friends had got places at Oxford and would be available for selection, and there was a promising pool of home-grown talent. British rowing was doing well in the early 1960s. A crew from Tideway Scullers had won silver at the 1964 Tokyo Olympics, and London University was producing a succession of championship-winning crews which, they liked to say, would crush either Oxford or Cambridge if they ever got the chance to row against us, although it was an unshakable tradition that neither Oxford nor Cambridge ever rowed against another crew over the Boat Race course. My first act after we had settled on the coaching team was to announce that we would accept a challenge from any of the top crews in the country over the full course in the weeks of training leading up to the Boat Race.

Then we had the Mackenzie letter. Five days before Sam was due to take over as Blue Boat coach, Jim Rogers,* who was coxing Isis, approached Ronnie and me with a letter that had been written by Sam to Jim's father, an Alabama business-man. He had fowarded it to Jim with 'Is this guy nuts or am I?' scrawled over the top of it. The letter said that Sam would soon have responsibility for crew selection and implied that he could be influenced to promote Jim to the Blue Boat to replace Mike Leigh, the present cox. Sam had provided the number of his bank account in Henley.

Ronnie and I found Sam after that day's outing. He had been coaching Isis. We asked him to join us in the back of Ronnie's VW minibus.

---

* Jim coxed the Blue Boat to victory next year. This is the same Jim Rogers who later became George Soros's original partner and, after he left Soros, a famous investor and motorbiker, author of the best-selling *Investment Biker* and various other books combining investment with adventure.

I produced the letter. 'Sam, this letter is open to serious misinterpretation. People could say you are selling seats in the Blue Boat.'

Sam, six foot six of solid sinew, snatched the letter from me with a hand the size of a ham.

'Strewth, Miles, you can't think that's serious. It's a joke, a bloody joke.'

'Sam,' chipped in Ronnie, 'we'd like to believe that, but if it's a joke why give the number of your bank account?'

An hour later the minibus was rocking from side to side as Sam threw his mighty frame about, pounded anything he could find to pound and said he could see no reason to resign. Rowing in a Boat Race is one thing but being threatened by the strongest oarsman the world had ever seen in the back of a minibus was a scary experience. Finally we told Sam that if he didn't resign we would have to resign him. He eased his huge frame out of the minibus muttering oaths and telling us we could do what we wanted.

Next day we announced that, owing to a misunderstanding, Sam had decided to resign as an Oxford coach. The press were all over us as Sam was always good copy, but we agreed to say no more and eventually the fuss died down. I was sorry. I liked Sam and I would have loved to have been coached by him. We now had six weeks to the Boat Race and no coach. Ronnie, imperturbable as ever, got permission from Radley to take another four weeks off teaching, and Lawton Fage, a calm, smiling presence who had rowed in Ronnie's 1959 crew, filled in the remaining two-week gap. By then Ronnie had laid such a solid grounding that we were rowing on autopilot.

We knew we had something special, but we also knew that odd things happen in Boat Races, and overconfidence has resulted in many fine and favoured crews being beaten on the day by a weaker crew. The race is different to a timed trial; it is two crews next to each other over more than four miles of winding tidal river with psychology playing as big a part as physique.

Tideway Scullers, a crew of powerful adult oarsmen and indisputably the fastest in England, challenged us to a race over the Boat Race course. We accepted and two weeks before the Boat Race found ourselves on the stake boat at Putney looking across at one of the top crews in the world packed with oarsmen who nine months earlier had won Olympic silver in Tokyo. There had been a lot of talk in the Putney boathouses about the race, and the Scullers had let it be known that they were glad finally to have the opportunity to put one of the Boat Race crews in its place.

I can remember just about every stroke of the race. As had happened so often, we were led off the start but, as was always the way with Ronnie's crews, we knew we were fitter. Just like in the 1963 Boat Race, we were down by just over a length after the first four minutes. Getting back was going to be difficult. We had a crew of Olympic medallists ahead of us, not the 1963 Cambridge crew.

For the next seventeen minutes we swapped the lead. As we approached the finish we were just ahead, and they came at us like madmen. Both crews were flying. They began to close. In the words of *The Times*: 'As they came to the Brewery [a landmark close to the finish] it seemed just possible that they might get on terms. But Trippe [our

stroke] was not having it and Oxford came in at a blister-
ing pace to finish in 17 minutes 37 seconds, four seconds
ahead of the Tideway Scullers. This was a great triumph for
Oxford and must do much to restore the image of the Boat
Race.' Richard Burnell, the *Times* correspondent, himself an
Olympic gold medallist and one who had been critical of
the breaks we had made with tradition, had begun his report,
'Boat Race practice at Putney tends to be prosaic enough.
Just occasionally it has moments of real excitement. This was
one of them. I have never seen a finer row over the Boat
Race course, or a better race.'

The record for the Boat Race course had been set by
Cambridge in 1948 at 17 minutes 50 seconds. Our 17min
37sec had just broken that record by thirteen seconds.

After that the Boat Race itself seemed destined to be an
anticlimax. We knew that on paper we had the beating of
Cambridge, but on a number of occasions the tensions of
Boat Race day have caused an oarsman to black out, allowing
the other crew to sail past. That is one reason why psychology
plays such a large part in the race. We worried that that could
happen to us. One of our crew had blacked out in a race a
couple of years earlier, and we prayed that he would not go
over the edge this time.

The race was held on a very hot day for spring. I had won
the toss and we were once more on the Surrey station on the
outside of the first bend. Cambridge were again thought to be
planning a fast start. As it was, we led them from the start and
moved steadily away. We won by four lengths in a respectable
time, the third-fastest ever, but when we saw Ronnie after
the race he was clearly disappointed. He had been hoping for

a margin larger than the six lengths by which we had lost in 1964. So had we.

The strange thing was that the race was the opposite of the one against the Scullers. Then we had been flying the whole way with the boat in full song throughout. This time, against Cambridge, it felt as if we were going through treacle. Several of us, including me, didn't remember the second half of the race at all; it had been simple drudgery. And at the end, far from feeling ready to race back – as we had against the Scullers – we could hardly summon the energy to row ashore.

We had probably peaked too early; we had probably over-warmed up; we had probably done too much in the days leading up to the race. But we would never know exactly why we had not had a better row. Despite that, the *Daily Telegraph* in its report on the race said, 'This could be the best Oxford crew of all time, though we have seen them going faster than today.'

I stepped out of the boat at Mortlake after the 1965 Boat Race and knew I would not be stepping back into a racing shell ever again.

PART III

THE GROWN-UP WORLD

15

On the Beach in Greece

The first thing I did on leaving Oxford was put off getting a job. Instead I became a beach bum in Greece. I saw an advertisement for a replacement minibus driver for Murison Small in Corfu. Colin Murison Small and a firm called Continental Villas invented foreign villa holidays and the chalet girls who went with them. They rented villas and chalets in Greece and the Alps, recruited girls who wanted something more exciting than secretarial college, told them to cook moussaka and fondue, provided cases of strong local wine, and sold the package to the English middle classes for villa parties. A brilliant idea.

Colin Murison Small's girls were known as Muribirds. There were three Murivillas in Corfu, all close together just up the hill from Corfu town. The villas had a capacity of fifteen punters, six chalet girls and two drivers. There was a VW minibus and a Fiat to take the punters to the beach for the day and into town or up to a hill-top taverna in the evening. I was to be a Muriboy, as the drivers were known.

I went out to replace a previous Muriboy who had dived into the deep end of a swimming pool after too much ouzo. The pool had had no water in it. We crossed at the airport. He looked like a mummy with most of his limbs wrapped in plaster and a bandage at a rakish angle across his head. 'Oh, hello, you must be Miles,' he called from his wheelchair. 'You'll have a fantastic time.'

All the women I have ever fallen for have been the same type – brown hair, medium height, good figure – and there in the departure lounge at Luton Airport waiting to board the Corfu flight was a medium-height brunette with the grace of a butterfly. I found a way of starting a conversation with her and discovered that she too was bound for Corfu and on the same plane as me. And she was going out as a replacement Muribird. I discovered over Marseille that she had a fiancé, a brilliant young barrister, but by the time we had started our descent into Corfu I further discovered that she couldn't decide whether she really wanted to get married, so she had gone away for the summer to give her the time and perspective to think it over. Better news. I shall call her Diana.

Life as a Muriboy was good. Corfu in the mid-1960s was still the island that Gerald Durrell had written about with such charm in *My Family and Other Animals*, an island whose beauty had not yet been scarred by budget air travel. I soon learned my way around, although locating the bumpy goat tracks that led down to Corfu's long yellow-sand beaches took a little time. On beaches where today stand hundred-room hotels and ranks of jet skis there was nothing but a donkey and a lonely bar. After breakfast I would drop the punters off at one of these beaches, where they would spend the day drinking ouzo and burning in the sun, while I popped off to Corfu Town to buy supplies for the villas and to hang out with the Spiros.

St Spiridon is the patron saint of Corfu. Since his body arrived there following the fall of Constantinople it has kept the plague at bay and twice repulsed the invading Turk. The Corfiots repay him by naming their first-born sons Spiro. As a result half the male population has the same name. But, just as in Wales you have Dai the baker and Dai the miner, in Corfu I soon got to know Spiro the electrician, Spiro the builder, Spiro the carpenter, Spiro the taxi driver, and Spiro who went to the airport every day to 'watch the movement'.

The Spiros were very friendly. They plied me with drinks and entertained me to long lunches in the course of which we would argue vehemently about politics. At that stage in my life I was flirting with communism, a creed the Corfiots, with memories of the terrible civil war of the late 1940s, found abhorrent. In exchange I facilitated access to the female punters. Many of the women who came on Muriholidays were single and looking for romance. Some were not finding romance in England. The Greek taste in women is not the same as that of the English. The Spiros could not understand my attraction for Diana, whose graceful and willowy figure they regarded as far too thin. What was more she was a brunette. The Spiros liked women with lots of blonde hair and plenty of meat on their bones. They were not fussy about the other things.

The Muribirds served dinner at a long olive-shaded trestle table in the garden of the largest villa. On changeover days while the new punters were eating I let the Spiros in.

They hid at the bottom of the garden smoking Papastratos. At the end of dinner, while coffee and Metaxa, the cheap Greek brandy that tastes of burned cork, were being served, the punters would get up from the table and wander around. At this point the Spiros leaped from the bushes and presented themselves. It was seldom long before the blondest and fattest of the women was borne back into the bushes. Sometimes Spiro the electrician, ever the romantic, would balance a giant blonde on the tiny pillion at the back of his moped and take her off, squealing and wobbling, to a bar. Everyone was happy, and I was the most popular man in Corfu.

The Spiros at work

I had justified my decision not to get a proper job on leaving Oxford by announcing to my family and anyone else who asked that I was 'writing a book'. This seemed like an excellent substitute. In addition to my slender baggage I took with me to Corfu a small, somewhat dented portable Olivetti Lettera 22 typewriter, which had followed me through university. I loved my Olivetti. On the days when I stayed on a beach with the punters rather than going off to argue about communism with the Spiros I would find a seat and a table in some shade near the bar, order a Fix beer, light up a Papastratos and insert a sheet of paper into the Olivetti.

I was good at beginning novels; in the course of the summer I began ten or fifteen of them. However, they had a habit of stalling after the first chapter. I would create characters, often based on people I knew, and invent situations, usually based on things about which I had no first-hand knowledge. I worried that if I based the situation on something from my personal experience that might be too boring, so I dreamed up more exciting situations that people would want to read about. I sat there in the shade, straw hat on my head, cigarette burning in the ashtray, sometimes two at the same time, a bottle of lager warming in the sun, tap-tapping away at the Olivetti, every inch a novelist.

As page after page of onion-skin paper came out of the typewriter I stacked them under the Fix so they didn't blow away. Once a week I sat down to read the latest wodge. Few novels got further than one wodge. I realised after reading through ten pages of beer-stained onion-skin that if I, the author, was unconvinced by the situation, readers were certainly not going to be. Occasionally a novel reached a second wodge but none ever made it to a third.

Life could hardly have been better. I usually slept under the stars on the flat roof of one of the villas. London and a real job seemed a world away. My horizon was bounded by the Ionian Sea and Diana. Her initial reticence had all but disappeared, and the brilliant barrister fiancé, let us call him Martin, seemed to be dropping out of her consciousness. We lived in the moment, and Martin was far away. The days drifted by, and there was little need to count them – days of Diana, bouzouki music, tap-tapping on the Olivetti, chatting with the Spiros and dancing at Nicky's, a nightclub a short walk from the villas overlooking Pontikonisi, or Mouse Island, a view so romantic when lit by the Greek moon that you could have fallen in love with a cushion.

Then, disaster. News came from London that one of the chalet girls in Tolon had had to return to London and, as Corfu was thought to be overstaffed, Diana was to be transferred there. Tolon was hundreds of miles away in the Peloponnese. The other five chalet girls were fun and pretty, but without Diana Corfu was going to lose its sparkle. I took her to the airport for the flight to Athens, from where she would travel on by Murivan to Tolon, and said a sad goodbye. Both of us had things we wanted to say but were not yet ready to. Our relationship was close to the tipping point but had not quite reached it. The timing of her move could not have been worse.

Then, a miracle. I persuaded Murison Small in London to transfer me to Tolon too. I was instructed to drive the minibus the 700 kilometres from Corfu to Athens, where I was to pick up a group of punters at the airport and take them on to Tolon. This was wonderful. I would have only a two-week gap without Diana.

There was a problem. The brakes on the minibus were shot, and the road from Igoumenitsa, the ferry port on the mainland opposite Corfu, to Athens was a mountainous one. Before setting off I took the VW to a garage. '*Ta frena. Kaput*,' said I in my best Greek. An hour later a smiling man in greasy overalls popped out from under the VW to assure me that *ta frena* were *poli kala* – the brakes were very good.

I set off with two punters who wanted to see Athens. One, Carole, was a psychotherapist seeking romance in Greece who had made it clear that I, not a Spiro, was the person she was seeking romance with. I had mentioned to her as often as I could the existence of Diana, but as there was no Diana to be seen, she took this as a challenge. I was glad that Norman, a delightfully funny Manchester accountant, also wanted to make the trip, so I would not be alone with Carole for the nine or ten hours the journey was likely to take from the time we landed in Igoumenitsa.

The first part of our journey consisted of a long climb up a windy road to the mountain resort of Ioannina. Halfway up it became clear that the brakes were far from *poli kala*. When I pressed the brake pedal there was no firm pressure back but just a squodgy feeling as the pedal went down and further down as brake fluid was expelled. I stopped and crawled under the minibus. Most of the tape that the garage man had wrapped around the tube was now hanging down, dripping.

I told Carole and Norman the situation we were in and said that I would plough on and hope for the best while using the gears to brake the van, but we had a lot of mountain roads ahead of us and at the end we would be driving through rush-hour Athens traffic. The journey would not be without risk, and I would quite understand if they wanted to return to the safety of Corfu, in which case I would be happy to drive them to the Ioannina bus station. They left the minibus for a conference and when they returned announced that they would both go on with me. I am proud of that drive. The ten-hour journey took us fourteen hours, as going faster than 50 mph would have been suicidal. Whenever we passed a garage, and they were scarce in those barren hills, I stopped and bought brake fluid to put in the reservoir and a spare for after that. For the next ten miles or so the brakes would more or less function, particularly if I didn't use them except when absolutely vital, but after a bit the fluid would once more have been squeezed out and we would hurtle on brake-less round the hairpins of western Greece. Coming into Athens at 10 p.m. was a further challenge. If I went too slow a queue of hooting traffic built up behind us, and if I went at a normal speed I knew I would have no hope of bringing the minibus to a halt if the lights went red at a crossing.

How happy we were to ghost to a halt outside the Muriflat in Athens. Next day I asked the Athens Muribird to come to a garage with me. She spoke excellent Greek and explained that the brakes were *poli kaki* – very bad – but she was also able to tell them not to patch the tube but to replace it with another. They found one that fitted and an hour later I sped off with a smile on my face and the squeal of brakes when we came to a corner.

Tolon proved to be a mini-version of Corfu. The two Murivillas were next to each other on a long beach on the outskirts of a tiny village consisting of a handful of houses and a couple of tavernas. There were, it is true, no Spiros, but I soon made friends with a number of the fishermen who frequented the tavernas and found myself being asked to Greek weddings and family parties. How good it was to see Diana. She and I put our mattresses on the roof of one of the villas, where we were undisturbed by anyone else. In the morning we would get up early before the punters were about, drink coffee and fresh orange juice on the roof, and gaze across at Aphrodite's Breasts, a pair of hills on an island half a mile off Tolon beach.

On the beach at Tolon

But the season was winding down. Diana had come out for two months, and it was now time for her to head back to England. One evening after she had finished looking after the punters she and I took a walk down the starlit beach.

'Diana?'

'Yes.'

'Will you marry me?'

'Oh darling, I don't know, I don't know. I don't know what I feel about Martin and I don't know what I feel about you.

If now was the only moment the answer would be yes. But how will it be when we get back to England? My parents are really keen on my marrying Martin.'

Diana's father was a judge, and I knew from our talks how big an influence he was on her life. I could imagine his reaction if Diana told him she was chucking the brilliant young barrister for a jobless Muriboy.

We agreed that trying to decide while we were in Greece made no sense. She would get on with her life without feeling she had a commitment to me and be free to see Martin, while I would get on with mine on the same basis, and when I came back to England we would get together and see how things went.

I drove Diana to Athens airport along with a group of departing punters. At the check-in desk we promised to write to each other; she gave me her special smile, which always seemed to start small and demure and finish up as a grin, and then, with one last shy wave, she disappeared into the departure lounge.

Three weeks later the season was over, and it was time for the Muristaff to check out and return to England. However, I had received word from England that the VW was needed by Murison Small in Verbier in the Swiss Alps for the winter season. I was to drive it to Geneva and drop it off, for it to be picked up later by a winter Muriboy. In fact, I was told by head office, if I wanted to be a Muriboy for the winter season I would be welcome. I was tempted – the summer had been wonderful – but some semblance of sense inserted itself into my brain and I realised that a summer on the beach was one thing, but if I did a winter as well it could be habit-forming. Reluctantly I said no.

The villas closed at the end of September, and the VW needed to be in Geneva by the end of November. I could see no reason to hurry back to the jobless reality of England so I decided to take my time. I would go back to Corfu. Two days later as I drove the VW off the ferry there I saw a knot of people waving at me. It was the Spiros. I was so pleased to see them and touched that even though I had no more blondes to pimp, four of them had come to meet me.

The next couple of weeks passed in a blur of long lunches, longer political discussions and nights at clubs getting ready to close for the season. I met an American woman called Bridget who had been floating around Greece for the summer and was preparing to return to London and then go back to America. I offered her a lift to Geneva and said we could take the train to London from there. She accepted. I said goodbye to the Spiros with sadness; there was much hugging on the dock before we left on the ferry across to Italy.

The drive to Geneva was bad. We left Florence an hour before the sluice gates in the Valdarno Dam above the city were opened to save it from breaking under the weight of water from days of torrential rain. Two hours after we left, central Florence suffered the worst flood in modern Italian history. It was under twenty feet of water, and two million paintings were submerged – as would we have been if we had overslept. We tried crossing the Alps but ran into an early snowstorm, which made the roads impassable until the next day, when we bought chains and tried again.

The Volkswagen leaked, and the water froze as it dripped on to our thin summer clothes. Bridget rubbed my hands as I drove to stop them going numb. When we finally reached the French border post on the Col du Mont-Cenis we were waved through with cries of '*Bon voyage*' from the border guards, who could not believe that anyone would be stupid enough to set out so unprepared. The French had done a better job of clearing the snow than the Italians, so soon I was able to take the chains off and speed on at 55 mph towards Albertville and Geneva. Even a puncture and an icy half-hour replacing one bald tyre with an even balder one did not dampen our spirits.

A day later we were in Geneva. I said goodbye to my faithful minibus, leaving it in a car park to be collected later. Bridget and I caught a train from Geneva to Paris and on to Calais and London.

My Greek summer was over.

16

My Brilliant Career

I was now back in London. It was filled with people who had jobs and places to live. I had neither. It was tempting to call up Murison Small and ask them when the next flight to Geneva was. And then there was Diana. On my second day in London I called her. As soon as I heard her soft voice on the phone memories of the summer overwhelmed me. We agreed that I would take her out to dinner in two days' time. That was good. What was not good was that first I was to have a drink with Mr and Mrs Bowman, her parents. They lived in a set of apartments in the Inner Temple.

Diana greeted me at the door. We hugged and kissed. She giggled nervously and led me into a room which was more like a library than a sitting room. Her parents were sitting in armchairs. They looked at me as I came in. Eventually Mr Bowman got to his feet and extended a hand.

'Good evening, Mr Morgan. I've heard about you.'

'Daddy, it's Morland. Not Morgan,' whispered Diana.

'Good evening, sir,' I said in as grown-up a way as I could muster. Mr Bowman was not a large man, but he had a terrifying intensity about him. 'And I've heard a lot about you, sir, from Diana. It's a pleasure to be here. Thank you.'

I was so eager to please that if I had had a tail I would have wagged it.

'Yes. I expect you drink?'

I looked around to see what they were drinking. Not a glass to be seen.

'Thank you so much, sir. Yes, maybe a small gin and tonic?'

'Gin and tonic?' said Mr Bowman as if I had just asked for heroin. He stalked over to a table in the corner on which there were three bottles. He picked them up one by one, each time stopping to scrutinise the label as if he had never seen it before.

'No gin,' he announced. 'Sherry?'

'Yes, please. Wonderful, wonderful. I love sherry.'

He gave me a withering look.

'So. Diana tells us you left Oxford six months ago and have been –' he paused and looked at Diana '– driving a bus since then. Very unusual. And now what?'

'Yes, yes, sir. I wasn't really driving a bus. I've been working very hard on a book. And I'm thinking of becoming a barrister.'

'Book, eh? Huh. And now you're to be a barrister? When do you start your law course? You've already lost six months since you left university and chose to go and be a bus driver.'

I considered lying but knew the judge would find me out. Thank God I was not up in front of him in court.

'I, um, sort of quite soon, sir.'

'Really? And, if I may ask, young man, where are you doing your course?'

'Ah, yes. Well, sir, there are so many good courses I want to make sure I do the best one. So I've been looking into them. Maybe you could give me some advice.'

'Bah, they're all the same. There's no earthly point in wasting time trying to choose between them. They're crammers. Just get on with it. It's you who have to do the work, you know. Don't think the course is going to do it for you.'

In the course of the next half-hour I was stripped bare by Mr Bowman's questions. Whatever it is that people do to put others at their ease, Mr Bowman was doing the opposite.

At last, my cheeks sore from the rictus grin I had kept on my face, a look which must have convinced Mr Bowman that I was even more stupid than my sycophantic conversation had already led him to believe, Diana said in a bright voice, 'Well, Daddy, this is such fun, but I think we need to go. Miles is taking me out to dinner.'

As we left Mr Bowman gave me another of his withering looks.

'Goodnight, Mr Morgan. May I suggest you do not delay starting your course any further? There are many excellent, excellent and hard-working young men, not much older than you, who are already qualified as barristers. You will be hard put to catch up with them. Goodnight, Mr Morgan.'

Never have I been happier to leave a room.

As we walked to my car, Diana slipped her arm through mine. 'There, that wasn't so bad, was it? I know Daddy can be a bit of a bear, but I'm sure he really liked you.'

I was speechless.

We went to the Bistro Vino in South Kensington, where one of the waiters was a friend from Oxford and I knew I could get an affordable dinner. I was hoping that the rough wine and the smoky atmosphere would take us back to Greece, but it didn't. Conversation was cordial but the magic was not there. Diana had broken off her engagement with the brilliant young barrister when she came back from Greece – this I knew from a letter I had received in Corfu – but I suspected she had been under heavy attack from Mr Bowman.

We avoided discussing the future apart from my assuring her that I would soon be starting law classes.

'I thought you'd decided against that,' she said in a quiet voice.

'Well, I had, but maybe it would be a good thing to do after all. Your dad may be right.'

I dropped her home at eleven. God knows what Mr Bowman would have done if I had kept her out later than that. We agreed to go to the cinema the next night and to have dinner afterwards. I was hoping that once we became used to each other's company again the old flame would ignite. The next night we met at the cinema. Later we walked to a little Italian restaurant. Diana was quiet. She looked tense.

'Oh, Miles. It was terrible last night.'

'Darling, what? Tell me.'

'Daddy. He was waiting for me when I got home.'

'Well, what did he say?'

'Oh, Miles. He said I was making an imperial idiot of myself. Those were his exact words. An imperial idiot.'

'Oh. I see.'

'No, I don't expect you do. What did I think I was doing throwing myself away on this feckless fool who didn't even have a job or the prospect of one and breaking my engagement with Martin, one of the most promising young legal brains of his generation? Feckless fool, I'm afraid that was what he said.'

'Gosh. Wow. Well I mean your dad doesn't even know me. That's a bit hard. I mean I am going to get a job.'

'I know, darling, but you can see his point.'

I could.

We saw each other another two times, but they were uncomfortable meetings. Diana was unhappy and defensive. Her father was a big figure in her life, and although she did not pass on any more of his comments we both knew that the romance of the summer that had meant so much to both of us was sadly no more than that, a romance of the summer. After that we did not meet again, but I would often think of her and her butterfly grace and her demure smile and sipping coffee on the roof in Tolon as the sun rose over Aphrodite's Breasts.

Then there was the job. At one time I had been toying with the idea of becoming a journalist and had indeed spent the whole of the 1964 summer vacation from Oxford working as one. At that time the most powerful and professional newspaper empire was the Express Group controlled by Lord Beaverbrook, a right-wing Canadian who had been close to Winston Churchill and saw himself as the king-maker in British politics.

I managed to get a job working for three months on the newsdesk of the *Sunday Express*, a paper completely unlike the sad relic it has become today. In 1964 it had a circulation of five million and was twelve years into the thirty-two-year editorship of the legendary and irascible John Junor, a man who suffered fools not at all and a newspaper genius with an eye for spotting talent. I was bewitched by Fleet Street. Beaverbrook loved to hire left-wing journalists at high salaries and nudge them into writing for his right-wing newspapers. A political columnist on the *Sunday Express* was the brilliant Alan Watkins, a lifetime left-winger and a particularly acute observer of the absurdities and hypocrisies of British politics. Alan used to take me along to El Vino's, a Fleet Street drinking den where women were not allowed to stand at the bar and political journalists met to tell each other stories. I hovered at Alan's elbow, intoxicated by the excitement of listening to the great men whose columns I had been reading for years.

I was tutored by Brian Vine in submitting my expenses. Brian went on to become managing editor of the *Daily Mail*, although his most famous period was as New York correspondent for the *Daily Express*, a job from which he is reputed to have been recalled when the management in London heard that he was keeping a string of racehorses on his expense account. Brian saw me submitting a claim for the reimbursement of some Tube and bus expenses.

'Dear boy, at the *Express* we never submit Tube and bus expenses,' Brian told me, scanning my form through his monocle.

'Oh, sorry, but I don't want to be out of pocket. I'm pretty broke.' I was trying to live on the fifteen pounds a week that the *Express* was paying me, of which I had eleven pounds and ten shillings left after they deducted tax.

'Out of pocket? We are never out of pocket. You're on a national newspaper now. Give a taxi driver a couple of bob and ask him for some blank receipts. Then you can fill them in yourself. Dear boy, you can get around on a bicycle for all I care but on the *Express* we always charge for a taxi. Unless you want to charge for a limousine.'

The deputy news editor was Dudley Smith. When he was not doing that he was Member of Parliament for Brentford and Chiswick. An election was due in October 1964 so Dudley took leave of absence from the paper to campaign. I was asked to sit in his seat while he was away and cover as many of his duties as I could. The most frightening of these was to read all the newspapers – there were nine dailies at that time – by 9 a.m. every morning and to cut out the best version of each story and present these in a folder to John Junor, the editor, by 10 a.m.

Everyone lived in terror of Junor but he was always charming to me. My innocence about the ways of Fleet Street may have appeased him. I would tiptoe into his huge corner office on the third floor of the black-glass *Express* building and put the daily folder in front of him. He would usually be on the phone. As I tried to escape he would wave a hand and motion me to sit down. Then, when he had finished his conversation, he would look at me over his glasses and say, 'Och, well, laddie, what's happening today? What does the mighty *Times* think is important, eh?'

One day Alan Watkins asked me into the office which he shared with another political reporter.

'Now look, Miles, there's an election coming up in six weeks' time. All the other papers have pollsters doing work for them, Gallup, National Opinion Polls, people like that, so they can tell their readers who's going to win. We've got nothing. So we're going to do our own *Sunday Express* poll, and I'd like you to take care of it. I'd like you to get in touch with our stringers in the 250 most marginal constituencies, the ones which could possibly change hands, and find out who's going to win the election in that constituency and what the most important issues are.'

I assumed this was a make-work project to keep me busy and give me something interesting to do before I went back to Oxford in early September. Nevertheless I had a form printed up, which I sent to the *Sunday Express* stringers in the relevant constituencies. Alan had given me a list of constituencies and I got the stringers' details from the news editor's secretary. In your judgement, I asked the local stringers, who will win the election in your constituency? And, I asked, what are the most important local issues? I named several, such as inflation, cost of living, immigration and housing.

The forms were duly posted with a return envelope marked with my name. All national newspapers employ stringers, usually reporters for local newspapers who get a small retainer from the national in return for being available to send them a report if there is a local incident worthy of national coverage. They can go for years without being contacted. After ten days eighty of my two hundred and fifty forms had been returned. I set about calling the non-repliers.

'Hello, is that the *Western Telegraph*?'

'Yes, *Western Telegraph* here.'

'May I speak to Rhys Davies please?'

'Ah, now, we've got two of those. There's one in the print shop and there's young Rhys who runs messages. It won't be him you're after.'

'Er, no. Thank you. *Sunday Express* here. I'm looking for a Mr Rhys Davies on the newsdesk.'

'Oh, poor boy, no. That's terrible. He was a lovely boy. Liked a party.'

'Sorry?'

'Oh, you didn't know then? Poor lad. We lost him six months ago. Had a heart attack and hardly fifty. But he did like his drink. Terrible business.'

'I'm so sorry. Could you put me through to the newsdesk in any case?'

I would then speak to whoever picked up the phone. It may have been the star reporter or the messenger boy. I had a 170 calls to make and this was no time to examine people's credentials. I'd explain who I was and how I had been hoping to speak to Rhys but could they help me instead? Usually they were only too delighted to give me a detailed rundown of exactly what they thought would happen, and I would fill in the form accordingly. In some cases the newspaper where the stringer was meant to work had ceased to exist so there was no one to speak to.

I had a week left to finish my poll and seventy forms were still uncompleted. I did not want to get caught doing them myself in the office so I took the forms home to my five-pound-a-week bedsit in Earl's Court and filled half of them in sitting on my bed and half at the Troubadour coffee bar in the Old Brompton Road. I had no idea who was going to win in Carmarthen West or Maldon, but as this was just a make-work project, I could not see that it mattered.

The *Sunday Express* was closed on Mondays so the following Tuesday I handed my sheaf of forms over to Alan. He gave them a brief look and me a quick 'Thanks, Miles' and stacked them on a table by his desk. I imagined it would be a short journey from there to the waste-paper basket.

I left the paper two days later to return to Oxford before term started. That Sunday I bought the *Sunday Express* curious to see if Alan had mentioned my 'poll' in the 'Crossbencher' column that he had made famous. I turned first to that without checking the rest of the paper. No mention. Ah well. So it did go in the waste-paper basket. I then had a quick look at the front page and did a double-take. There, topping the lead story, in letters an inch high, was the headline TORIES TO WIN BY 26. It began, 'The *Sunday Express* team of political analysts has been conducting an in-depth survey into voting trends throughout the country. Every marginal constituency has been assessed . . .'

The poll created something of a sensation and was widely reported on the television news and comment programmes. Most of the other polls were pointing to a hung Parliament or a Labour victory. No one but the *Sunday Express* saw the Tories winning by that kind of margin. There was particular surprise at some of the analysts' findings. Who had suspected that immigration was an issue in North Norfolk and that defence was on the minds of the good folk of Berwick? These of course were forms I had filled in at random at one in the morning in the Troubadour.

A month later Harold Wilson and Labour won the election with a majority of five.

I had loved my time on Fleet Street. It was a wonderful place to work. The people were witty, original and seldom took themselves or anything else too seriously. Every journalist knew extraordinary stories that never found their way into the papers, and being privy to those was exciting. But journalism was a cynical profession. Time after time the *Express* would print stories that were not strictly untrue but presented in such a way that they gave a false impression and usually ruined someone's life in the process. Despite that when I got back from Greece I contacted various newspapers and asked if they had a job on their City pages, thinking these were likely to be less cynical than the general news pages.

I had met Kenneth Fleet in El Vino's in 1964. He was one of the great Fleet Street City editors of the era and did much to move British financial journalism away from sycophantic puff stories towards investigative reporting. He was starting a new column on the *Telegraph* called 'Questor'. This was modelled on the 'Lex' column in the *Financial Times*, which reviewed four or five company stories every day and delighted in puncturing corporate reputations. Fleet remembered me and asked me to come in to see him. Despite the fact that my ignorance of matters financial was total, he offered me a job on the new column. I said I would think about it and get back to him; I was very honoured to be given such an opportunity.

I had also thought about a career in television. Two years earlier I had captained the Lincoln team on *University*

Challenge. While at Granada, which made the show, I got to know the man who was producing *University Challenge*, and he took a liking to me, introducing me to the woman who ran the Scripts Department at Granada. Despite its mundane name this was responsible for programme development and thus critical to the company's future. She and I hit it off instantly. She was very bright and very funny, and offered me a job at Granada. This was tempting. In those days television was glamorous. Again I said I would think about it.

The job on the *Telegraph* paid £850 a year and the job with Granada £925. I thought I ought to look around and see if I could find something that paid a little more as I did not want to rely on handouts from Tom and Ma and I would find it hard to get by on less than £1,000, so in December I made the trip to Oxford to see the Oxford University Appointments Board. 'Mr Morland, most of our jobs went six months ago to people who graduated in June, as you did. What is it you say you have been doing since then?'

'Foreign research. I have been abroad researching a book project but I have decided to put that to one side and concentrate on getting a job.'

The adviser pulled out various files and went through them shaking his head. 'That's been filled. No, one of ours took that. They're no longer looking.' After fifteen minutes he had three suggestions. There was still an opening at Unilever as a graduate trainee, probably in Nigeria; there was a job in insurance as an average adjuster; and there was a firm called John Govett, which managed investment trusts in the City, which needed an investment analyst.

Nigeria, which had just got its independence and was busy getting rid of the British, did not appeal. Insurance sounded boring, and I had no idea what an average adjuster was, so that left John Govett. They sounded boring too, and I did not know what an investment analyst was either, but on the file was a letter from someone I knew, Duncan Fitzwilliams, who a year earlier had joined Foreign and Colonial, John Govett's neighbours in London Wall and a similar firm, saying how much he enjoyed his work and recommending the job at John Govett.

I went to see them. It was a small firm employing about fifteen people. The interview process was not an arduous one; the firm had five partners of whom I saw three. I stressed the fact that I knew nothing about the financial world and had no idea what the difference between a stock and a bond was.

'Don't worry, Morland; you'll be amazed how quickly you'll pick it up,' I was told by Derek Baer, one of the partners. 'None of us knew anything either when we started. Now, I see on your curriculum vitae that you rowed in the Boat Race. What was that like?'

It was clearly my rowing blue rather than my potential financial acumen that intrigued them. They offered me the job at £1,100 a year and I took it.

17

Gassed in Washington, Married in London

I have always wished I had had a proper training in the financial world instead of being left to pick it up on the job at John Govett. Despite a lifetime of dealing with investments, I still find myself bluffing my way around a balance sheet. I soon went from John Govett to Schroders, then one of the great London merchant banks, where I was assigned to the American desk, responsible for managing their US investments, which I found far more interesting than the parochial world of British investing. Schroders assumed I had had some training at John Govett, so the bluffing continued.

The American investment world was huge and fascinating. It had brilliant companies like Kodak, Xerox, IBM and Polaroid, far more exciting than the dinosaurs of British industry. I changed jobs again and joined the London office of one of the oldest of the big New York investment banks,

Kuhn, Loeb.* They sent me to New York for six months' acclimatisation at their head office.

In 1970 the USA was in turmoil. Thousands of young people were being drafted every month to fight in the Vietnam War. Demonstrations against the war were brutally suppressed by the police, while the draft, which became increasingly difficult to evade, meant that few families in the US did not have a member involved in the war. Despite or maybe because of the turmoil, New York was an exciting place to be. This was the era of flower power and love-ins. One weekend in May 1970 I caught a train to Washington from New York with a group of young friends from KL to join a demonstration against Nixon's invasion of Cambodia, a country on whose seven million people the US dropped 2.7 million tons of bombs compared with the 2.0 million tons dropped by the Allies in all of World War II. A million of us massed in front of the White House, sang songs, some of which I knew from the Aldermaston marches, and listened to speeches from 'Hanoi Jane' Fonda and Dr Benjamin Spock, the baby doctor. Then we sat down at a major crossroads and stopped the traffic. The police, instead of beating us up, as we had been expecting, treated us with humour and tolerance as they dragged us off.

---

* Kuhn, Loeb and J. P. Morgan were once the two dominant firms on Wall Street. In the first half of the twentieth century KL had transformed America. Two partners, Otto Kahn and Jacob Schiff, had been the main financiers of the US railroad system and another, Paul Warburg, created the Federal Reserve. When I worked there it was living off its reputation, and later it suffered the ignominy of a forced merger with what its partners saw as the upstart firm of Lehman Brothers.

Bored with stopping the traffic, we decided to storm the White House. All around it yellow school buses had been parked nose to tail to form a barrier. Platoons of National Guardsmen were on the lawn of the White House chatting and eating sandwiches. With cries of 'No more war, no more war' we ran at the empty buses and began climbing up and over them. On the lawn the National Guardsmen put on their gas masks and prepared to fire CS gas canisters. *Pfooff, pfooff, pfooff* – soon the air was dense with tear gas. I had never been gassed before and never since.

Tear gas is astonishingly effective. Your eyes tear up immediately (hence the name) and you are forced to shut them; you cough uncontrollably; your nose blocks and your skin stings. We clambered blindly off the buses and ran as far away as we could. People with water were wetting handkerchiefs and holding them over their faces. Some people were peeing on handkerchiefs and using them. I just ran.

That evening thousands of us streamed back to Union Station to catch trains back to New York. I had somehow been reunited with my gang despite the fact we had been scattered by the gas. It had been a very hot day for May with shade temperatures into the nineties and we were looking forward to the air-conditioned coolness of the trains. When we were allowed to board a train we found that the temperature inside was so hot it was close to unbearable. A conductor came by and we asked him what was wrong with the air conditioning.

'Son,' he said, 'Penn Central don't like passengers, and they particularly don't like you kids, and they sure as hell don't like their trains being used for your demonstrations. This train has been sat out in the heat all day. I'm told they put the heating on and the driver has instructions not to use the air conditioning. I'm sorry, but there ain't nothing I can do.'

The conductor was in a thick blue serge suit and close to melting. There must have been over a hundred people in our carriage, none of us over thirty, and unlike the conductor we had no need to keep our clothes on. We stripped down to our underwear, opened six-packs of beer, sang anti-war songs and danced our sweaty and near-naked way to New York. A month later, on 21 June, in the biggest collapse in corporate history, Penn Central filed for bankruptcy.

One afternoon I was sitting in the research department of Kuhn, Loeb flicking idly through telexes from the London office when someone shouted that I had a call. I picked up the nearest phone.

'Hello,' said a bright American female voice. 'It's been difficult tracking you down. No one knows who you are. Is this Miles?'

'Yes.'

'Hello again, I'm Debby. We haven't met, but my friend Stephan tells me that you're a nice guy and you've just arrived in New York and you don't know anyone. He said I should invite you to dinner. How does Thursday look?'

My Thursday was as empty as my Wednesday and my Friday, and so three days later I found myself ringing the bell of a handsome brownstone in the East 70s. Debby was a bewitching woman, the daughter of a Wall Street banking titan. She was married to a successful English investment banker famous for his easy-going charm. However, they had been together for several years and for Debby the charm was wearing thin. She was having an affair with Stephan, who worked at Kuhn, Loeb. Stephan was an elegant aristocratic German who did a bit of investment banking in the morning and spent the afternoon making love to the wives of Wall Street bankers while their husbands were doing deals.

One afternoon Stephan had said to Debby, 'Oh, by the way, there is this nice young English boy who has come to work at KL. It's a bit sad but he knows nobody in New York. You should ask him to dinner.' And so she did. When Debby called I had asked if Stephan was going to be there. 'No, sweetie,' she said. 'He's not exactly welcome in the house with my husband.'

There were sixteen people there. As we had drinks I was overawed by my fellow guests' sheer glossiness and elegance. Then I noticed a woman with long brown hair who was standing on the edge of a group not saying anything. I made my way over to her and introduced myself. 'Yes, Debby told me about you. You're the brilliant English investment banker who's just joined Kuhn, Loeb.' Tony Thorne, my boss-to-be in London, would have been surprised to hear his new junior equity salesman described that way. She was called Guislaine. I was delighted to find I was sitting next to her at dinner.

We chatted away happily, and I asked Guislaine where her exotic name came from. She told me she had a French father, Guy, and that the 's' in Guislaine was silent. Her mother, she said, was Irish-Australian, a writer and singer and artist and, as I discovered later, an enchanter of men. Things took a backward step when I learned that Guislaine was married to someone called Bobby, the black sheep of a rich Long Island family, but improved when I learned that he was twice her age and she was his fourth wife. They had been separated for over two years.

I asked her to dinner the next night. She accepted. I wanted to appear cool and not too Wall-Streety so I booked a table at Elaine's in the East 80s, then just starting to gain a reputation as a literary haunt where you might meet Woody Allen rather than go to for the food. I picked her up in a taxi. I announced myself to the person at the desk and said, 'Morland, for two.' 'Sir, no, we've got you at a table for eight.' Just as I was about to remonstrate Guislaine chipped in: 'Oh, sorry. I meant to tell you. I asked a few other people along as well. Hope you don't mind.' I did mind. I had been looking forward to an intimate *diner à deux* and suddenly I was going to be sharing Guislaine with six other people. 'Thought it might be more fun for you,' she said.

We were at a large round table and I was not even sitting next to her but two away. Between us was Stephan with a tall blonde model, while the rest of the table were friends of Guislaine. Everyone was polite to me and asked questions about what I was doing and where I came from, but all I wanted to do was to talk quietly to Guislaine.

Finally, as coffee was being served, I leaned forward and waved at Guislaine through the cigarette smoke and the Valpolicella bottles.

'Yes?' she said, smiling.

'Will you marry me?'

'What?'

Stephan raised an elegant eyebrow and intervened: 'No, Miles, no. Please. Not here. This is not cool.'

'Will you marry me?'

'Don't be silly. I'm still married to someone else.'

Before I could take in what was happening there was a pushing-back of chairs and a paying of bills and a putting-on of coats. Two minutes later there was a slamming of cab doors and I found myself alone on Upper Second Avenue.

The next day Stephan took me out for a drink after work. We sat in Delmonico's on Wall Street drinking his favourite bourbon, Wild Turkey, on the rocks with a twist of orange peel.

I asked him what I should do about Guislaine.

'Ah, Miles, you English boys. Always in such a rush. Don't crowd them. The girls don't like it. Let them come to you. There are lots of women in New York; you have the summer ahead of you. Take it easy. Guislaine is a lovely woman but don't hurry.'

He ordered another Wild Turkey.

'And, Miles . . .' He leaned forward.

'Yes.' I leaned forward too. I was about to learn Stephan's secret.

'No more of this silly marriage talk.'

I persisted with Guislaine though not with the marriage talk. We spent weekends with friends in Southampton; we saw each other almost every night. I was due to go back to London in August, so I sent a telex to Tony Thorne, explaining that I had fallen in love and asking if I could stay in New York a bit longer. Of course, telexed Tony. A happy employee was a good employee. Would another two months be enough?

I had never felt this way about a woman before. With Diana I had never been certain; with Guislaine I was. But then things began to go wrong between us. It was no one's fault but soon we could not be together without twisting knives in wounds. We stopped seeing each other, and in November I returned to London. I heard from Stephan, who would visit the London office from time to time when he was 'working on deals', that Guislaine had a new boyfriend and that he had moved in with her. I wrote Guislaine a couple of chatty letters and received brief but friendly replies. The following June I was going to New York for a week to visit head office, so I called Guislaine a week before I left.

'Hello, Guislaine? It's Miles.'

'Oh, Miles, hello. What a surprise. How are you?'

'Just great. Look, I'm going to be in New York next week. I've heard from Stephan that you have a boyfriend and I hope that's all good, but it would be lovely to see you. How about lunch?'

'Yes. Why not? That would be nice.'

We agreed to meet at one o'clock at an old haunt of ours, Gino's, an Italian restaurant diagonally across the street from Bloomingdale's. It managed to be noisy, busy and cosy at the same time.

I caught the Lexington Avenue subway up from Wall Street and arrived fifteen minutes early. I sat at a table and ordered a vodka Martini on the rocks. Guislaine arrived. Food arrived, wine arrived; food went, wine went, and for three hours the two of us sat there talking nonsense but happier than we had ever been. All we lacked was a chorus of violins in the background.

Next day I had to return to England, but the following weekend I was back in New York, this time not for business but to see Guislaine. The weekend went quickly, and a week after that, on 16 September 1971, Guislaine packed up and came to live with me in London. Six months later, on 10 March 1972, we did get married.

It was almost bigamy as her divorce from Bobby took a long time to come through. We were told it would happen in January so we felt confident sending out wedding invitations for March, but by February she was still legally married to Bobby. Guislaine and I then made a quick trip to New York as I had to go there on business. One night we went to a movie and then for a hamburger at P. J. Clarke's on Third and 55th. As we went to our table, Guislaine hissed, 'It's Bobby. Over there. At the bar.' And so it was. Her husband was sitting by himself at the bar drinking Scotch on the rocks.

'Shall we say hello?' I asked.

'No. I don't want to talk to him.'

'Maybe he could help get the divorce expedited.'

'Doubt it.'

A few minutes later Bobby rose unsteadily to his feet and began to negotiate his way through the crowded bar to the men's room. As he passed our table he looked down.

'Why, Guislaine. I'll be damned. How are you?'

'Hello, Bobby,' said Guislaine.

'Mind if I sit down?' he said, lowering himself into a chair. 'Well, I hear you're marrying some English guy, Miles Quintin Morland the third, for his money.'

'That's me,' I said.

'Oh, hi. How're you doing?' Bobby shook my hand warmly.

'By the way,' I said, 'I'm a fraud. I'm not the third, and I don't have any money.'

Bobby rocked with laughter as if this were the funniest thing he had ever heard.

'Oh, that's great, man,' he gasped 'No money and not the third. You gotta like it. What're you drinking?'

Bobby and I got on splendidly, but after half an hour Guislaine, who had been looking increasingly uneasy, suggested he leave.

'Sure, sure,' said Bobby. 'I was on my way to the john anyway. Good luck, guys. No money . . . I love it.'

And that was the first and last time I met my predecessor as Guislaine's husband. A week later, at the end of February, her divorce came through.

Two years later Tasha was born. I had gone to the hospital to be by Guislaine's side but was unprepared for fatherhood. I picked Tasha up gingerly. I looked at this amazing, tiny-but-perfect creature in wonder. My daughter. After a minute or so, terrified that Tasha might break if I held her wrong, I handed her back to her mother.

England in the early 1970s was as depressing as a country could be. The febrile excitement of Swinging London and the 1960s – when if you lived in London you felt anyone could do anything – had given way to a time when you felt no one could do anything. The financial world in which I worked had all but ground to a halt by 1973. During the three-day week we sat in an office lit by candles. Guislaine and I decided we would move back to America and try our luck there.

Wall Street was an exciting place compared with the City of London. The hottest firms in New York were the new, fast-growing 'research boutiques', which specialised in supplying research to the huge investing institutions. In return the investing institutions channelled their buy and sell orders through the boutiques rather than the more traditional investment banks, which had little to offer in the way of insight and advice. The buy and sell orders generated commission, and at that time Wall Street commission rates were fixed, allowing everyone to make a healthy living. However, in early 1975 fixed commission rates were to be abolished, and rates were likely to plunge once they became negotiable. In that environment, I decided, the firms that prospered would be the specialist research boutiques which had something additional to offer.

I bought myself a ticket to New York and cold-called three of the top research boutiques: Wainwright; Spencer, Trask; and Mitchell, Hutchins. I also had an interview set up by a friend at Goldman, Sachs, then one of the coming firms but lower in the pecking order than Wall Street aristocrats like Morgan Stanley and Kuhn, Loeb. The first interview was at Goldman; this was not a success. 'No, I'm afraid we have nothing for you. You don't have enough qualifications for Goldman. And can I give you a piece of advice?' 'Yes, please.' 'Get your shoes shined before you go to an interview.'

I took this advice and presented myself with gleaming shoes at Wainwright and Spencer, Trask. They were intrigued but unwilling to offer me a job in the US, where I had no useful connections. If I wanted to join their London offices they might have an opening.

Mitchell, Hutchins was my last chance. This was the hottest of all the boutiques and the number-one investment research firm in the US. I arrived at 9 a.m. for an interview with Bill Lorenz, their top equity salesman. Bill was quite unlike anyone I had met on Wall Street before: informal, quick, funny, brilliant and a lateral thinker. The interview was like a furious ping-pong game as we bounced ideas off each other. When our hour was up Bill asked me to wait in his office for a moment while he went off to talk with someone else. Ten minutes later he was back.

'Hey, Miles, when are you going back?'

'I've got a six o'clock plane today.'

'No, you haven't. I'll get my secretary to change it to tomorrow morning. We've got you set up with a day of interviews here.'

I was taken to lunch in the Downtown Athletic Club by Jed and Marty, two senior Mitchell, Hutchins people. Jed had flown a helicopter gunship during his Vietnam War service.

'Miles,' said Jed, 'why do you want to come here, where you know no one, when you've already got a great franchise in London, where you know everyone? I don't get it.'

It was a good question. I tried to explain how dismal 1973 London was.

'Jed,' said Marty, 'give him a break. Don't be such a hard-ass. England sucks. OK?'

By five o'clock I had had nine interviews and was giddy with exhaustion and jet lag. I was shown into the office of John Engels, the head of sales. Surely I was going to get a job offer.

'Look, Miles, sorry. Can't talk now. Too much going on. Meet you at seven. Carlyle bar. OK?'

At seven, exhausted but exhilarated, I was at the bar in the Carlyle. Mitchell, Hutchins was markedly different in style to the formality of Kuhn, Loeb. It had the energy of a sports team but the ethos of an ivory tower.

John tapped me on the arm. 'Hi, Miles, let's find a table. This is Dick Falk.'

Dick, it turned out, was John's backup.

'What are you drinking?'

'Oh, it's been a long day and I've got a bit of jet lag. Just an orange juice.'

'An orange juice? Don't be a pussy. Have a proper drink.'

'Oh, OK. Wild Turkey on the rocks.'

'That's m' boy.'

John and Dick both ordered beers. They sat there sipping while I gulped down my Wild Turkey. John ordered me another one. The chat was just general Wall Street stuff about the changes taking place, the likely effects of negotiated rates and the consolidation of the industry that would follow that. I was desperate to hear whether I had a job or not but didn't feel it was up to me to bring the subject up so I had another Wild Turkey.

John looked at his watch. 'Hey, let's grab some dinner.'

Dinner was in an Italian restaurant three blocks away from the Carlyle. I bumped into a fire hydrant on the way there and hoped that neither John nor Dick noticed. Walking and talking were both becoming difficult.

As soon as the antipasti were served – along with another bourbon, which had been ordered for me – John and Dick turned tough.

'Look, Miles, you're an interesting guy but we'd be crazy to hire you to work over here,' said Dick.

'He's right,' John chimed in. 'We've got the top talent on Wall Street beating on our door. We can have anyone we like, all the top producers. These are guys with a proven record. And you? Yeah, as Dick says, you're smart and I like you, but, hey, can you imagine what it would be like if we sent a Limey like you down to call on clients in Texas. Wooo-eee, with an accent like yours they'd think you were a faggot.'

Normally I would have tried to defend myself against such a verbal battering but I just smiled. I was past talking.

'Do you know how tough it is at Mitchell, Hutchins?' John asked.

I smiled again and tried to cut up my veal piccata.

John looked at Dick and shook his head. 'Dick, this is one cool guy.'

If John had realised I was too drunk to articulate anything other than grunts by this time he might have been less impressed.

'Feller,' said John, reaching his hand out to shake mine, 'we'd like to offer you a job. Welcome to Mitchell, Hutchins.'

I later learned that John and Dick's be-nice-and-then-beat-them-up routine was one they had practised well. Five hours later I was on my way to JFK Airport, head thumping and stomach churning from the night's drinking. I had to stop the cab on the Van Wyck Expressway and get out to throw up by the side of the road. When I reached the airport I called John from a payphone and accepted the job.

Mitchell, Hutchins was all I expected. That is more than can be said for my analysis of the industry. Negotiated commission rates brought a revolution to Wall Street in 1975, just as the Big Bang did years later to London. Commission rates plummeted far further than anyone had forecast. Mitchell,

Hutchins' future, and my analysis, had been predicated on the assumption that people would be prepared to pay extra for added value such as Mitchell, Hutchins' outstanding research. They weren't.

All three of the brilliant research boutiques that interviewed me failed and were forced into mergers, while the big boring firms survived and ultimately prospered. In 1977 Mitchell, Hutchins merged with the giant firm of Paine, Webber. It was like Cartier merging with Woolworths. I found myself reporting not to John Engels, whom I had come to like and respect, but to bland Midwesterners in stretch polyester suits. The best and the brightest of Mitchell, Hutchins made for the door. I followed them and went to Morgan Stanley, then just starting to flex its muscles as a global powerhouse, for five hard but exhilarating years.

By then, Guislaine and I had moved out of New York to Bedford, a leafy Westchester village an hour's commute from New York. It was here that Georgia was born. Guislaine had started labour at about noon and arrived in hospital an hour or so later. By four o'clock she was making little progress, the contractions coming at wider intervals. At half past five her obstetrician, a charming man called Dr Cohen, slipped back into her room.

'How are we doing?' he asked.

'OK,' said Guislaine, who had stopped her breathing exercises as these were just for when the contractions came. 'But I don't think much is happening.'

Dr Cohen examined her. 'Yes, you're doing well,' he said, 'but this baby looks as if it's going to take its time.'

'Should I be induced now I've started?'

'We'll see,' said Dr Cohen. 'No hurry. By the way, there's something I need to tell you.'

'What?' said Guislaine and I in unison. When a doctor says he has something to tell you it is seldom good news.

'I have tickets for the opera.'

'Oh.'

'Tonight. At the Met in New York. *Madame Butterfly*. I'm going to have to run because it's curtain-up at 7.30. But I'll pop in when I'm back. Should be around midnight. You'll be in good hands and I don't think baby's going to arrive before I get back.'

At midnight Dr Cohen slid around the door wearing a white tuxedo. The opera, we learned, had been a triumph. Guislaine was tired, bored and wondering what was going on as the contractions had more or less petered out. I wondered whether Dr Cohen had slipped her something to slow the process down so he could get to the opera without worrying.

'Don't worry,' he said, hanging his jacket on the back of my chair and examining Guislaine. 'We'll give you something to help baby on its way. We'll have baby out before you know it.'

He administered something to induce labour, and at 4 a.m. little Georgia popped out, bright and bawling. Guislaine had been in labour for sixteen hours and was exhausted. The long delay after labour started had a nice consequence for me: it meant that Georgia was born on 18 December with the result that we shared a birthday.

Living in America was easy. New York was fun; we liked the contrast between nights at Studio 54, the greatest club the world has ever seen, and at GG Barnum's, its transsexual neighbour, and our comfortable existence in Westchester; we had nice American friends; the girls were in a nice local school in Bedford; everything was nice. But there was an edge that was lacking. We also thought it would be good to give the girls the chance to be English if they wanted to.

When we left London, Edward Heath's disastrous years were about to give way to another equally disastrous spell of Harold Wilson. Now Margaret Thatcher was in power. England in 1982 was finding an energy that had deserted it during the Heath/Wilson years. For the first time in my life-time England was looking forward not back. In 1982 I got a call from John Engels, who was now head of equities at First Boston, another global powerhouse, which had become the dominant firm on Wall Street in mergers and acquisitions.

'Hey, Miles. Ever thought about going back to England?'

Guislaine and I had originally come to New York for two years; we had now been there for nine. John was offering me the opportunity to run First Boston's office in London. First Boston had formed CSFB, a joint venture with Credit Suisse, the giant Swiss bank, to deal in the Eurobond markets and carry out corporate finance. This was a huge operation; by many measures CSFB was the leading firm in the Euromarket. The business of dealing in stocks and shares, the equity busi-ness, was not part of the joint venture but conducted by First Boston on its own. This was the business that John was asking me to go and run.

I took the job, and by April 1982 Guislaine, Tasha, Georgia and I were back in England. I was working hard at First Boston, under pressure from John to expand the office and double our business. I came home late most evenings and slumped silently in front of the television hoping that the white noise would give me the chance to empty my brain of work and to gather energy before dinner. I might have been tired but I was happy with the way things were going; we were starting to make good progress at First Boston and I was pleased with our new life, our new house, my new job and the opportunity to catch up with old friends. Things were good. And then one weekend Guislaine told me she wanted a divorce.

I felt as if I had been hit by a train. I thought we had a good marriage; it was now thirteen years old. Our friends thought we were the perfect couple. What was going on? I literally did not understand it. I understand it better today. I was so wrapped up in what I was doing and in my job that I had little energy and attention left over for Guislaine. I took her for granted. While I was bursting with adrenalin and energy she felt she had been parked on the sidelines.

At the time though I could not believe that this would lead to a real break-up. We went to talk to Dr John Cobb, a highly reputed therapist. I had been looking forward to the meeting as a drowning man might spot a life raft. Dr Cobb would explain to Guislaine that with a little work – and I was ready to do whatever work it took – we could set the marriage back on a stable foundation. The closer the meeting got the more excited I became. Everything was about to be cleared up. Guislaine would come to her senses.

The meeting was on a cold Thursday afternoon at four o'clock. I had been delayed at the office by a call from New York and arrived fifteen minutes late. It looked as if Guislaine and Dr Cobb had already been talking for some time. Now was my chance to explain that I loved Guislaine; I'd do whatever it took to restore the marriage; and all I needed was for her to have an open mind. I explained this to Dr Cobb, knowing he would explain it to her.

'Miles,' he said in a quiet voice, 'thank you for coming, although it's a pity you couldn't be here on time. Guislaine and I have been talking. I've seen many people with far worse problems than the ones you two have work them out and put their marriages back together.'

'Yes. Yes,' I said, restraining myself from punching the air. Guislaine was about to be told how easy it would be for us to repair things.

'But,' Cobb continued, 'in these cases both parties have wanted to make it work. Without that commitment it won't. It's apparent that Guislaine does not want the marriage to continue. One person alone can't repair a marriage. Under the circumstances you may have to prepare yourself for how you end your marriage with grace rather than how you repair it.'

Initially I did not understand what Cobb was saying. I assumed that the words were directed at Guislaine, and he was telling her that here was this nice guy who loved her and of course we would be able to work things out. But that was not what he was saying. I had never till that time understood the cliché about feeling the earth open up to swallow you, but now I did. Cobb and Guislaine went on talking; I was numb and heard nothing.

Afterwards I stumbled out, silent, into the street with Guislaine. We drove home to Richmond without a word being said. The next morning we told Tasha and Georgia over breakfast. I remember the tears running down my face as I said I was going to be moving out and Guislaine telling me in French not to cry in front of the children.

Divorce has no heroes. Ours was a disaster. Guislaine hired a series of lawyers, one a man with the apt name of Tooth but who was rumoured to prefer his nickname of Jaws, whose strategy was to make the process as unpleasant as possible for the husband. His efficiency in stirring up acrimony where little existed before was unrivalled.

It was a miserable time, but out of the misery came some good. I wanted somewhere to take Tasha and Georgia at weekends. I had moved out of the house on Ham Common and was living in a small flat in Chelsea with one bedroom and a fold-out sofa for the children in the sitting room. One weekend I found myself with nothing to do. I have always loved Romanesque and early Gothic cathedrals, believing them to be the finest works of art of Western man, and I had never seen the great cathedrals of East Anglia, so I set off to spend a weekend visiting Ely, Norwich and Peterborough cathedrals. In between Norwich and Ely I took a detour along the north Norfolk coast. I had never been there before. The marshes and the creeks and the little sailing villages with their flint and brick houses took me back to Tollesbury and the Blackwater estuary in Essex. I had been happy there. The wild, elemental Norfolk coast was balm to my bruised soul.

Next weekend I was back in Norfolk with Tasha and Georgia. I had spoken to estate agents and we looked at houses. Then we saw Shipley House, a red-brick Queen Anne-style house with a small garden in Westgate Street in Blakeney, one of the prettiest of the north Norfolk villages.

Shipley House was two tiny fishermen's cottages which had been joined together and had a posh brick front added.

I fell for it instantly. I looked at the girls, tired and restless after a day's house-hunting. They had perked up.

'This one's a yes, Daddy,' they both said. I bought it.

I would retreat to the house at weekends like a wounded animal. As soon as I got near Blakeney I would turn off the car radio, wind down the window and smell the air coming in from the sea and the marshes. I felt my spirits lighten. And the girls liked it. Initially I had no furniture, just a bed in my bedroom, a folding card table and one chair, supplemented by a garden table with two benches.

Tasha asked if she could spend her twelfth birthday there. I was delighted. I rented a minibus and drove up with Tasha and five of her friends from Putney High School, all girls. I told them to bring sleeping bags as they would be sleeping on the floor. I had a sixteen-foot Wayfarer sailing dinghy designed for three people. All seven of us went out in the dinghy with girls falling over the side, girls dragging in the water behind and girls rocking the boat from side to side. Before we went out I mentioned to Perry, the son of Stratton Long, the ships' chandler from whom I had bought the Wayfarer, that I had six girls sleeping on the floor in Shipley that night. When we got back I found six mattresses stacked in the sitting room. Perry had been around the village and collected them for us. At the time I hardly knew him. I realised then that Blakeney, and Norfolk, were special.

Guislaine had become interested in therapy, triggered by the visits we had made to Dr Cobb, and gained some insights into our marriage which may have put things in a different perspective. We began to see more of each other. The weather between us changed, the clouds blew away and we remembered why we loved each other. Almost three years after our break-up we remarried.

I was still working hard at First Boston but the weather there had also changed. CSFB, our much larger affiliate, was in the same building. It was staffed by brilliant people and run by a Napoleonic German, Hans-Joerg Rudloff, who thought that the way to get the best out of your employees was to create as much tension as possible between them. I liked being independent of CSFB. I had become a partner of First Boston in New York and reported there, not to Rudloff.

But First Boston was in trouble. It kept on making gigantic financial bets and getting them wrong. Credit Suisse usually bailed it out, but by 1989 it was obvious that the days of independence were over and that the whole of First Boston was going to be taken over by Credit Suisse. I had no wish to work for Credit Suisse so in June 1989 chucked up my job. My partners at First Boston thought I must have secret plans to go and work for one of its competitors because otherwise why would I walk away from a partnership at a great Wall Street firm? One of my partners offered to put me in touch with a psychiatrist.

The truth was I had no idea what I was going to do with the rest of my life. My sole ambition was to be free and not to work for anyone else ever again. Guislaine, who had remarried a well paid banker, now found herself attached to an unemployed man who seemed in no hurry to get a job. Luckily my salary, though a fraction of what bankers later came to be paid, had allowed us to pay off our mortgage and put aside money for the children's education. We had enough money saved to survive for a couple of years, but after that I was going to need to find a way of earning a living. Guislaine must have worried about what I was going to do, how I was going to support the family and what my not working meant for us as a couple. She was as much affected by my resignation as I was, but she never gave me anything but support and encouragement.

How well I remember the intoxicating feeling of freedom that came with giving up my job. It was like how coming home from school for the holidays had been. The first thing I wanted to do after twenty-two years chained to a desk shouting down a phone was travel, move around, explore, have adventures . . . But Guislaine hates the idea of travelling and moving around; she likes being places, not getting to them.

'Why don't we go on a walk?' she said.

'Yes, that could be fun. But we'd need to start and finish somewhere. We couldn't just walk aimlessly about. Walks need a beginning and an end.'

After a few false starts we hit on the perfect walk: Mediterranean to Atlantic, sea to sea. We would walk across France. We would start by dipping our feet in the Mediterranean then shoulder our packs and strike out for the Atlantic, some 500 kilometres away. I stretched a bit of string on the map across the waist between France and Spain to find the shortest way but this took us over the Pyrenees. No, thank you. We wanted to amble gently through fields and along placid streams. We had no interest in climbing Europe's second-largest mountain range. I moved the bit of string a little to the north, where the Pyrenees would be no more than a blur on the horizon, and there, we had our route. We would start at Gruissan-Plage, near Narbonne, on the Mediterranean, and we would hit the Atlantic at, well, just about anywhere the wind blew us but probably somewhere north of Biarritz.

We were equally excited and equally appalled by the magnitude of the undertaking. We were going to walk with backpacks the whole way, no cheating and no cadging lifts, but were hopelessly unfit; we had not walked much further than from a restaurant to a waiting taxi in recent years. Neither of us remembered ever having had a backpack, while Guislaine, being half-French, did not believe in outdoor exercise and had never even owned a pair of tennis shoes. This would be a huge physical challenge for her. I at least had been fit in my rowing days.

We had only remarried a year or two before. Would this adventure blow our revived marriage apart? Or bring us closer together?

I walked out of First Boston at the end of June 1989 and a week later Guislaine and I landed in Toulouse. We got a train and then a taxi to Gruissan-Plage, where we dipped our feet in the Mediterranean. Twenty-seven days and 550 kilometres later we ran down the last great dune before the Atlantic at Capbreton, cast our packs on the sand and stood hugging in the Atlantic surf, tears streaming down our faces, as happy as we had ever been.

I later wrote a book about our walk and what had led up to it. Most authors hate their publishers; I loved mine. Instead of positioning the book as a cutesy travel book they promoted it as a lifestyle book: 'frustrated middle-aged bloke gives up job and buys backpack'. The world is filled with blokes who'd love to give up their job and buy a backpack. Thanks to this brilliant marketing many of these frustrated people bought the book, or their wives bought it and gave it to them. *The Man Who Broke Out of the Bank* got to number five on the *Sunday Times* best-seller list and came out in the US and a number of other countries in translation. I treasure the Japanese edition, which has a drawing of Guislaine and me walking along a French country lane on the cover. We are both coal-black.

The Walk showed me that now I was free my options were infinite. I had spent twenty-two years half-asleep working for other people. Now I resolved that, unless driven to it by bankruptcy, I would not work for anyone else ever again. I was free. I could do anything I wanted. The question was what.

18

The Garden Shed

I now needed to earn some money or I would find myself having to knock at the door of Morgan Stanley or Merrill Lynch and ask for a job. I thought about becoming a writer. *The Man Who Broke Out of the Bank* helped to plug the hole in our bank balance so we could survive a little longer, and I did odd pieces of journalism, which brought in a tiny amount of extra money. I was astonished to find out how badly journalists are paid. People who have worked in the financial world are always astonished to find out what people who work in other areas are paid.

I thought of other things to do. I have always been obsessed by stock markets. Once you get to understand a little about them they can become absorbing, like an infuriatingly complex game whose rules change as soon as you think you've learned them. They are about big emotions – fear, greed and panic – and have little to do with numbers. My other obsession is being bloody-minded. I hate being told what to do, which could explain why boarding school was such a failure, and I love doing the opposite of what other people think is a sensible idea. Maybe one day I shall write a book called *The Expert Is Always Wrong*. Because experts are experts in what worked yesterday, they are challenged and proved wrong by something new which comes along and upsets the world in which they got their doctorate. This is why none of them foresaw the end of communism or the advent of the Arab Spring.

When I was at First Boston I had become involved in what later came to be called emerging markets. In the 1980s few non-anglophone countries had functioning stock markets; places like Spain, Austria, Portugal, Greece and Finland had markets with one or two stocks that traded very occasionally. Such markets had become moribund during years of nationalisation and socialist orthodoxy, but as privatisation became the way of the future, they would be needed again. It was apparent that pioneer investors, people like George Soros and Jim Rogers, who did their research and invested early in these fledgling markets, later did extremely well when the markets were discovered by other investors. I was intrigued. What was the next set of markets waiting to be discovered? I needed to do some research.

Shortly after the Walk Guislaine and I sold our grown-up house on a London square and moved to the 'This one's a yes' house in Blakeney that the children and I had bought a few years earlier. By now it was more or less fully furnished. Living there full time was going to be very different to using it as a weekend house.

Guislaine and I loved Blakeney with its wild big sky, its giant flocks of winter geese and duck, sea lavender, the marsh and the creeks, and beyond, a long dune which separates a fifteen-mile beach of sand and shingle from the marshes. In summer the sand shimmers like a beach in the Bahamas and in winter the North Sea crashes brown and angry on the shingle. Year round a colony of several hundred grey and white seals with whiskered Labrador faces stations itself on the sands of Blakeney Point.

Blakeney had grown rich in the thirteenth and fourteenth centuries on the wool trade with Holland, but then the harbour silted up, the trade died out, the railway never came, and Blakeney, along with its neighbours Cley and Morston, was left unspoiled. It has been going gently downhill for 600 years, although today it has enough dinghy-sailors, marsh-walkers, and bird-watchers to keep it ticking along. Once a day the tide floods in along the creek and everyone rushes down to launch their dinghies; two hours later they are close-tacking back up the creek hoping to get home before the falling tide strands them on the mud. Just like Tollesbury so many years ago.

Despite the lack of a job I needed somewhere to work in case I found something to do. We put up a shed in the garden. This became my office. I spent most of 1990 getting in touch by mail – no email then – with stock markets all around the world, everywhere from Iceland to Fiji to Ghana. For the seeker of the next markets to emerge it soon became apparent that most had already been discovered. The Far East and South East Asia were top of everyone's list; Latin America had been well explored; India and Pakistan were coming on to investors' screens; and above all Russia and the countries of Eastern Europe that had shaken off communism were acting as a magnet to pioneering investors. My old firms CSFB and Morgan Stanley were thundering into Russia and Eastern Europe. Where Napoleon and Hitler had failed, Hans-Joerg Rudloff and his CSFB troops hoped to succeed. These were not places for an unemployed bloke in a Norfolk garden shed to compete with the heavy squad from Wall Street and the City.

However, my research threw up an interesting fact. Two parts of the world were being shunned by everyone. No one wanted to invest in Africa or the Middle East. Africa was perceived as an economic black hole and the Middle East as a hotbed of Islamic terrorists. No one from outside had any interest in investing there. This insight did not hit suddenly but gradually crept up on me as I found out more and more about fledgling markets around the world.

In 1990 Africa and the Middle East were true virgin territory. Bingo, Miles, I thought. These are the places for you. I mentioned the idea to one or two people and was greeted with derision: there were no functioning stock markets; there was nothing worth investing in; what a waste of time. Go to Thailand, Brazil, Argentina. So, carried along on a tide of derision, I set off for Africa and the Middle East.

I knew the Middle East from my childhood but had never been to Africa. I contacted companies, stock market officials, finance ministers and privatisation overseers. But just turning up and saying, 'Hi, I'm Miles,' was not going to impress the local Big Men, and if Africa and the Middle East have one thing in common it is that they are places where you need to be a Big Man or you are nothing. I was not a Big Man so I needed to be a company. Thus Blakeney Management Ltd was born. I appointed myself chairman and designated the garden shed its international headquarters. It had no other employees, but no one in Africa or the Middle East knew that; in 1990 they couldn't google me or Blakeney Management because Google did not exist. At this point I was not sure how I was going to make a living out of discovering African stock markets, particularly as the experts told me there weren't any that functioned.

Visiting African markets in those first years was intoxicating. In 1990 the Cairo Stock Exchange, for instance, was a grand circular marble hall with ornate pillars in which sat three old men wearing fezzes, sipping Arabic coffee and dreaming of 1955. They were wondering whether there was going to be a trade that week. The answer was almost certainly not. Hundreds of companies were listed, but most were now owned in their entirety by the government as a result of Nasser's nationalisations, so there were no shares in public hands to trade. Of the few which did trade I had read that only one, Suez Cement, was open to foreigners.

I asked one of the three be-fezzed brokers if I could buy some shares in Suez Cement. He looked at me as if I had just lowered my trousers and asked my interpreter to repeat the question; it seemed I was the first foreign investor he had ever met. He summoned the other two brokers. For five minutes the three elderly men shouted at each other and gesticulated at me. The youngest of the three, a man possibly in his early nineties, then wrapped his arm around my interpreter and whispered urgently into his ear. Following this he bowed to me and gave me a big smile. 'You are welcome, mister, most welcome.' 'Good. Can I buy some shares in Suez Cement?' I asked the interpreter. 'Of course, no problem. He say always you can buy these shares.' 'Thank you, excellent. Well, let's buy a hundred to start with just to see if this is going to work.'

The interpreter conveyed the request to the broker, who spoke quickly to the interpreter and then flashed me another smile and a couple more 'most welcomes'.

'Is not possible today,' said the interpreter. 'You, foreigner.'

'Yes, yes, I know I foreigner. But Suez Cement is open to foreigners.'

'Of course, no problem, mister. But not possible.'

'Why?'

Another hurried consultation. Fezzes wagged dangerously.

'Technical problem.'

At that time the only functioning markets in Africa were Johannesburg and Harare but neither was accessible to foreign investors. Harare was open only to Zimbabwe residents until late 1993, and Johannesburg had put itself off limits because no one would invest in a country that practised apartheid.

I trotted off to Accra, Casablanca, Nairobi, Amman, Abidjan, Bahrain, Oman, Tunis and any other place that purported to have a stock market. In most places the people I met could not work out what I was up to. They assumed I was attempting to seize control of local companies because why else would I be asking these questions about them? The idea of a foreign investor just buying some shares in the hope that they might go up in value was completely unknown to them. But when I turned up again a month or two later people were intrigued to see the nosey foreigner back and began to open up; I forged a number of friendships, which continue to this day, with smart young people who, like me, were starting their own firms to do things on the stock market.

I needed to make a living and, wondering if anyone would pay me for the knowledge I was building up, went to see some of the emerging-market investors I knew from my days working for Wall Street firms. The first serious investor I approached was the legendary Barton Biggs, founder of Morgan Stanley Asset Management and a fanatical investor in emerging markets. I knew Barton from my time at Morgan Stanley. We had lunch in a Morgan Stanley dining room on Sixth Avenue at noon. You had to be quick with Barton because at 12.45 p.m. he went to the gym.

'So whaddya like, Miles?' Barton did not do small talk.

'Well, I've been doing work on African and Middle Eastern markets – been visiting companies, talking to the locals.'

'Jesus, they have markets in those countries? Do any of them work?'

'Yup. I mean they're not exactly Bangkok or Hong Kong, but things are stirring. There's no one, but no one, out there doing research apart from me, so a lot of these stocks are selling at the wrong price. Some are ridiculously expensive relative to their earnings but most are absurdly cheap. You can buy any stock you like in Ghana for three times earnings.* It's absurd. It's money sitting on the table waiting to be picked up.'

'So what are the companies? All mining companies?'

'No. Banks, breweries, consumer companies, the normal stuff. Barton, I was rather hoping I could sign Morgan Stanley up as a consulting client. From time to time I'm going to come across some money-making ideas in my area and I'll pass these on to my consulting clients.'

---

* A price: earnings ratio is a common way of assessing the value of a stock; other things being equal, ten to fifteen times earnings might be considered normal. Three is a steal.

'Well, we're sure as hell not going to dick around in the Côte d'Ivoire or Ghana ourselves so why don't you dick around for us and tell us what you find? Sure, we'll sign up.'

'Thanks, Barton.'

Thanks, indeed. I had my first client. Could this be a new career?

It was the dick-around factor that gave me my new business. My second client was the Soros group, not George Soros himself, but someone universally known as the Prince of Darkness, who worked for him at the time. A few months later I had fifteen consulting clients, including many of the big hedge funds and leading emerging-market investors of those days, for whom I was happily dicking around in the Côte d'Ivoire and elsewhere. I was not only making a reasonable living out of the consulting fees they paid me – enough so we now had a little more money coming in than going out every month – but I was having more fun than I ever had in the days when I worked for others.

Many of these flea-bite markets were keen to develop but did not know how. Some asked my advice as I had now watched a number of markets move from embryo to a functioning state and was happy to share this knowledge with stock market people in places like Tunisia and Ghana. In 1993 *Euromoney* magazine called me the 'father of the Casablanca bourse'. This title would have been as big a surprise to the Moroccans as it did to me, but to be fair I had been the first person to get anglophone foreigners to invest in that market.

My first visit to the Casablanca bourse had been in 1991. Half a dozen men in suits drank tea, read the Casablanca papers and told jokes in front of whiteboards with a few numbers and names scrawled on them. There was no trading

that I could see. The *chef de bourse* ushered me into his office
with grave courtesy. He spoke no English; my French was
good for reading a menu but not a balance sheet. I asked
him how many stocks were traded on the bourse and what
the volume of trading was. He rose slowly to his feet and
shuffled over to a pile of leather-bound ledgers on a table.
He bent slowly down and blew dust off the top one. When
he was satisfied it was dust-free he picked it up and handed
the heavy book to me. '*Regardez, monsieur.*' Inside, inscribed
in blue ink, were details of recent trades. Judging from how
faded the ink was when I turned to the previous page, it was
a long time between trades.

I revisited the Casablanca bourse several times and went to
see companies. Getting to talk to the managements of these
companies was not easy. In London or New York companies
have departments to deal with actual and potential investors.
Moroccan companies had no investor relations departments
in those days and saw no reason to share information with
a nosy foreigner whose motives were unclear. An Iranian
woman friend of mine in London had a gay Moroccan
friend, Abbas, in the fashion business who came from a grand
family. Most Moroccan companies at that time were owned
and managed by members of such families, and Abbas was
related to many of them. He was puzzled as to why I wanted
to see his cousins – the boring ones in business. Most of the
Europeans he knew wanted to experience the louche side
of Moroccan life, but he took me literally by the hand and
trotted me in to see chief executives and government ministers. He was related to most of those too.

I asked them questions in schoolboy French. Their natural good manners prevented them from telling me to mind

my own business but it was obvious they thought I had no business enquiring as to how sales were going or what profits they might report. I wrote a long research report for my consulting clients on ONA, the Moroccan conglomerate that dominated the local business scene and whose largest shareholder was the King. Guesswork led me to suggest in the report that the company was far more profitable than it let on as its accounts did not include the results of many of its subsidiaries. I recommended to my consulting clients that they buy shares in it. Some of them did. They were the first foreign investors in the Moroccan market. The chief executive of ONA, when I next went to see him, was not pleased.

'Where did you get the information in your report? Who told you?'

It had not occurred to him that even the most amateurish of analysts, and few analysts were more amateur than I, did not need an insider leaking information to work out that the profits from a number of ONA's connected companies were not showing up in the accounts. However, the effect of foreigners buying into ONA was to push the stock price sharply up, thereby enriching the chief executive and indeed the King. Next time I went to visit I was more warmly received. And a year later ONA began to report consolidated earnings.

19

No Dinner in Bucharest

Visiting Moroccan and other African companies had yet to become a full-time job, but the wanderlust generated by twenty-two years chained to a desk was growing. I wanted to see everything and to go to all the places I had never been. While I had been gathering information on African and Middle Eastern companies the world was blowing up. Poland in mid-1989 had already abandoned communism, but the Russians, led now by Mr Gorbachev, instead of sending in the tanks – as they had done in Hungary in 1956 and Czechoslovakia in 1968 – had stood by with their hands in their pockets whistling. East Germany was in a ferment. Every Monday in October there was a riot in Leipzig. The first one had been 5,000 people, then 10,000. Erich Honecker, the hard-faced leader of East Germany, was reported to be talking about shooting rioters, but still the numbers of demonstrators mounted. By mid-October there were 100,000 people, then 300,000. Dresden was rioting too. East Berlin was a powder keg. But no one was shot or arrested. This was a new script. Communism was crumbling as we watched.

I love a good riot. I've been heckled by fascists on the Aldermaston march, arrested in Oxford at the time of the Cuban missile crisis, tear-gassed in Washington with a million other people after Nixon bombed Cambodia; I've narrowly avoided having my head split open by hard hats supporting the Vietnam War on Wall Street, thrown ball bearings under police horses' hooves in Grosvenor Square, come out against the invasion of Iraq in Hyde Park, and chucked tomatoes at Dubya in London. Well, actually I didn't chuck any tomatoes because the police wouldn't let anyone get within tomato-chucking range, but I gave it a try.

I have always liked being a witness to history; I want to see things first hand. Here was one of the biggest events in the history of the twentieth century going on in Europe, and I wanted to go and have a look for myself. How to go and where to go? In 1946 Ernie Bevin, the foreign secretary in the Labour government that had just ousted Churchill's Tories, is reported to have said, 'I dream of the day when a man can go to Victoria Station and buy himself a ticket to anywhere in the world.' At that time almost all borders were closed to non-official travel and if you wanted to travel you took the train.

That is what I would do: I would go to Victoria Station and buy myself a ticket to Eastern Europe. I would see the riots first hand and with any luck be part of them. Travelling by train I would meet people. There is nothing like sharing your sausage with someone in a long-distance train compartment to bridge a language barrier.

Everyone was going to East Germany. It was all over every newspaper. The rest of Eastern Europe might as well not have existed. Nothing appeared about Czechoslovakia, Romania and Bulgaria, all three still communist states. No riots were being reported in these countries. The secret police appeared to have everyone there firmly under control. I decided to bypass East Germany. I had a feeling that by the time I got there the Berlin Wall might have come down and I would have missed the fun, so I would go and have a look at the places where the fun was just beginning.

I bought myself a train ticket from London to Paris via the cross-Channel ferry and then from Paris to Prague, changing in Cologne, stopping off in Prague for a few days, and then on to Budapest for another stopover, and finally on to Romania and Bucharest. I would fly back from Bucharest in a couple of weeks. I then scurried off to the Czech, Hungarian and Romanian embassies to get tourist visas. There were no queues. No one else was asking for tourist visas.

Czechoslovakia and Hungary seemed to be functioning normally whereas Romania was functioning not at all. Nicolae Ceausescu was the most hard line of the Eastern European rulers. His rule was absolute but the Romanian economy was in ruins. The local currency, the leu, was now useful only to stuff pillows, but using foreign money was an offence that would get you ten years in a Romanian jail. The parallel currency, the guidebook told me, was Kent cigarettes. A packet of Kent bought you a favour or paid for a meal; a carton would buy you a village. It had to be Kent; it was no use proffering Marlboro or Winston. No one wanted those. Kent had become the Romanian currency. No one ever smoked a Kent; it was like setting fire to a fiver. I bought two cartons of Kent and tucked them in the bottom of my luggage. I was now a Romanian millionaire.

I had a couple of hours between the boat train getting into the Gare du Nord on the night of Wednesday 8 November 1989 and the night train leaving the same station at 11.30 p.m. for Cologne. I found a brasserie outside the station, had oysters, coq au vin and a *pichet* of Beaujolais, lit a Marlboro, and sat back with a feeling of great well-being combined with excitement. I had no idea what to expect but I knew I would have an adventure. I felt I was in a film watching myself. Very Graham Greene.

Some time in the small hours we chunkled into Cologne station, where I needed to change for the train to Prague in half an hour. I had expected the station to be empty at this time in the morning. The opposite was true. The *Bahnhof* was electric with noise and tumult. Hordes of singing young people linked arms and waved banners. The announcement boards showed that special trains were being put on for Berlin. Everyone was laughing and smiling and everyone was everyone's friend. People were hugging each other and crying. I had no way of knowing what the news was and spoke no German. I tried stopping a couple of people and asking what was going on. They laughed, waved their cans of beer and chanted, 'Berlin, Berlin.' Maybe I should buy a ticket to Berlin and join them? I almost did but instead boarded my train to Prague. This train would avoid East Germany, taking a southern route through Frankfurt and Nuremberg, and cross into Czechoslovakia in the early afternoon.

When we got to the border we sailed through the German side without doing anything other than showing our passports. Several kilometres later we stopped at the Czech customs post. This was the Iron Curtain. The track had run through a barbed-wire corridor all the way from the German side. Blue-uniformed officers flooded on to the train. My compartment had two other people in it, both Czech, one of whom spoke a little English. We had become sausage friends. My spicy Cologne station salami was better than his Czech donkey sausage. He had asked me what the purpose of my trip was, and when I told him I was just going along to see what was happening he looked at me with bafflement.

The officers came into our compartment and examined our documents, mine in particular. They were polite and efficient. They asked me where I was going in Czech and my sausage friend translated: 'Praha.' 'Purpose your visit?' 'Tourist.' The officers looked at each other and shrugged.

Twenty minutes later the train moved on. The scenery in communist Czech Bohemia did not look that different to the countryside of the capitalist German Bavaria we had just left, although to my surprise the fields were smaller; I had assumed that with collectivisation the fields would be enormous. There were more chickens, ponies, cows and dogs running around free. The houses were smaller. This appeared to be a holiday district as there were rows of tiny A-frame wooden houses with little vegetable plots around them, maybe dachas for junior members of the *nomenklatura*.

At about five o'clock in the evening we pulled into Prague station. According to the guidebook I had a walk of no more than 200 yards to the Esplanade Hotel. Outside the station was like an old Jack the Ripper movie of London: damp fog, yellow street lights, people flitting past in thick coats with the collars up, flat caps, fedoras, the muffled sound of little traffic and the squeal of a tram.

The Esplanade had pretensions to grandeur but was run-down. The lobby was dark wood and brocaded furniture, but the brocade was frayed and the wood dull. I had never seen so many suspicious-looking people. Everyone appeared to be a spy. There were men in leather overcoats down to their ankles, the coats either slightly too big or just a bit too tight in the armpits. There were a few women with permed hair and too much lipstick. One had a cigarette holder.

I smiled with happiness. I was still smiling when I checked in. No one else was. A stern matron took me up to my room without offering to help me with my bags, handed me a key so big it might have been used to lock up the Count of Monte Cristo and left me alone in communist Czechoslovakia.

I decided to go for a walk and then get some dinner later. The hotel was less than half a mile from Wenceslas Square. That was the obvious destination. I was delighted to be in Prague but feeling a twinge of envy that I was not in the thick of the action in Berlin. Everything looked very quiet. There had been no mention of Prague in the Western press so I assumed that the contagion that had ripped through Poland and was setting Germany on fire had not yet touched Czechoslovakia.

Wenceslas Square is not a square but a grand boule-vard running downhill from the National Museum. If you swapped the Arc de Triomphe for the museum you could be in the Champs-Elysées. Five minutes later I was at the top end of the square. The yellow fog made it difficult to see more than a hundred yards. From the downhill end, several hundred yards away, there was a noise. I walked towards it. As I descended the fog began to clear and the noise got louder.

It was people shouting. The whole of the bottom third of the square was packed with yelling demonstrators. I hurried down to see what was up. The demonstrators had surrounded two police Skodas. They were rocking them from side to side and threatening to overturn them. The policemen inside looked terrified. The crowd was growing every minute as people rushed in from neighbouring streets.

I was desperate to know what was happening but I spoke no Czech. There was a café to one side of the tumult. A waiter was standing outside. Perhaps he spoke some English. I approached him. 'Please. You speak English?' I asked.

He looked around.

'Little.'

'What's happening? What are they demonstrating about?'

'No, no, you go now. Nothing. Nothing.' He was very jumpy and kept looking around to see if anyone was watching him talking to the red-haired foreigner in his funny foreign clothes.

'But what are they demonstrating about?'

'No demonstrazion. Small, small manifestazion. Nothing. Please, you go.'

I thanked him and moved towards where the rioting was going on. This 'small manifestazion' must have had over 100,000 increasingly excited people. I was seeing the first anti-communist demonstration in Czechoslovakia since the Prague Spring of 1968.

Then, from the streets at the very bottom of the square, sirens sounded. Not one siren but an orchestra of them. I stood on a café chair to see what was happening. Armoured personnel carriers and heavy army lorries were moving in.

Brown-uniformed rifle-carrying soldiers jumped out of the vehicles and formed up in line all the way across the square. It must have been 200 yards from side to side. They began to march, shoulders almost touching, up the square. The rioters who a moment ago had been about to capsize the two trapped police cars backed away uphill to get away from the advancing soldiers. I did not want to miss the action but neither did I want to get bayoneted for rioting so I pushed back into the entrance of the café and tried to look as foreign as possible.

The soldiers tramped unstoppably past. No one stood up to them or resisted. The police cars were now free and disappeared with a squeal of tyres off to the south end of the square. The rioters were evaporating. They slid into side streets; they escaped through the open north end by the museum. Fifteen minutes after the sirens had sounded, the square was all but empty of civilians.

This demonstration was never reported. If you look in Wikipedia the first Czech riot was on 19 November. The one I had just seen was on 9 November. All the reporters were in Berlin or Leipzig.

Based on what I had just witnessed, my conclusion was that the Czech government still had a tight rein on things and the people no stomach for a fight. How wrong I was. I left Prague two days later on the 11th. Two weeks after that half a million people were demonstrating in Wenceslas Square, and on 28 November, less than three weeks after the riot that I had witnessed, the communist government surrendered, agreed to hold elections and hand over power to whomever the people chose to elect. I had seen the first wrinkle of what later came to be called the Velvet Revolution.

I returned to my hotel room and had some excellent Czech beer, veal stew and dumplings sent up by room service. I had not slept much on the train and was exhausted. I wished I could find out what was going on elsewhere in Eastern Europe. What was the news from East Germany? I turned on the television. It had two channels, both state run. At 9 p.m. the news came on. I would not be able to understand what they were saying but I hoped I could get an idea what was happening.

Sure enough, the lead story was of a riot. People were waving banners and placards. Was this East Berlin? I looked more closely. The placards were in English: ABORTION IS MURDER. Later, when I reached Budapest and could buy a copy of the *Herald Tribune*, I learned that a few hours earlier that day the Berlin Wall had come down. There were no pictures of that on Czech television. The day the wall fell, the moment of icon at the end of over forty years of Eastern European communism, the lead story on Czech television was of an anti-abortion demo in Los Angeles.

I spent another two days padding around Prague but sightseeing was boring after the excitement of the Wenceslas Square riot. I stood on the Charles Bridge and watched the people flow past in their thick winter coats and mufflers. It was clear and sunny; the yellow fog had evaporated along with the demonstrators. I climbed the hill to look at Prague Castle. I tried to get into St Vitus's Cathedral but it was closed for maintenance. I bought a sausage in Old Town Square and sat in the sun eating it with a glass of Czech lager.

Next day I took the train to Budapest. Hungary had effectively abandoned communism with the fall of János Kádár in 1988. Elections had been held and new parties created to take part in a genuinely democratic process. I had been to Budapest once before, for a weekend in 1986. I had gone with a woman who became a friend for life; we had seen the sights, listened to Gypsy music, eaten too much Hungarian foie gras, and drunk Bull's Blood and Tokay. Even then Hungary did not seem repressively communist.

I was happy to be back in Budapest because it is a charming and fascinating city with charming and fascinating people, but I didn't see how I was going to have any adventures there. No one was going to demonstrate in Budapest because there was nothing to demonstrate about. The country was on track to become as democratic as Western Europe.

I was booked into the Gellert, maybe not the most modern hotel in Budapest but certainly the grandest, an art nouveau palace facing the Danube at the foot of the Buda Hill. The Hungarians love their spas. Attached to the Gellert and immediately behind it are the grandest baths in Budapest, where anyone, not just hotel guests, can steam and splosh in marbled and pillared galleries filled with evil-smelling sulphurous water. The Gellert staff behaved as if they had learned their trade in the last days of the Austro-Hungarian empire. Forty years of communism had not erased their courtesy. When a party of loden-clad Germans with shotguns in shiny leather cases had finished checking in, a grave-looking concierge with a moustache in which birds could nest, bowed to me, took my passport and said, 'Herr Morland, my name is Imry and it is my privilege to welcome you to the Gellert. Your pleasure is my concern.'

As in post-demo Prague, I did some sightseeing. Budapest has a lot to see, but I was here to watch people riot, not sit in fur coats in cafés eating cream-filled buns. After two days I set off to catch the morning train to Bucharest, capital of Romania. No one knew what was happening in Romania. It appeared that Ceausescu, the last of the hard-line communist dictators, was trying to insulate the country from the wind blowing through the rest of Eastern Europe. I was hoping to find out if the people were still cowed or if the brave and the young were taking to the streets to demonstrate.

Imry supervised the carrying of my modest suitcase to the taxi.

'Sir, it has been a great pleasure having you as our guest at the Gellert and I hope we will see you again soon. May I enquire where you are going?'

'Bucharest.'

'Bucharest?' Imry's mighty moustache trembled. 'Bucharest? I wish you the best of voyages. It may not be the best time for a visit, but I assume that you will be staying in the Intercontinental?'

'Yes, I will.'

'Of course, Herr Morland. You have chosen well. Please tell Bogdan, the head concierge there, that Imry of the Gellert sends his compliments. He will make sure you are well looked after.'

I thrust a fistful of forint into Imry's hand and set off for Bucharest.

When I got to the station it became apparent that the train I was going to catch did not begin in Budapest. I was booked on the Berlin–Sofia Express, which started its journey in newly liberated East Berlin and would finish up in Bulgaria, the far side of Romania. My trip, Budapest to Bucharest, would be but two stops on that journey. As I stood on the platform waiting for the train to come in I could see that there were no more than four or five other people intending to board.

I had a reserved seat in the first-class car. The rest of the train was crammed with Bulgarian workers going home for Christmas, but I was the only person in my compart-ment. I had sausage, I had ham and tomatoes, I had biscuits, apples, two bars of excellent Hungarian chocolate, a bottle of Bull's Blood wine and a Swiss Army Knife with which to cut the sausage and open the wine. What more could a man want?

The train crept and jiggled through the great Hungarian plain that runs south-east from Budapest. The land was as flat as the American Midwest. Small towns and villages flicked by, some with art deco buildings in startling colours; peasants walked behind plough horses, chickens ran from the train, old women looked up from their washing and waved. I had a long journey ahead of me. The train had left Budapest at 7 a.m. and was scheduled to arrive in Bucharest just before midnight.

I pulled out the only book I had brought with me, *Middlemarch*. I had never read it and had thought that its 800 pages should last me through the trip. For some unaccountable reason some people refer to it as the greatest of English novels. For me it was one of the most irritating. Why did Dorothea put up with the appalling Casaubon? If ever a man was in need of my mother's universal remedy of a kick up the backside it was Casaubon.

In the middle of the day the train pulled in to Lokoshaza and stopped. Doors banged, there was shouting, and a few minutes later a Hungarian official came into my compartment. He looked bored. 'Passport.' I gave it to him. He flicked through the pages, nodded and handed it back before going on to the next compartment. Half an hour later the train pulled out of Lokoshaza and proceeded slowly towards Romania. I assumed there would be a Romanian checkpoint in a kilometre or two and then we would be on our way to Bucharest. The train passed between a wire fence which ran continuously on either side. That must be the actual border. We gathered speed. I looked for differences in the countryside. The fields seemed bigger, the houses and roads more run-down. Five minutes elapsed, then ten and no border post. Perhaps the Hungarian one sufficed for both.

I was reluctantly readdressing myself to Dorothea and Casaubon when we entered a town and began to slow. We came to a halt. The signs announced this was Curtici. It was a big junction with five or six tracks running through it. There was a platform to the right of the train. I hoped the wait would not be too long. Fifteen minutes elapsed and then I heard footsteps down the corridor and could hear the people in the next-door compartment being checked. My door was thrown open. Two uniformed officers came in. They had smart grey-blue uniforms, big peaked caps and large pistols in holsters at their waists. They did not smile. The senior one barked at me in Romanian. I shrugged. 'English,' said I, pointing at myself. The official barked more Romanian. '*Parlez Français?*' I tried. The two spoke quickly to each other, then the junior one leaned out of the window and shouted down the platform. A minute later two rouged and lipsticked women in leather miniskirts marched into the compartment. They must have been in their early twenties.

'Good morning, mister. This Romanian border. We are interpreters,' said one of the women, gesturing at herself and her companion. They seemed friendly enough.

'Passport please.'

I handed over my passport. The senior man took it, matched me against the photograph and then began very slowly leafing through each page.

The junior one opened my briefcase and started to take its contents out item by item, laying them out on the seat opposite. I had a copy of *Private Eye* with a picture of a near-naked Mrs Thatcher playing volleyball with Ronald Reagan on the cover. Thank God it did not have any Ceausescu jokes in it. This was scanned and put in a leather satchel. I had a copy of the *Herald Tribune* with photographs of the wall coming down in Berlin. The officer was more interested in the *Trib* than *Private Eye*. He handed the paper to one of the women and rapped something at her. She scrutinised the paper and began slowly to translate the story about the fall of the wall. The officer was not pleased. It too went in his satchel.

I dug into the bottom of my suitcase and pulled out a carton of Kent.

'Please, miss,' I said, handing the carton to the older of the two interpreters, 'this is a gift from me to you and the officers.'

The woman looked startled at first, then took the carton and handed it to Senior. He put down my passport and looked at me with a completely expressionless face. Oh God, I thought. Now I've really blown it.

He shook the carton lightly as if weighing it, put it in the satchel, gave me a slight nod and went back to examining my passport.

Everything was then pulled out of my suitcase. I had not had an opportunity to go to a laundry since leaving London. I winced as the officers pulled out dirty underpants, filthy handkerchiefs and scrumpled shirts, and dropped them with distaste on the seat.

Senior had finished going through my passport and was asking me questions through the interpreters.

'Where you go?'

'Bucharest.'

'What purpose?'

'Tourism.'

'Tourism? Why tourism?'

'Um, I've heard that Bucharest is a beautiful city that has been rebuilt under President Ceausescu, and I want to see for myself.'

'What profession you have?'

I had a good answer to this one. There is one profession that is despised in the West but held in universal respect in backward countries.

'Economist.'

Senior nodded and looked at me with a smidgen more respect.

Junior had emptied out all my filthy clothes. He now picked up the suitcase and began probing it to see if there were hidden compartments. One of the girls smiled at me. Maybe the Kent was working.

Senior gestured at *Middlemarch*. 'What that book?'

'English literature.'

'What is subject?'

Good question. I felt that this was not the time to be flippant or to discuss Casaubon's many failings as a human being.

'Economics.'

Senior nodded and spoke to one of the girls. Reluctantly she picked it up and began haltingly to translate the first words: 'Who that cares much to know the history of man and how the mysterious mixture behaves under the varying experiments of Time has not dwelt at least briefly on the life of St Theresa . . .' Senior was not impressed. He snatched the book from her hand, gave it a riffling and dropped it on the seat then gave some orders to Junior and the girls.

'You stay here please now,' one of the girls said, and the four of them marched out of the compartment with my passport.

I repacked my suitcase and restored order in my briefcase. We had been stopped now for nearly an hour. I could hear from shouts and jeers down the train that the Bulgarians were getting restless. I tried reading *Middlemarch*. That didn't work.

Another twenty minutes elapsed and then I heard footsteps down the corridor. Finally I was going to get my passport back and we would be on our way. It sounded as if there more than four people this time.

Senior came in first followed by one of the interpreters. The others waited outside. 'You go back,' he said.

'What? Go back to Hungary? Why? Look, I've got a valid visa from your consulate in London. Look there in the passport. I'm allowed in. It's valid for three months. Have a look. What's the problem? I don't understand.' I addressed this to the older and more sympathetic of the girls. She shook her head.

'Mister, you go back to Hungary.'

Senior handed me my passport and pointed at the visa. There, stamped in red across it, was ANULO. I did not need a translator for that.

He slid the door back and beckoned. Two brown-uniformed soldiers with what looked to me like AK-47s came into the compartment. One gestured with his gun for me to pick up my things. I was marched out to the end of the corridor, but instead of turning right on to the platform the door to the left was opened.

'Goodbye, mister,' said one of the girls. 'You must get down on track now. The soldiers they take you. Goodbye.'

One of the armed soldiers got down on the track ahead of me. The other remained behind with the gun pointed at the small of my back. I put my luggage on the floor of the train and clambered down the steps the four or five feet on to the track. The girls handed me my two bags and waved good-bye. The other soldier climbed down and gestured with his gun that I should walk across the tracks. Another long train was waiting at the far platform; it was pointed in the opposite direction. We would have a hundred-yard walk around the end of the train to get on the platform. As I began the walk the Berlin–Sofia Express from which I had just been off-loaded inched forward. Hundreds of Bulgarians leaned out of the windows and shouted, jeered and whistled as the soldiers led away the Western spy for whom their train had been so long held up.

We reached the end of the other train and then the end of the platform. Where were they taking me? One walked ahead, the other behind with his gun inches away from my

back. I followed the leader up on to the platform. I could see
from the signboards on the side of the train that this was the
Bucharest–Warsaw Express. Judging from its insignia it was
Polish. I was marched down the platform. Curious passengers
looked out of the windows. I had not noticed this train arrive
but had the impression it had been there for a long time. The
passengers were looking impatient.

Halfway down the train was a first-class carriage. Armed
soldiers with German shepherd dogs stood at the doors either
end. I was poked on to the train and marched along to an
empty compartment. It appeared the whole carriage had
been cleared for me. I sat down with my luggage. The soldiers
withdrew to the other side of the door but remained there on
guard. Ten minutes later a border official came in.

'Passport.'

I gave it to him. 'What's going on? I haven't done anything.
What is this?'

The officer looked at me and shrugged. He spoke no
English and I had lost the girls in the miniskirts. He took my
passport and left. I saw him go into an office on the platform.
There were three or four other people in there. One began a
long telephone call while waving my passport up and down.
Then he hung up and put the passport down on the desk.
The men began a conversation. What would happen if the
train decided to pull out? I had no papers. I could spend the
rest of my life stateless, shuttling backwards and forwards on
the Bucharest–Warsaw Express.

Half an hour elapsed. The men in the office drank tea.
Then I saw one answer the phone. Another long conversation. The call ended, and the man who had originally taken

my passport got up and boarded the train. Without a word he handed it back to me. The two soldiers guarding me marched smartly off the train, and fifteen seconds later a whistle blew and the train pulled out in the direction of Budapest and Warsaw. It was more than three hours since the Sofia train had first arrived in Curtici.

At 8 p.m. that night I was back at the Gellert.

'Herr Morland, welcome back,' said Imry. 'You did not like Bucharest?'

'I don't think it liked me. Could I have a room, please?'

Imry glanced briefly at the ledger. 'Herr Morland, your old room awaits you. Allow me to escort you.'

When I got to my room I called Guislaine. She sounded distraught.

'Thank God you called. We've been so worried. Where are you? Are you OK?'

'Yup, I'm fine, but I've had an interesting day. I'm back in Budapest.'

'I'm so glad.'

'Why? What's going on?'

'It's been all over the news and the evening papers. Romania has closed its borders to everyone. The airports have been closed, and no one is allowed in or out of the country. We were worried you were inside and had been trapped.'

With the help of the next day's *Herald Tribune* I pieced together what had happened. Ceausescu had been at the Romanian Communist Party conference, the last he would ever hold as it turned out, electing himself president for another five years. His survival depended on insulating Romania from the wind of democracy so he gave orders to close the borders. Nearly everyone who wanted to travel to Romania that day would have done so by plane, but they could not as the airports were summarily closed. I must have been the only foreigner on the Sofia train who intended to get off in Romania, but I did have a legal visa. That is what the phone calls and the mystery had been about. Legal visa or not, neither I nor any other foreigner was going to be allowed into the country. The attempts to insulate the country did not work. Five weeks after my visit to Curtici, Nicolae and Elena Ceausescu were summarily tried and shot by their own secret police.

Four months later I got another visa for Romania and spent two weeks visiting Transylvania and Moldova, doing a story for a London newspaper. What a beautiful country. The people were desperately poor. Bread and water were available but little else. I was based in Sibiu, a handsome city that commands one of the Carpathian passes. Every afternoon little vans skidded into the main square *parmp-parmping* their horns. People would jostle and push to get whatever it was that the vans were carrying. At first I assumed it was food. I was wrong. These were editions of hastily run-off newspapers. For forty years the Romanians had been starved of news and truth. Now everyone was turning out a newspaper and expressing an opinion. People seized the papers and fell to discussing and arguing about the opinions in them. Forget food, they were intoxicated by freedom.

PART IV

I BUY A MOTORBIKE

20

Transit to Turkey

In 1991 I celebrated my menopause by buying a motorbike. I'd always wanted one. I crept off to Wimbledon and took some lessons, and a month later passed the test on a hired bike little bigger than a moped. After that, whenever I was in a car on a winding country road, I would dream that I was gliding round the corners on a steeply banked bike. I began secretly reading *Motorcycle News*. I knew exactly what I wanted. At forty-seven, I didn't see myself crouched over the tank of a Japanese racer or on a butched-up off-road bike; I wanted a powerful long-legged touring machine that would allow me to sit up straight and would keep on going for ever. A bike to go places on and to have adventures on.

One afternoon, just back from a trip to call on some Egyptian companies, I found myself standing outside BMW Park Lane. I knew little about motorbikes apart from titbits half-remembered from *Motorcycle News*, but I walked boldly in and up to the biggest bike, a steel-grey BMW

R100RT – a massive creature with fairings, slanting wind-screen and an engine that looked as if it belonged in an industrial museum.

'Have you got any of these in stock?' I asked the salesman, trying to sound knowledgeable.

'Several. What colour do you want?'

'I'll take the grey,' said I in my gruffest voice. 'And I'll be back tomorrow to pick it up. Oh, and I'll have a helmet as well. Extra large.'

Next day at 4 p.m. I returned. Terrified. I'd never been on anything bigger than the tiny bike on which I had taken my test a year earlier and had no idea how to ride a bike weigh-ing the best part of half a ton. The salesman stood there with a smile on his face waiting for me to ride off.

'You're OK with this, are you?'

'No problem, I'm cool,' said I, hoping that the sweat patches on my shirt weren't visible. The BMW was 1,000 cc, ten times as powerful as my test bike. Riding it out into Park Lane rush-hour traffic was a scary prospect. The salesman showed me the controls; I fired up the bike and gingerly steered the Beast out of the garage and off down the bus lane. The traffic chaos of Hyde Park Corner loomed up ahead. The Beast didn't shrug. It took me gently round the bends and as I opened the throttle a touch and banked into Belgrave Square I could feel my excitement growing.

That weekend I drove it up to Norfolk and back, and found that despite its size and power it was as sweet and docile as a pony. I was enchanted by the physicality of riding a bike – you did it all by weight. And the sense of freedom. This was what open-cockpit flying must have been like. Riding a bike, you become a different driver. You start to use senses that are asleep in a car. When I got off the motorway and on to an empty road and felt the Beast bank and swoop into bends with the grace of a butterfly, that gave me a feeling I had never had in a car.

Another dream had been a journey across Europe, not for sightseeing but for the sake of the journey. Anyone who asked 'What's the point of that?' wouldn't understand any more than I could fathom why people run marathons. The week-end after buying the bike, I set off for Istanbul. Guislaine understood. She worried but she understood. We talked about her flying out to join me in Istanbul but didn't want to tempt providence by making firm plans in case I didn't make it.

I had intended to leave on Monday morning, but the European weather forecast – 'France very stormy: heavy rain accompanied by winds as high as 100 kph' – meant that I fled down the M2 for Calais at daybreak on an October Sunday hoping to stay ahead of the storm. I had yet to ride in the rain and wasn't looking forward to it. The weather and I hit France at the same time. I arrived in Nancy that night, twelve hours after leaving Chelsea, exhausted from a day fighting gale-force winds and vicious rain.

But for a few moments that afternoon the rain had stopped and a pale autumnal sun had come out long enough to dry the road as we – the Beast and I – came down the Meuse Valley. I had tried thinking of the bike as a 'she', but it just didn't work. It was about as feminine as Walter Matthau, so the Beast it remained. My heart danced. The road curved gently along the valley, and as the surface dried, the bike began to find its footing round the corners. I even found myself in the middle of the Liège–Rome vintage car rally, and for an hour the Beast and I glided along as the poplars *whoosh-whooshed* by, escorted by Delahayes and Frazer-Nashes.

I had no exact route as I wasn't sure how far I'd be able to go each day. I had imagined that about four hours in the saddle would be enough, but a bike-riding neighbour told me that he had once covered 500 miles in a day. We'd see. Istanbul was well over 2,000 miles away; I had two weeks to get there and back, and I wanted a couple of days' rest in Istanbul. I would have to average further than London to Edinburgh each day.

I decided on the northern route out, France, Germany, Switzerland, Austria, Hungary and then dropping down through my old friend Romania – where I hoped this time my visa would be honoured – and finally on to Bulgaria and over the mountains into Turkey. I intended to take the southern route back, across Greece and through Italy, using the ferry across the Adriatic to bypass a Yugoslavia torn by civil war.

Next morning I woke to the sound of cars splashing through water in the street. The dawn sky over Nancy was thick with rain clouds and the wind still moaned. I contemplated giving up: No one apart from Guislaine knows I'm doing this. I must be mad. Why don't I just go home and get warm and dry? but I decided to continue. I would give it another day, and if it was still hellish then I'd creep quietly back to England. With some dread I put my wet biking over-clothes back on and nosed the Beast out into the rain.

Dodging through the mist-shrouded mountains of the Vosges, I found the views dramatic and the driving terrifying.

On a bike the front brake is the one that stops you and has all the power, the back being an auxiliary. This works well in the dry. In the wet, if you hit the front brake while you are going round a corner you can send yourself over a precipice.

Things got worse when we crossed the border into Germany and found ourselves sucked into the autobahn system bypassing Freiburg. The road was a narrow two lanes each way with a slippery concrete surface and traffic in the slow lane going at 75 mph. Overtaking in these conditions was hard. I discovered that a big truck creates a quarter-mile wake of turbulence which builds to a climax as you pull out to pass it, and just after you do, you get sucked the other way and buffeted by a crosswind.

Then it changed. The rain stopped, the sun came out, the road dried and we were in the Black Forest. Bikers from all over Europe come to ride here just for the fun of it. It was a strange but gratifying feeling to find myself part of a new fellowship. As big bikers pass on the open road they salute each other. At first I found myself returning their salutes with a kind of royal wave, until I realised how gauche this made me seem. The appropriate acknowledgement was a two-inch lift of the outside hand and an upward flick of the two outside fingers. Lunch in the weak sun by Lake Konstanz, and then once more the rain came down. This set the pattern for the next few days: just as I was wondering how much more punishment I could take, everything would come right and there would be an hour or two of biking ecstasy.

I avoided motorways where I could. They make for boring riding at best, and even where they pass through scenery as beautiful as that between Innsbruck and Vienna, you don't have the spare concentration to admire the views. My rule became that when it was wet I stayed on the motorways and covered the miles, and when it cleared up I sought out the small roads and the mountain passes.

I left the autobahns for the Alpine road up through the ski resorts of Lech and Zurs to the Arlberg Pass and down to St Anton. The Arlberg is the watershed of Europe. To the west of it everything drains into the Rhine and the North Sea; to the east everything flows down into the Danube and the Black Sea. The sparse traffic was left behind like sweet wrappings. The bike rose and fell like a lapwing on the long mountain bends. Brake, change down, bank to the right, change down again, let the bike almost fall sideways as the bend tightens, just a touch of throttle to pick her up before she goes over, now some more throttle to bring her upright, and then over and bank to the left for the next bend. Perhaps the best moments were those instants on long S-bends when I flowed out of one curve and brought the bike up and into the opposite bank for the next. It's close to the feeling of slaloming down a field of fresh powder snow.

If those were the high points, things didn't get much worse than the four stomach-clenching hours from the Hungarian border at Nadlac to Sibiu in Romania, where I hoped to spend the night. There weren't many private cars on the roads in Romania. The traffic consisted of locally made diesel lorries, which sputtered and coughed and left bits behind them in the road, agricultural machinery, horse-drawn wagons and weary peasants plodding from one village to the next.

The main road was just wide enough for a tractor to over-take a hay wagon. In the rain its already slippery surface was made worse by a top dressing of diesel oil and donkey drop-pings from the wagons. This produced a surface on which riding something with two wheels required skills which I was not sure I had yet learned. When night fell it became worse. The tractors and carts had no lights, and my normally power-ful headlight wasn't much use through a smear of mud.

But when I arrived I felt like a star. There was a hotel in Sibiu, the Imperator Romaniul, which Nico Ceausescu, the dictator's son, had had restored. Every surface was marble or mahogany. The Beast, a rarity in Romania, was parked in a place of honour under the main hotel canopy and soon attracted a crowd of around fifty. The old-fashioned archi-tecture of its great finned engine was something they could appreciate.

Next morning another crowd had gathered. I felt like a medieval knight preparing for battle as I slipped on helmet, over-trousers and gloves, stowed my luggage in the panniers and inserted the folded map in the transparent cover of the tank bag. The more knowledgeable kept up a commentary: 'Now he's turning on the petrol. Look at those carburettors.' The Beast's star quality was a blessing. There were between 200 and 300 cars in the queues at the infrequent petrol stations. I drove up to the front each time, and instead of the other drivers objecting, as they had every right to, they got out of their cars to admire the Beast.

By the time I reached Bucharest, the rioting miners who had been disrupting the city for the two previous weeks had gone home and I was able to photograph the bike in front of the blackened parliament building until President Iliescu's motorcade came out; the guards, who had been quarrelling about who was going to sit on the Beast and have their picture taken, hurriedly shooed me away. That night, after five days on the road, I reached the Black Sea at Varna in Bulgaria. I had crossed Europe, sea to sea.

All along the coast were neat white hotels set in lush gardens and a shoreline of rocky coves and sandy beaches. I biked to dinner in the next village just in T-shirt and jeans – no helmet, no gloves, no jacket. I had a wonderful illicit feeling of freedom with the wind on my cheeks and bare arms for the first time on the trip. It was here that Ovid had been exiled for eight years of moaning after he wrote *Ars Amatoria*. What was he on about? Next morning I saw his point. A great storm had rolled in from the Black Sea. I looked out with a mixture of excitement and terror and was thankful that I only had 300 miles to cover that day to reach Istanbul.

Bikers develop a blind person's sensitivity to road surfaces – the slipperiness of the white line in the middle, the join left by a road mender, the qualities of grip of different types of tarmac and concrete. This new skill was severely tested when I took the shorter, inland route to the border through the mountains. The road ran through forest and over heath, the surface varying from leaf pulp to sheep droppings. In places the road had collapsed over a cliff edge, and the Beast and I had to pick our way over the debris. The cold was intense. I had stopped in a bus shelter in Varna to put on a sweater. I hid from the rain under a cliff to put on a second. By the time I reached the Turkish border at the high mountain pass beyond Malko Tarnovo I had on five layers and the noise of chattering teeth echoed around my helmet. I sang to keep my spirits up, but that fogged the visor.

There was a two-hour delay at the border while Turkish officials sipped tea and bullied Bulgarians on their way to Istanbul. I felt as if I were entering the Ottoman empire. I was sent to a special room to get a visa; a mustachioed officer flicked through my passport and then left the room with it. After fifteen minutes I asked where he had taken it. 'Toilet.' I hoped he had enough paper and was relieved when, after another twenty minutes, he brought it back with its pages intact and gave me a visa.

I often thought during the journey out that things couldn't get worse. Each time I was soon proved wrong. I still don't like to remember the four hours from the border to Istanbul. Although the road was narrow, it was the main artery connecting Turkey with Europe and a thundering procession of speeding trucks. The rain never let up while the cold and wind increased. Water had penetrated my over-clothes, and I felt as if I was sitting in cold rice pudding. Each time a truck swept past in the opposite direction it was like standing on the edge of a station platform as an express went through. I was hit by a wall of solid air and tossed about like a canoe in the rapids.

At last I was in the suburbs of Istanbul and after the buffeting I had received relieved to be in slower-moving rush-hour traffic, even Turkish rush-hour traffic. I had no idea where I was until suddenly the sparkle of light on water popped up on the right – the Bosphorus. I could get my bearings and orientate myself. I had biked from the other side of the English Channel to within sight of Asia. Then it was easy, past the six minarets of the Blue Mosque, the Galata Bridge and up the hill to the Pera Palace Hotel, which was built in 1892 to accommodate the first passengers from the Orient Express, and hadn't changed since Agatha Christie wrote *Murder on the Orient Express* in Room 411.

I was received with courtesy by Hakan at the hotel desk when I stumbled in dripping, steaming and stinking in bike suit and helmet, trailed by a flunkey carrying my pannier bags. I had no booking – to have booked before I knew I would make it to Istanbul might have tempted providence – but was escorted up in the 1892 lift, the only lift I know with a sofa in it, to a magnificent room on the top floor with Turkish rugs on the floor, a marble bathroom and a view over the Golden Horn.

Next morning I met Guislaine off the plane from London and we had a weekend of bazaars and mosques and little fish restaurants. It rained most of the time but we didn't care. The Beast stayed in the Pera Palace garage, apart from a trip to the Blue Mosque to pose for photographs. Guislaine was worried when I told her how bad conditions had been on the journey out.

'How awful. Just looking at you I can see you've suffered. You must have been miserable.'

That made me think.

'You know, I was tired, cold, uncomfortable and often terrified, but I was never unhappy. I was never miserable. I wouldn't say I enjoyed it all, but it was a great thing to do, and the bits that were good were fantastic.'

The next morning I headed off at dawn for the return trip into the obligatory thunderstorm. I felt like a refugee from the Book of Job. But surely nothing could hurt me now. We, the Beast and I, had even survived a dust storm in

Bulgaria. Hadn't we seen it all? Not quite. The storm leaving Istanbul was so violent that it brought an avalanche of rocks and mud down from the mountains on to the motorway, which had to be closed and traffic diverted to the coast road. This was flooded a foot deep. How could we get through this? I put my head down, engaged second gear and prayed. Clouds of hissing steam as brown slush washed over the hot engine, mud on the visor, bow waves from passing trucks, but the Beast chugged through without a hiccup. We lost the horn though, its Teutonic klaxon reduced thereafter to a mere burp.

And that was the last trial. It was as if I was being tested, and the rest of the way home was a reward for surviving. The sun came out and the wind dropped. The Beast and I coasted along the Aegean, swept up through the Pindus Mountains on a road that seemed to float in the sky, and came down to the Ionian Sea on the other side of Greece. I took breakfast in an olive grove and then a ferry trip up a tranquil Adriatic as thunder rumbled over warring Yugoslavia. There followed a night in Stresa on Lake Maggiore and a pink dawn as I crossed the roof of Europe, the Simplon Pass. That was the best of them all, two hours of swooping bends that danced around the flanks of the mountain.

The plan had been to stop for the night in Paris and then drive on to Calais the next morning, but the adrenalin was so high when I came down from the Simplon that I didn't want to stop. We cruised past Paris at dusk on the Périphérique and kept going.

Seventeen hours after leaving Lake Maggiore, the Beast and I skidded on to the midnight boat from Calais. At 3 a.m.

we banked gently into a deserted Parliament Square after twenty hours in the saddle and 800 miles on the road in one day. Three more to go.

Along the Embankment we were slaloming from side to side in triumph, Europe twice crossed and 5,000 miles behind us. I had my visor up and was singing with joy while the tears rolled down my face. I hoped a policeman would stop me.

'Now, now, sir. Going somewhere, are we?'

'No, officer, I've been.'

Shortly after an account of this trip appeared in the *Sunday Telegraph* I received the letter below (the names have been changed):

Nov 25th 1991
Dear Mr Morland,

I ask forgiveness for burdening you with this letter, yet I write it with some compulsion for your article on 'The Beast' in the Sunday Telegraph 24 November opened my eyes in a manner which has given me a considerable degree of solace.

My son Paul, a Metropolitan policeman aged 28, of Bow Street and then Heathrow, also owned a much beloved BMW R100RS bought from Coopers of Park Lane, after having three or four of the same make previously. He had considerable experience and had done two Police motorcycle courses. Like you, he was lyrical in his attitude towards his machine and enjoyed every minute riding it, servicing it, or even standing gazing adoringly at it.

Until reading of the almost ethereal joy it gave you, I could not imagine how such a huge and powerful – and frightening – piece of machinery could become so compulsive as to rate second only to his young wife of less than two years. To me, it was a monster, a machine that seemed more likely to be master than mastered, so that one day standing alongside it outside this house, I banged my fist on its saddle, saying: 'I hate this bloody thing, it's a death trap'. Patiently, Paul said, as he had said often before: 'No Dad, it's not, it's the most marvellous thing I've ever owned . . . I'm quite safe on it . . . I don't take chances . . . I've had lots of experience and two Police courses . . . there's nothing for you to worry about.' He turned and put on his helmet, then looked at me over his shoulder: 'Of course, Dad, none of us can handle a cowboy coming round a bend on the wrong side of the road.'

Ten days later, at 11.18 at night on 2 August 1990, that is exactly what killed him. Coming off duty at Heathrow, a 20-year-old in a ten-year-old Capri, lost control on a bend in Clockhouse Lane, near Staines, hit the nearside kerb and, at about 50 mph, slewed across the road so that Paul could not avoid it, despite later investigation indicating that he had braked and was only doing 14½ mph. The BMW front wheel went into the car and killed the driver, the petrol tank exploded and the two dead boys were pulled out of the inferno by courageous passers-by before being burned.

We, and his wife, know that he would never have given up his beloved BMW and that he was fully aware of risks, but to me – until I read your proud and happy piece of writing – it was incomprehensible that he should prefer it to their car. So, as I have said, your opening my eyes has provided a queer sort of solace, that my lovely son would prefer to die as he did than by the shotgun of a bandit – he had already won the High Commissioner's Highest Award for Bravery for chasing and disarming a bank robber in the Strand in London, after being knocked to the ground and the gun placed at his head.

So, thank you for writing it. I hope it gives you a sort of pride to know that, with my Son, you are part of a unique and perhaps-to-be-envied sect.

Here's wishing you happy and safe riding.

Yours sincerely,
David Freeman
Miles Morland Esq.,
c/o Sunday Telegraph,
London

21

The Great Ghana Trade

By 1992 Blakeney Management had outgrown the garden shed, and I needed to be in London to see my consulting clients. Shortly after the Walk, while we were moving to Norfolk, I had bought a houseboat on the Thames in Chelsea, the *Rudyard Kipling*, as a London pied-à-terre, or perhaps pied-à-l'eau.

Sadly, the house in Blakeney had to go. Now that my business was starting to move forward we needed to be somewhere within an hour or so of London. In 1992 we sold Blakeney and moved to a creaking old house in a village in the Vale of the White Horse, between Wantage and Lambourn in Oxfordshire. The village sat at the foot of the downs, along the crest of which ran the Ridgeway, dating back to the Stone Age. This was horse country. Each village had a couple of trainers who would lead their strings of horses up every morning to where the springy chalk-grown turf on top of the downs made ideal training gallops.

It was pretty, but I have never been a country person or a horse person. I like the sea. I missed Blakeney and left part of my soul there. Guislaine, who has never been as attached to the sea as I, liked our new country existence and soon settled in. I used to spend three or four nights a week in London on the houseboat doing Blakeney Management work; Guislaine, who had initially regarded the boat with detachment but had later become an enthusiastic, if nervous, boatie, would join me for half of that time and spend the rest happily lost in the country.

I acquired a real office, the ground floor of a little building on the quay of the houseboat moorings, and Pips Wooderson came to work with me as my assistant. Life was as good as it could be. I loved scurrying around Africa and the Middle East talking to businessmen, politicians, journalists and stock-market people. There was still no one else doing it and I was regarded as a curiosity, but what fun I was having finding things out. I would have lunch from time to time with friends who still worked for big investment banks. The stories were the same: overwork, pressure, intrigue, politics, memos and meetings, arguments over bonuses, clumsy Americans show-ing the ignorant Europeans 'how to do it'.

How happy I was not to be part of that. Much of what I was now doing belonged more in the pages of Evelyn Waugh than in the City of London, nothing more so than the Great Ghana Trade of 1993. My best friend in West Africa was Ken Ofori-Atta, a charming and aristocratic Ashanti who had been to Yale, worked on Wall Street, and now, in his thirties, gone back to Ghana to found Databank, the first real invest-ment bank in the country.

Ken's grandfather had been Nana Sir Ofori-Atta, the Okyenhene or King of the Akyem Abuakwa, a people who are kin to the Ashanti and acknowledge the overlordship of the Asantahene, the Ashanti king. Nana Sir Ofori-Atta had had 25 wives and 126 children. When he died in 1943 several of his pageboys went missing. The British authorities instituted an enquiry and found that they had been dispatched to accompany the Okyenhene into the afterworld, the tradition being that such a great man could not arrive unattended when he went to meet his ancestors. With blasphemous disregard for local custom the British authorities arrested three members of the family and hanged them for the murder of the boys.

Ken was more interested in taking Ghana into the modern world than in burying pageboys. He knew everyone in Ghana and was generous in his introductions. In return I would sit in the office with him and Keli Gadzekpo, his partner, and give them advice on how to build an investment firm. On the office walls were pictures of his grandfather and of Malcolm X, the American black power leader.

One day we drove to Kumasi, the Ashanti capital, a long and bumpy drive from Accra through the forest. On our way back, women jumped out of the forest like Italians with their baskets of porcini in autumn, and waved coconuts, tied in bunches of five or six and suspended on palm fronds threaded through their shells, at us.

'Angie told me to buy some for dinner tonight,' said Ken.

He asked his driver to stop and stepped out of the car. I followed him. He stood there immaculate in his dark blue suit and Hermès tie, blue shirt with white collar, and gleaming shoes. Soon three or four women surrounded him thrusting their coconuts at him. The coconuts had funny pointy shells. Then I realised that they were moving around.

These were no coconuts; they were the giant Ghanaian land snails I had heard about. They were the size of chickens. Ken bought a couple of bunches and threw them in the back of the Peugeot station wagon. We drove on. I was in the back seat. From time to time I would see snail horns and slug-like faces the size of tennis balls trying to climb over into my seat. I shuddered.

'Jesus, Ken. How do you cook those?'

'Miles, I'm not sure. I've never been in the kitchen. But they are delicious.'

'I don't mind the odd escargot but I'll pass. Thank God you didn't invite me to dinner at your house tonight. I really wouldn't want to eat those.'

Ken laughed. 'Miles, what do you think you ate in the palm-nut soup last night.'

'No.'

'Yes.'

The palm-nut soup had been thick and dark brown in colour. It was viscous and filled with fibrous matter. I resolved to feed Ken a kipper when he was next in London, possibly with jellied eels to follow.

Ken introduced me to many important businessmen and politicians. One afternoon I had a meeting with Dr Kwesi Botchwey, who had been finance minister of Ghana for over ten years and was respected across the continent. I was ushered into his office, but Dr Botchwey did not look particularly pleased to see me. This was because Ken was associated with the Ashanti-led New Patriotic Party (NPP), which was in opposition to Dr Botchwey's NDC. I was desperate to think of something that would make Dr Botchwey take me seriously. Ken had told me that Ghana was under strong pressure from the World Bank to privatise and that Jim Wolfensohn, its president, was visiting Ghana in a few months' time. If no progress had been made on privatisation by then it was possible that the World Bank would withdraw its support from Ghana.

Ken and I were cooking up a scheme. We knew it could not work but it might at least get us noticed. He had told me that Dr Botchwey had been talking to S. G. Warburg, the respected British investment bank, about a scheme to sell off the government's holdings in seven of the biggest companies on the Ghana Stock Exchange including Unilever Ghana and several of the banks.

'Your Excellency,' I said to Dr Botchwey, 'I can help you with your plan to privatise the government's stock-market holdings.'

'Yes.' Dr Botchwey looked at me suspiciously. 'What?'

'Well, at present I understand you have mandated an international bank to do it. They will take many months to produce a prospectus, many more months to mount a market-ing campaign, and finally, in maybe a year's time, place the shares, for which they will charge you a fee of some 6 to 7 per cent. You will not get your money till next year.'

'Mr Morland, I cannot comment on our plans. They are confidential.'

'Well, Your Excellency, my firm, Blakeney, will do it for you both more quickly and more cheaply than Warburgs or whichever other advisers you are talking to. I know the people active in African markets better than the international banks because those people are consulting clients of Blakeney

Management. Moreover, I will charge you nothing. Blakeney is paid by its clients.'

Dr Botchwey looked out of the window, yawned, explored his right ear and then looked back at me.

'What is this Blackney?'

'Blakeney, Your Excellency, is a highly respected consulting firm known throughout the United States and Europe for its African research. Most of the biggest emerging-market investment institutions look to Blakeney for guidance on investing in Africa. I am its chief executive.' I did not think it necessary to tell Dr B that I was also its only executive.

'So what would this Blackney do and how long till the government receives its money?'

As this whole exercise was fantasy, there was little risk in making a bold promise.

'Your Excellency, we have consulting clients eager to invest in Ghana. From the time Blakeney receives your mandate, the firm will put its entire resources behind the initiative. I can promise you that it will take us less than a month to place the shares with our clients, at the end of which period you will receive your money at no cost to you.'

'Thank you, Mr Morland. Goodbye. I have another meeting.'

Two weeks later I was back in London. The Ghana trip had been a success although Blakeney was still far from being taken seriously in Africa. The phone rang. It was a terrible line. Pips told me someone was calling from Ghana and put them through. Eventually I realised I was talking to Dr Botchwey's deputy.

'Mr Morland, you will remember what you said to Dr Botchwey about selling our holdings on the exchange. We have been in conversation with Mr Ofori-Atta following your meeting with the minister.'

Now what?

'Yes, yes, I remember well. It was an honour to meet the minister.'

'Mr Morland, we accept your proposal. Mr Ofori-Atta will handle all matters in Ghana. All you need to do is to produce the buyers for the shares. You will remember that you informed Dr Botchwey that this would not be a problem and that your firm had clients eager to invest in Ghana.'

'Um, yes, absolutely. Yes. It may take a little time. Maybe three months.'

'No, Mr Morland, one month. The government needs to be paid in one month, as you promised Dr Botchwey.'

'Of course, of course. No problem. I'll get my people to work on it right away.' I hung up. 'Jesus Christ . . .'

Pips looked at me.

'Miles, are you all right? You look as if you'd just had a shock. Would you like a glass of water?'

I had done some research on the shares the government wished to sell. They constituted 25 per cent of the value of the entire Ghana stock exchange. To the best of my knowledge no one had ever placed more than about 5 per cent of the value of a stock exchange in one go. Also and again to the best of my knowledge, no foreign institution had up to now ever bought a single share on the Ghanaian exchange. Yes, I had just had a shock.

Fortunately, after a previous visit to Ghana I had written a seventy-page report on the companies listed on the exchange saying how cheap they were. I had sent this to my consulting clients and it had elicited a couple of questions and some mild interest. No one had asked me how they might go about actually buying some of these bargains, and if they had the liquidity on the exchange was so poor that their chances of putting much money to work were small.

Now everything was different. The world-famous firm of Blakeney Management with its one-room office on a quay in Chelsea had a mandate to sell a quarter of the entire exchange. Although the value of this package of shares was tiny by international standards, about $50 million, it would provide enough liquidity to float a battleship.

I called Ken.

'Hi, guy,' he said. 'Did the deputy minister call you? Isn't it great? Your pitch went over so well.' I had omitted to tell Ken that my pitch was only vaguely rooted in reality.

'Yes, yes. It's great. May take a bit of work though.'

'Don't worry, Miles. We'll handle this end of it. For reasons of transparency they want the trade to go through the exchange. The government will be the seller and your clients will be the buyers. We've just joined the exchange so this will be our first trade. We'll get on with setting up the Ghana end. All you need to do is give us the identity of the buyers.'

Simple really. I had one possibility. One of my clients was a powerful and aggressive New York hedge fund. Let's call them Stone Partners. I didn't talk to Micky Stone himself but to Jack, one of his associates, who was in charge of exotic markets. I needed a lead buyer and Stone could be it. Two days later I was in New York in Jack's office.

I explained that I had a unique mandate from the government of Ghana to sell a package of ridiculously cheaply valued shares. 'Jack, I've had a lot of interest in these shares from my other clients. There's big demand out there for the new markets, and Ghana is as cheap as it gets.'

Jack had a copy of my report on his desk. I saw it had been well thumbed and annotated. Stone liked doing things that were off the map. They prided themselves on doing big macho trades and loved doing things that other people didn't dare to.

'Miles, I've been to see Micky. I showed him the report. Micky's hot for frontier markets. We've had a great run in the large markets and he thinks the crap is gonna get off the floor and start dancing. We like this trade. Tell you what. I'm going to jump on the plane to wherever you fly to in Ghana, check it out, see some of the companies, talk to your Ghanaian broker buddy, and if we still like the trade when I get back, we'll do it.'

I resisted the temptation to jump over the desk and hug Jack. I tried to look cool and uninterested.

'Well, OK. But as I say we've seen a lot of interest in this trade. If you decided you wanted to do it after your visit, how much of the $50 million would you want to do? You'd have to take a share of the whole package. I'm afraid we couldn't allow you to cherry-pick the shares you liked best.'

'Mate –' Jack was Australian '– we don't piss about. We'll take the whole lot. Don't want other people muscling in on the trade.'

'Hmm, OK, Jack. Lemme think about that. The Ghanaians are keen on spreading the shares among a number of different buyers – but, hey, I think we might be able to make this work.'

'Too right, mate – you're gonna make it work. But look, no worries, if we do the trade it'll be split among five or six of our accounts. It'll look like five different buyers. That should satisfy your Ghanaian buddies.'

I was now in a tricky position. I had other clients I was due to see in New York and needed a fallback in case Stone decided not to do the trade, but I didn't want to excite people too much and then tell them they couldn't take part. Luckily my other clients were generally more measured and careful. I went to see them, got some polite interest but found no one who was ready to commit. They asked to be kept in touch.

A week later Jack made his trip to Accra. I had asked Ken to take good care of him, but there had been some misunderstandings. Jack was accustomed to being treated like a deity when he arrived in an emerging market. He expected to be met at the airport and glad-handed throughout his stay. He had taken his wife along with him to 'show her Africa', to which neither of them had ever been. Ken, on the other hand, was an aristocratic Ashanti who was delighted to take Jack around to see the companies, but it had never occurred to him that he was meant to be Jack's butler.

Despite Jack's annoyance at the lack of limos at the airport and the fact that he and his wife were expected to make their own plans for dinner, the trip was a success from a business point of view. Ken phoned and told me that Jack wanted to go ahead with the trade. We now had the mechanics of the trade to set up. Someone needed to arrange for the transfer of $50 million to Ghana and simultaneously take custody of the shares released by the government. Stone had a close relationship with Salomon Brothers – Solly as they were universally known – the firm made famous in Michael Lewis's book *Liar's Poker*. Solly were not the biggest investment bank but they were certainly the toughest and most aggressive. They went where others didn't dare.

Jack, after a quick moan about how he had not been looked after the way he expected, said he was ready to do the trade and suggested using Solly to set it up and do the custody. I was delighted because my ignorance of the mechanics of such an unusual deal was complete.

'Sure, Jack. Great idea. Do you want me to talk to them?'

'No worries, mate. I'll handle it. I'll talk to Billy.' Billy was a Solly partner already famous for his exploits in the Russian markets. 'This'll be child's play for him.'

I could not believe it, but little by little this trade was coming together. We had a buyer, Jack's five different Stone accounts; we had a seller, the government of Ghana; we had a broker to execute the trade, Ken Ofori-Atta; and now we had someone to take care of moving the money and taking custody of the securities on behalf of Stone, the mighty Salomon Brothers. The deputy finance minister was calling Ken daily and asking when the trade was going to happen. We scheduled it for a Thursday two weeks out to allow Solly time to set up the transfer and custody arrangements. That was two weeks before the scheduled visit of Jim Wolfensohn, the head of the World Bank. Our trade would allow the government of Ghana to show him that they were serious about privatisation.

I was a happy man. Or I was until the phone rang on Wednesday, eight days before the trade was due to happen. It was Jack, calling from New York.

'Hey, Miles, mate.'

'Hi, Jack, what's up?'

'Micky's spooked about the way some of these emerging markets are acting.'

'Sorry to hear that. Still, Ghana should be OK. It's insulated from the big markets. It shouldn't affect our trade.'

'Miles, sorry, mate, but there isn't going to be a Ghana trade. Well, not for us. But don't worry. Billy owes us a few favours and this is chicken feed for Solly. So I told him to find some buyers for the trade himself. Hope that's OK with you. Bye.'

The bastard. Now, not only didn't I have a buyer but my carefully nurtured trade was about to go walkabout in the wilderness. Billy had never been anywhere near Ghana and knew nothing about the package of shares. If he attempted to place them it would be chaos. The Ghanaians would hunt me down and have me fed to the snails. I needed to get the trade back under my control and to place the shares with my other clients, all of whom at least were now familiar with Ghana thanks to my report and could be counted on not to try and resell them into a non-functioning stock market as soon as they had bought them. God knows if it could be done, but that was the only hope.

I called Billy in New York only to find he was in Ecuador chasing down an Ecuadorean bond trade. There were no mobile phones in those days. I finally reached him on Friday afternoon in his hotel in Quito. I explained that the shares needed to be placed in firm hands.

'Hey, Miles. Whatever. Y' know, I like this trade. These shares are great value but it's your trade, my friend. Tell you what. Lemme keep $10 million worth for Solly's account and for a few of our friends and you do the rest.'

'Thanks, Billy. That's great.'

All I needed to do now was, in the next five days, find buyers for $40 million of Ghanaian shares among people who had never owned an African share before. It was lucky that I had been to see my other clients as an insurance policy when Stone had committed to the trade. There was of course no email. Everything had to be done by phone and fax. The phone lines to Ghana seldom worked. Pips had raw fingers from continually dialling Ken. I went to see my London clients. I phoned my American and European clients, and then I phoned them again. Somehow the trade began coming together.

On Thursday morning Ken, as scheduled, in his first ever trade on the Ghana stock exchange, walked on to the floor and traded one quarter of the value of the entire exchange. No one had ever done that before, anywhere. The seller was the government of Ghana. The buyers were identified as clients of Blakeney Management. Their names were not made public, but they were a high-quality group of institutions, some of the biggest and most respected names in the world of emerging-market investing – far more respected than Stone. I could not believe it, but the Great Ghana Trade had become a reality.

I was exhausted but exhilarated.

The next day the *Financial Times* ran a quarter-page story on the trade. Blakeney Management, of whom no one had ever heard, was mentioned as if it was a well known firm. The aftermath of the trade also worked well. The Ghanaian government got its money on time, and Mr Wolfensohn was pleased. Those of my clients who participated in the trade decided to take a closer look at Ghana and began buying more shares there, which in turn encouraged the locals to follow them into their own market. As a result the market more or less tripled in the next year, giving Blackney Management a lot of happy clients who made a lot of money.

And next time I went to call on people in Accra or Lagos they knew who we were. Blackney had street cred in Africa.

22

Man Has Accident in Muscat

Most careers are a series of random accidents to which we later try to lend logic. I had one such accident at the end of 1993. The consulting business was going well; the Great Ghana Trade had caused a stir, and I was now turning away consulting clients. One afternoon two tall men called Nigel shimmied into my office on the quay. One was Nigel Pilkington, a friend since First Boston days. He brought with him the equally tall and elegant figure of Nigel Cayzer.

'Know anything about Oman?' said Nigel Cayzer.

'Funnily enough, yes. I do know a bit. All the Gulf stock markets are closed to foreign investors, but one of these days they'll have to open up so I thought I'd find out about them in advance. Then when they do open I'll be ready. So yes, I've done some work on the Muscat Securities Market and it looks interesting.'

'Good boy,' said Nigel P, giving an I-told-you-so look to Nigel C.

'Well, that is a good thing,' said Nigel C. 'You appear to be the only man outside the Gulf who has ever heard of the Muscat Securities Market. You see, I know the Omanis pretty well, and the chap in charge of the stock market is a very go-ahead person called Muhammad Musa, who's also the minister for development. He wants to open their market to foreigners but he doesn't want to let the whole world invest there because it's a small market and he worries they might get swamped.'

'That makes sense. A number of countries, like Brazil and Korea, have done it by stages,' I said.

'Exactly,' said Nigel C. 'Muhammad has been studying what they did and would like to do the same thing. He'd like someone to raise $50 million for a fund for foreigners to invest in Oman. That fund would be given an exclusive licence. They would be the only foreigners permitted to invest in the market and would also be allowed to invest in the other Gulf markets. What do you think?'

'It's a great idea. The Gulf markets are cheap, and there's a lot of oil money out there in the hands of the locals, which one of these days will find its way into their own markets. When that happens they'll blow the roof off. Running the Oman fund will be a nice piece of business for whoever you get to manage it. Anything I can do to help?'

'Well, yes,' said Nigel C. 'How would you like to raise the money and manage the fund?'

'Me??'

'Yes. How about it? We could work together. The Omanis would help.'

'Look, it's a great opportunity for someone, maybe Foreign & Colonial or Genesis, but I'm not a money manager; I'm just a consultant. You have to be registered with IMRO to manage money. I'm not.'

Consultants advise investors as to what to do, and the investors may or may not take the consultants' advice. A money manager, on the other hand, is entrusted with a chunk of investors' money, either retail money from individuals, or institutional money from entities like pension funds and insurance companies, to look after. The manager makes the decisions as to what to buy or sell and gets paid a management fee relative to the size of the assets.

I refrained from saying that my money-management skills dated back to the era of bowler hats. The last time I had been a money manager had been on Schroders' investment desk some twenty years earlier. 'Sorry. I'd love to help but I can't.'

The Nigels shimmied off into the Chelsea night.

Later that evening Nigel Pilkington rang. He had a knack of making everything sound simple. 'Miles,' he said, 'you should do this. It's a great opportunity. And I'd help. It would be great to be working together again.'

'But I can't. I'm not registered with IMRO, and I'd need more people at Blakeney. I'm just one man and a Pips at present.'

'Yes, but you've got to start somewhere.'

He was right. Two months later, in late 1993, Blakeney Management was registered as a money manager with IMRO, the predecessor regulator to the FSA. I had hired Khaled Abdel-Majeed, an experienced Palestinian investment professional, as my partner, and we had mandated Barings, then the greatest power in emerging-market investment banking, to help us raise $50 million for the Oryx Fund, an Oman fund to be listed on the London Stock Exchange. The two Nigels were going to be on the board of directors along with a number of well known Omanis. I criss-crossed the US and Europe pitching to investors while Khaled spent time in Oman visiting local companies and getting to know them well.

Somehow this too came together despite my scepticism as to whether it was doable, and by June 1994 the Oryx Fund was a reality. Not only were we in business as a money manager but anyone who wanted to invest in the Gulf had to buy shares in the Oryx Fund; we were the only non-Gulf residents licensed to invest there.

Then I had another idea. A number of my consulting clients had from time to time asked me if I would manage some money for them and invest it all over Africa and the Middle East on their behalf. I had thanked them but turned them down as I was not licensed. Now I was, so I got back to them not just about the Oman market but also Africa and the rest of the Middle East. By the end of 1994 Blakeney Investors, a Luxembourg-registered trust, had been set up, and we had $17 million from ten different investors, an infinitesimal sum by money-management standards, but a beginning. I hired three more people to help as we had such a huge geographical area to cover and we were now a fully fledged emerging-market manager specialising in Africa and the Middle East. In fact we were the only emerging-market manager doing anything at all in these areas.

A year later we had another stroke of luck. One of our investors, John Walton, managed money for the Yale University Endowment Office. Yale's chief investment officer,

David Swensen, is the best-respected investor in the US after Warren Buffett, and under him the Yale Endowment had grown mightily to over $20 billion and outperformed every other large endowment fund in the US. John introduced us to Swensen, and in 1995 we began managing money for Yale. This was the ultimate seal of approval. David Swensen later wrote the bible on managing institutional money, *Pioneering Portfolio Management*, in which he makes unflattering comments about most of the big money managers, whom he dismisses as 'asset-gatherers'. About Blakeney and me, on the other hand, he says nice things and refers to us as a new type of animal, a 'guerrilla investment manager'. We were flattered. Soon other money came in too, and in addition to Oryx and a similar fund we set up in 1997 in Lebanon – the only fund for foreign investors in the Beirut market – we were managing $300 million by 1998.

Our performance was terrific. Others were starting to discover the markets we had pioneered, and this was pushing up the prices of the stocks we owned. I had closed down the consulting business in 1994 as we could no longer give hedge funds disinterested advice on markets in which we had become the biggest foreign investor. I then made the classic mistake made by entrepreneurs who enjoy some early success. I got overconfident and made a near-fatal misjudgement.

Like so many entrepreneurs who have a success in one area I thought I could extend this to a related area. Drunk with my own brilliance after four years of stellar success, I decided that African companies were short of management and technical expertise, and if we could get control of some of them, as opposed to just being the passive investor we had been to date, I could bring in management and technical expertise from outside and enhance our investors' returns. On paper it was a brilliant idea.

With my clients' money and with some help from some old consulting clients who were happy to come along for the ride, Blakeney got control of four companies and I or my nominee went on the board. We did not run the companies on a day-to-day basis but controlled their strategies and had a decisive say in appointing their senior management. The four companies were: the Social Security Bank of Ghana, of which we bought 51 per cent from the government in a deal teed up by Ken; African Lakes, a Glasgow-based trading company so old that Dr Livingstone had gone to some of its early board meetings; African Plantations, in which we co-invested with Soros and the giant Moore Capital, a private company run by Dekel Golan, an entrepreneurial Israeli who was going to bring modern Israeli management and agricultural techniques to the tradition-bound business of growing tea and coffee in Africa; and lastly Lonrho Africa, an unrelated bundle of assets collected by the buccaneering Tiny Rowland, which, now that Tiny Rowland was dead, was without a strategy.

These were referred to collectively as Blakeney's strategic investments. We managed to exit one of them, the Ghanaian bank, with a modest profit after five years of very hard work and many sweaty days spent planning strategy in Accra. So brilliant were my strategic investment skills that the other three investments went all but bankrupt.

We sold African Lakes' existing businesses and used the proceeds to buy, at the top of the market, Africa On-Line, the continent's leading Internet service provider. Africa On-Line proved to have an insatiable hunger for money and very modest revenues. We eventually sold the company for virtually nothing. Meanwhile, Dekel Golan's modern agricultural techniques had locked African Plantations into a cycle of expansion by building dams, generators and irrigation systems at a time when the traditional tea and coffee growers were spending nothing and waiting for prices to recover to normal levels. We lost 100 per cent of our clients' money there.

Our strategy at Lonrho Africa was to sell off its unconnected subsidiaries – hotels, plantations, car dealerships and the rest of Tiny Rowland's ragbag of assets – to people who specialised in these businesses and return the cash to shareholders. The price we had paid to get control was a fraction of the value of the sum of the parts, but by the time we began looking for buyers, the crash of 1998 had taken place and no one wanted to buy anything in Africa. Meanwhile the interest incurred by the huge debt burden run up by the company to buy these assets was destroying its value. By the time we managed to execute our plan the stock was down 80 per cent.

Taken collectively, Miles's brilliant strategic investments were an investment catastrophe. Although the performance of the companies where I was not on the board and interfering in management was good, the performance of the strategic investments meant that the value of the portfolio as a whole declined sharply.

David Swensen, whom I had come to look upon as an investment godfather, called me from Yale in 2000.

'Miles?'

'Yes.'

'You should do some thinking about what you're good at and what you're not.'

'That's good advice. Thank you, David.'

'And you should do some attribution work.'

'Er, what's that?'

'You better find that out pretty fast too.'

I did. Attribution involved doing a calculation in which you split your portfolio into its constituent parts and worked out how each bit had performed so you could see to what you should attribute your performance. We divided the portfolio into Miles's brilliant strategic investments and the rest. The conclusion was inescapable. The closer Miles personally got to the management of a company, the worse it subsequently performed, a humbling thing to learn about yourself. But meanwhile our basic model of buying shares in underpriced companies on inefficient exchanges was working better than ever.

We called our clients and promised to make no more strategic investments and that Blakeney would never go on the board of an investee company ever again. We would revert to being a one-joke comedian, identifying bargains in inefficient markets. The trouble was, we had hardly any clients left to call. Most had taken their money away. Yale and a big UK pension fund had remained loyal, but apart from Oryx and the Lebanon fund we had set up, the fees from which were just about paying the bills, our general money under management had shrunk from $300 million to about $70 million.

I called everyone together – we were now twelve people – and told them that we were operating at break-even. 'Let's give it a year. If we can bring in two good new clients we'll stay open. If we can't we'll close the firm and see if anyone has any jobs left.'

At the end of the year we had brought in no new clients but were close to landing one, a New York foundation managed by a brilliant woman who knew us from the time she had worked at the Yale Endowment. She did not follow herd thinking and liked giving money to people who had learned from their mistakes. We decided to keep going for another quarter, and to our great relief a month later she gave us some money. It was only $18 million, but it gave us the confidence to stay in business.

Our performance was improving now that we had got back to doing what we were good at and nothing else. Over the next six years our back-to-basics strategy turned that $18 million into $112 million. Soon other money began coming in. Our performance was extraordinary. By 2003 we had reached $500 million under management and stopped accepting new money, and by 2007 we had turned that into $2 billion. None of this was achieved by magic, mirrors or taking stupid risks. By this time my partners at Blakeney were doing most of the work while I swanned around talking to clients, but we had all recognised how narrow our talents were. We had found out the hard way how bad we were when we strayed outside our area of expertise. Blakeney resolved to remain a one-joke comedian.

And so it has remained.

23

Beirut

The last time I had been to Beirut was 1952. My only sight since then of the city had been two years earlier, in 1992, stopping off on the way back from Damascus. I never left the airport, but from the air it had looked untouched by the civil war, as pretty and well tucked-in as Monte Carlo, white apartment blocks nestling on green hills. I had heard since that there was still an area downtown which needed rebuilding, but knew from the papers that now, almost three years after sixteen years of civil war had ended, Beirut was more or less back to normal, all but ready to re-assume its role as the Paris of the Middle East.

Even the Beirut stock market had come out from the hiding it had been in during the dark years, and was starting to function again, albeit on a small scale. I also knew the Lebanese were among the most resourceful and entrepreneurial people on earth. It would not be long before they were dancing till dawn once more. I decided to go and find out what was happening before everyone else did. Maybe

Blakeney Management should be investing there before everyone else discovered it.

My first inkling that things might not be quite back to normal was at the airport. While waiting in a ramshackle shed for our baggage, people actually talked to each other. 'What brings you to Beirut?' 'Oh, just checking it out.' 'Well, you'll find things are different now. Eighteen months ago it was bad. Even the airport didn't work.'

Outside the airport all was midnight dark. I had failed to arrange for a car to pick me up as I assumed it would be easy to grab a cab. There were four beaten-up cars on the taxi rank. A villainous man with a Saddam moustache grabbed my bag and pushed me into the one at the end of the queue. 'What your name?' 'Er, Morland. Bristol Hotel, please.' Nod of apparent understanding. Why does he want to know my name? I asked myself as the door was slammed and locked from the outside and we drove off into the darkness.

We clunked down the unlit and potholed road. There were no street lights, no traffic lights. The road appeared to be half of what had once been the airport motorway. After about two miles the driver braked violently, U-turned and accelerated into a maze of narrow streets. All dark. There were chinks of light from behind steel garage doors. The car slowed, accelerated, turned into an even smaller street, and all I could think of was the three Beirut hostages who had recently been released. I wondered as we bumped down another dark potholed street if I would be as stoical as they had been after three years chained to a radiator.

I did not know my way around Beirut but was sure that the airport lay to the south of the city, which meant that we

must be driving in through south Beirut, the most impover-
ished part and the heartland of Hezbollah. The taxi slowed.
The driver was looking hard in the darkness for an address. To
me the houses looked identical, pockmarked, steel-shuttered,
unlit. Oh, God. I could see no happy outcome to this.
Should I open the door – we were moving at no more than
15 mph – throw myself into the street and make a run for
it? But where to? I would be easily caught. And hadn't he
locked the door? Should I try and cosh the driver with my
Psion Organiser? And then what?

The car stopped. The driver looked round at me as if
sizing me up. He muttered something guttural in Arabic and
stepped out. I tried my door. Yes, it was locked. The time must
have been 1.30 a.m. The street was utterly dark and deserted.
The driver went up to one steel-shuttered door, which had a
crack of light showing around it. He banged on the shutter.
After about a minute and another bang the door was opened
a crack. Inside was another Saddam-moustached figure. The
two had a hurried conference. The driver had his back to me
but I saw him accept an object from the other man although
I could not see what it was. There was some movement. It
looked as if the driver was counting out money and handing it to the man. There was a hurried conversation; the steel
door clanged shut again, and the driver slid the object inside
his jacket.

I was looking at myself with a sense of detachment and
curiosity now. The driver had obviously picked up a gun and
I was about to be taken into captivity. How was I going to
behave? Was I going to be brave? Resourceful? Resigned?
The last seemed most likely.

The driver opened his door and slid into the front seat. He spat out of the window, reached inside his jacket where he had concealed the gun and turned to face me.

'Mister?'

'Yes,' I said in as manly a voice as I could muster.

'Mister.' He withdrew the object from inside his jacket and thrust it towards me. 'Cigarette?'

A packet of Marlboro Red was pointing straight at me.

'Thank you. Please. Oh yes. Yes, please.'

Never have I been so grateful for a cigarette.

We drove on through the black Hezbollah heartland, both of us smoking, and twenty minutes later we pulled up outside another dark, pockmarked building with a moustached ruffian outside it, who managed to open my door despite it being apparently locked.

'Monsieur, welcome to the Bristol Hotel.'

The Bristol was the best surviving hotel in central Beirut. Well, not quite central Beirut. There were no functioning hotels in central Beirut. The Bristol was in a Christian suburb. It was the first hotel I had been to since Romania in 1990 where the entire reception area was lit by one bulb.

Next morning I decided to go for a walk, sit at a pavement café, window-shop, choose between restaurants for lunch, snooze in a deckchair on the beach and see if I could find a few traces of the civil war. Would everything have been restored by now? Since the civil war had stopped the journalists had moved on to other trouble spots, and you read little about the Lebanon. I was curious as to what Beirut was like.

After breakfast I asked the hotel for a map. They gave me a scrunched-up old yellow thing which appeared to predate the war. After giving it my usual mapaholic's scrutiny, I marched up to the desk and said, 'How far to the Etoile?' On the map, L'Etoile, between l'avenue Gamelin and la rue Allenby, was clearly the centre of town. 'Monsieur?' 'L'Etoile, you know, the centre of town.' 'Etoile?' He shrugged. I could have been asking for directions to Xanadu. 'You want tour? Beirut, Baalbek, Byblos? What you like?' 'Thanks. I'll walk.'

I tried following the map but it soon became obvious that it had little relevance to the reality of Beirut as it was now. I would have to follow my nose instead. I strode off. Downhill had to take me to the sea.

I hit the corniche about a mile west of the St-Georges Hotel, venue for my ninth-birthday party in 1952. Everything looked normal. People were fishing off the rocks with long bendy rods; vendors were selling Arab flatbread shaped like purses; the sea and the coast were as blue and green as ever. I remembered the corniche from forty years ago. Apart from the fact it was now lined with smart new apartment blocks on the land side, the sea side had changed little from the days when Michael and I would swim there. I walked north. The next three hours left me with my mouth hanging open. Literally. The Allied soldiers who first went into Belsen must have felt the same sense of disbelief.

The entire heart of the city, an area the size of Hyde Park, had been destroyed. Approaching it from the gleaming corniche, first you walked past buildings which were empty, then ones scarred by bullets, then ones which had been shelled, and finally you stood in rubble. The St-Georges was at the end of the Green Line, the frontier between Muslim and Christian in Beirut. It stood, but how? It had no windows, no doors, and concrete blocks with loopholes for guns on the ground floor. A soldier stood in front, and the street, Beirut's Fifth Avenue, was a marsh of sand and mud.

I walked on in horror. I remembered Bucharest a month after its revolution. A few buildings had bullet pocks and that was it. In central Beirut the buildings with bullet pocks were the lucky ones because they at least had walls. It was as if the people either side of a line drawn along Piccadilly, Knightsbridge and the Cromwell Road had spent sixteen years trying to annihilate each other. In the centre nothing remained but rubbish and broken masonry. A hundred yards back a few walls stood with their edges picked away like a rotting Stilton. I found the Etoile. In the midst of the desolation stood a giant metal statue of a heroic family. It was perforated with bullet holes, the man minus both arms, the woman with her head shot away, an apt metaphor for the civil war.

There were the empty husks of churches and mosques. Hardly anything stood higher than a few feet off the ground. One of the few remaining buildings was a large shell-shaped edifice. I walked around it. It was a cinema whose walls had been destroyed. At the edges of the destruction still stood the remains of the grand hotels – the Hilton, the Phoenicia, the Holiday Inn – but the walls were more bullet hole than brick. The old souk area, once the shopping centre of the Middle East, was razed to the ground. Nothing stood. It was chained off, to be rebuilt at some unspecified date 'as it was'. Knowing the Beirutis, in ten years the houses would spring up again, sleeker and more elegant than ever; the bullet holes would be stuccoed over, the streets repaved, the lifts reinstalled, while the only fighting would be between Bulgari and Valentino.

It is trite but none the less true that one adapts quickly to even the most abnormal surroundings. When I left the hotel the next day and we skirted the downtown area on the way to lunch it was almost starting to look normal.

Beirut traffic was alarming. After sixteen years of shooting and being shot at the Beirutis clearly did not regard NO LEFT TURN, ONE WAY STREET or NO PARKING signs as anything other than noise. There were no traffic lights and no street lights. Every car was a potential taxi. When you waved your hand the nearest five cars mounted the pavement and pinned you against the wall in an attempt to get your custom. Each trip turned into a mini-kidnap, particularly as none of the drivers spoke English or understood where you wanted to go.

Away from the centre, life bopped along: streets, horses and shops all looked close to normal with maybe a stray bullet hole or taped-up window here and there. I had a long dinner in an exquisite French restaurant with Serge, a charming Romanian aristocrat connected to one of the French banks who had arranged some introductions for me in Beirut. Serge would have been at home in the Hamptons: he spoke every language, knew everyone and talked without pause. His family had lost their land in Romania; he had been brought up in Argentina, spent years at the Shah's court in Iran, knew Baghdad well and was now a typical Beiruti.

He told me about the social structure in Beirut and how it was adapting to the return of the Lebanese who had made their fortunes overseas during the sixteen years that the country was destroying itself. Those who had come home after making a pile in Brazil, Canada or France were at the centre of Beirut social life and invited everywhere. These were for the most part Christians or Sunnis. Those who had got rich in Nigeria and the Côte d'Ivoire often had more money and built bigger palaces but were shunned by the smart set. 'Nobody mixes with them,' said Serge. They were mainly Shi'a. Snobbery, like the cockroach, could survive the worst of wars.

All through the night I had heard powerful jets screaming over the city at just above rooftop level.

'Don't they close the airport at night?' I asked Serge.

'*Bien sûr.*' He laughed. 'That was not Air France; it was the Israelis. They like to implement their Law of Moses: ten eyes for an eye, fifteen Palestinian lives for one Israeli. The flights serve no purpose. It is the Israeli way of farting in our face – to show us who is stronger.'

'Why don't you shoot them down?'

'My dear man, what weapons do we have to shoot supersonic planes down with? Rifles? The Lebanese have been shooting at the bastards for ever. They've only got one in fifteen years.'

24

Blood in the New York Gutters

I was booked to fly back to London from New York on 12 September 2001 but owing to the events of the previous day all flights had been cancelled and, several days later, there was still no news as to when the airports would reopen. So I called up Cunard and asked if they had a boat going back to England. Yes, they said, the *QE2* was leaving for Southampton on 17 September from Boston, to which it had been diverted from New York.

I caught a train to Boston and next day marched along the gangway into the *QE2*. The last time I had been on an ocean liner had been sixty-one years earlier, when the *Circassia* of the Anchor Line had taken Ma and me to Bombay in 1950 on our way to Iran. The five-day Atlantic crossing in brilliant September sunshine had a surreal quality to it. Everyone on the ship knew that 9/11, as it had yet to be called, had changed the world, but no one yet knew how. No one even knew who was responsible, but the name of Osama bin Laden was circulating before we reached England.

I wrote what follows on the *QE2* and have not changed it since because I realised that things would look very different in hindsight to the way they did at the time. I didn't know what I was going to do with it but it felt good to write something.

I was living and working on Wall Street in 1970 while the World Trade Center was being built. The Vietnam War was going on, Nixon was bombing Cambodia and New York was bankrupt. The act of construction at that time of the world's tallest building by the world's most bankrupt city was one of breathtaking effrontery. The sheer irresponsibility of the act caused great irritation to the rest of the country and great delight to New Yorkers.

After Nixon bombed neutral Cambodia in May 1970, Wall Street became the focus for the outcry against the spread of the Vietnam War. A week earlier I had been in Washington demonstrating and getting gassed. Now when I went out from Kuhn, Loeb's office at 40, Wall, for a lunchtime sandwich I saw that the demonstrators had come to Wall Street. Every morning teenagers in bell-bottoms and flowery shirts gathered in downtown New York to march up Broad Street to the junction of Broad and Wall. Here they established themselves on the steps of Federal Hall, the spot where George Washington had been sworn in as America's first president. This was their rostrum.

At midday the hundreds of construction workers who were building the World Trade Center, then two enormous holes in the ground some half a mile away, broke for lunch. Grabbing spanners and wrenches they barrelled their way down Broadway and charged left into Wall Street, a phalanx of bare-armed, beer-gutted, hard-hatted menace. Their president was bombing the geeks and the gooks in Asia to show them the American Way, to teach them the meaning of freedom. Someone had to root out the commie freaks who were standing on the steps of Federal Hall and talking treason.

At ten past noon this wave of sweat and brawn broke on Wall Street. The sidewalks were crowded with workers like me taking their lunchtime breaks; the street itself was given over to the rampaging hard hats. The police stopped the traffic, kept the crowds back from the road, and then leaned back to watch the fun, thumbs tucked in gunbelts. The recapture of the Federal Hall steps was the first thing the hard hats wanted to do; a flying wedge of brawn, using wrenches as bludgeons, drove its way into the crowd of students. Some twenty steps lead up to the portico of the building; the speaker stood on the top step behind a microphone with the statue of America's first president at his back.

'Friends, we are here with a purpose. Don't let these thugs—'

Kerrrump. Hard hats cudgelled students to their knees and kicked them aside as they stormed the first ten steps.

'Friends, hold firm. This is the kind of violence that is tearing our country—'

Kerrangg. The microphone went spiralling into the air as the hard hats recaptured the top step.

This happened every day for almost a week. Every day blood ran red in the gutters. Students were kicked in the face as they lay on the ground. Two ham-forearmed men, standing no more than six feet from me, held a frail teenage girl by the arms while a third beer-gutted hard hat punched her in the breasts and face. An elderly partner of Lehman Brothers standing right in front of me on the edge of the sidewalk raised his fingers in a V-shaped peace sign in solidarity with the kids. He was struck on the crown by a wrench and fell to the ground with blood gushing from his head. Meanwhile the crowd on the sidewalk chanted and bayed. 'Kill the commie faggots . . . Pinko scumbags . . . Fuck the red mayor.' (Mayor John Lindsay, from the liberal, Rockefeller, wing of the Republican Party, a decent man who was overwhelmed by the impossibility of governing 1970 New York, was widely regarded by the hard hats as being a pinko.) While the violence stormed, the police swapped quips with people in the crowd and loosed off a kick or two themselves whenever a kid rolled within range.

The first demonstration was on Monday. On Tuesday and Wednesday some of the kids took refuge a couple of hundred yards away inside Trinity Church. The hard hats barrelled in there as well, dragged the kids out of the church, held them down and beat them on the gravestones of America's founding fathers. The pattern repeated itself on Thursday.

And then on Friday something extraordinary happened. Led by students from Harvard Law School, busloads of graduate students from the leading East Coast business and law schools came to demonstrate. They wore grey suits, waistcoats, button-down shirts and striped ties. They assembled at the foot of Broad Street and began the half-mile march to Federal Hall. They marched in silence. The crowd who had gathered to cheer the noon-time carnage shuffled their feet as the students marched past, with their well-polished shoes and neatly trimmed hair. The steps were mounted and the speeches began. At ten past noon the hard hats came rampaging round the corner into Wall Street, wrenches a-wave, to be faced with the sight of a Harvard law professor delivering a carefully argued indictment against Nixon to an audience of be-suited graduates. The hard hats paused and then came to an untidy halt. Where were the commie freaks? After five minutes of muttering and sporadic shouts of 'Hey, fuck you, shitheads' they dissolved into the crowd of lunchtime workers. They were seen no more on Wall Street.

By the time the Twin Towers were finished, Nixon had resigned in disgrace to be replaced by Gerry Ford. Far from standing for American unity and strength, the World Trade Center was seen by the 95 per cent of the country that did not live in New York as a symbol of that city's overweening arrogance. In the words, now legend, of the *Daily News* headline when bankrupt New York rattled its begging bowl under Washington's nose and was told to look elsewhere for funds: FORD TO NEW YORK: DROP DEAD.

It was not only the city that was bankrupt and was forced to reach an arrangement with its creditors. The financial services industry, which was meant to provide the tenants for the Twin Towers' 218 empty storeys, was also all but broke; it was certainly in no condition to sign long leases for shiny new space in buildings which were not even on Wall Street. For instance, in 1970 the mighty Morgan Stanley, whose shareholders' capital today is $20 billion, had capital of $18 million.

No one took a lease. To the great delight of the vast majority of Americans the World Trade Center went bankrupt before it even started. The city authorities in the shape of the Port Authority had to step in and take over ownership of the building. They too were unable to find tenants on a commercial basis so New York's left hand signed a series of long-term heavily discounted leases with New York's right hand, and the towers were duly filled with floor upon floor of low-paid clerical staff employed by various municipal and state bodies.

It is ironic that the World Trade Center, for so much of its early life a reminder of the wrenching disunities of the Vietnam War and of the gulf that divided New York from the rest of the country, should become in its death a symbol of unity and indeed of America itself. When the first building was struck, everyone who was watching, and within ten minutes everyone in New York was watching, thought it was a freak accident, a light plane that had wandered off course. The first true moment of horror came when the second building was struck in full and open view of ten million people. The watchers in the streets and from the upper floors of midtown skyscrapers realised then that this was no random event. Someone was out to get them. But, as the smoke rolled over the downtown city, there was also a jutting of the jaw. These buildings, like America itself, could endure anything anyone could throw at them; they had been built, so people informed each other, to withstand the impact of a Boeing 707.

There was no one watching who thought for an instant that these buildings might *fall down*. That the New York police and fire service were, on 11 September, as brave as men in combat is certain. But it is also certain that, as they charged, reckless for their own safety, into the Towers, they knew that they would have to brave smoke, flames and debris, but none of those men and women who entered the South Tower thought for a moment that the whole building would *fall down*. That was an impossibility.

And that was the moment of metaphor. A great lowing cry halfway between a groan and a shriek went up from ten million throats simultaneously as New Yorkers realised that they were witnessing an impossible horror. This was not like a building toppling over; it was not like a building being demolished when a charge of explosive knocks away its underpinnings. The top fifteen floors of the South Tower began to slide down and then they did not collapse, or fall. They and everything in them *vapourised*. After that first bellow of horror, there was a time, five seconds, maybe ten, of a silence more absolute than the city had ever known.

Accounts written by the first people to visit Hiroshima after it was destroyed by an atom bomb all remarked on the same thing: everything was covered in a thick coat of the finest grey-white powder, as fine as talc. Four hours after the first impact, I walked the five miles downtown to Ground Zero, as it was already being called by the newsreaders, driven by some feeling that I wanted to be a witness to an event which might change the history of the world. Everything there was covered in a thick coat of Hiroshima dust. Public, and indeed private, transport had ceased in the southern part of the city. The streets were emptier of traffic than they had ever been. A tired and sombre army of Wall Street workers marched north on fifteen-mile walks to get home; some carried the high-heeled shoes that they had exchanged on 14th Street for sneakers. Knots of watchers stood on the corners of the avenues looking south at a cloud of smoke bigger than, well, bigger than the World Trade Center.

By then the only traffic coming in to the area was a long stream of ambulances from Long Island, New Jersey and the outer boroughs. A hundred of them were lined up six blocks north of Seven World Trade Center, the nearest building of the complex still standing. This presented an extraordinary sight. Its outside was still pristine marble and glass. Through every one of its windows could be seen orange flames so bright and high that people, so used to seeing computer simulations, kept on asking each other if they were real. The building itself, externally so normal and solid-seeming, suddenly shifted and developed a distinct tilt to the east. Two hours later it too fell down.

Stretchers, gurneys and wheelchairs were drawn up on the road in front of the ambulances, ready for the survivors. Gradually the realisation dawned that there were no survivors from the Twin Towers. The people who had escaped before the holocaust had already joined the trudge north. Of those who were in the building, there were no living for the ambulances to treat. All the paramedics could do was look after sufferers from smoke inhalation and shock or those who had been struck by flying debris.

The building of the World Trade Center had brought residents back to downtown. The excavation for the foundations of the Center had been tipped as landfill into the Hudson River next to the Center to create Battery Park City, now home to many thousands of residents. They had by now been evacuated from their homes and formed a refugee army wandering between the police roadblocks that had closed every street, asking questions to which no one had answers. The police, and the firemen, all clothed in uniform white-grey Hiroshima dust, knew by now of the toll that had been exacted on those of their colleagues and partners who had been the first to reach the area. Despite this, they continued their jobs with endurance and good humour. A weary man was stopped by a policeman next to me at a roadblock on Harrison Street. 'You can't come through here, sir.' 'I'm trying to get to the Staten Island ferry. An officer told me if I came this way I could get to it by taking the West Side Highway.' 'I'm sorry, sir. The Staten Island ferry is running but it's not taking civilians.'

Civilians. That is what New Yorkers had become. Civilians? This was now war? Against whom?

25

Starting Again

By 2006 Blakeney Management had recovered from the setback of the late 1990s and put together six successful years as a result of our back-to-basics one-trick-pony strategy. Our success and the reasons for it did not go unnoticed. We had become known as the African markets pioneers, the people who had started it all, but others had started investing there too. That was gratifying but I was feeling restless. Visiting places like Egypt, Morocco and Nigeria in the early 1990s when no one else was going there and finding stock markets like classic cars left to rust in a garage was intoxicating. Fifteen years later these had become near-mainstream markets with crowds of analysts and other financial intermediaries. I liked going to places that others didn't. Going to places where Euromoney was holding investment conferences held less appeal.

I had been running Blakeney ever since it started in 1990. People would ask me how long I was going to go on for. For many years I had been saying, 'Well, I'll probably kick myself upstairs in three years' time,' but the three years stayed three years away. Then a moment came in 2006 when I was on the cross-trainer in the gym listening on the iPod to the Supremes singing 'Stop, In The Name Of Love' and stopping seemed like a good idea. Once that thought had lodged itself it seemed so obviously the right thing to do.

The next day I told my partners that I would be handing over the firm to them. I gave them 80 per cent of the business, by now a valuable one, as a gift, and kept 20 per cent as the founder. I also wrote to Blakeney's clients.

I will be giving up all executive responsibility at Blakeney. That means I will not take part in investment decisions, will not be responsible for keeping in touch with clients, will not look after administration, and will toss any communication I get from the FSA [the startlingly ineffective UK financial regulatory body of that time, since deceased, replaced by another equally idiotic body] unread into the bin. I will, however, remain closely interested in what Blakeney is doing. As non-executive chairman I shall show up on a regular basis and find out what the active partners are doing and why. And if from time to time the partners ask my opinion on an investment matter I will be happy to caw a couple of words of ancient wisdom from my branch.

I added,

I have no intention of retiring and even less of learning how to play golf. Freed of Blakeney duties I hope to spend more time nosing around those places where the tap water is not safe to drink. Africa and the Middle East have never been as ripe as they are today with investment possibilities. 'I like to think I have a good

investment nose and a willingness to search for raisins among the
turds.' (The words of Charlie Munger, Warren Buffett's partner,
not mine.) What excites me is visiting virgin investment territory.

I may invest a bit of my own money in some of these places
if I find a raisin or two or, if I stumble upon large opportunities,
I may act as an investment pimp and pass ideas along to friends
with greater resources than I.

The idea is not to make money; it is to go on learning and
have fun. Playing golf makes you old; learning keeps you young.

Once again, as in 1989, I found myself without a daytime
job. And once again that set me off travelling to places unvis-
ited by investors to see what was hiding beyond the horizons
of the known investment world. I went off to countries like
Ethiopia, Angola, Syria, Palestine, Sudan, Libya, Vietnam,
Kyrgyzstan, Azerbaijan, Georgia and Iran. In some I had
connections, in others I didn't, but everywhere I went I was
greeted with friendliness. The rule seemed to be that the
more the American government disliked a country the nicer
the people were. Nowhere were people more welcoming
than in Iran, Syria and Palestine.

In all of these countries there were opportunities, but I
kept being drawn back to Africa, and once again I was struck
by how wide the perception gap was between the reality of
what was happening in places like Angola and Ethiopia and
how they were perceived in the West. In 1990 countries like
Nigeria, Egypt and Ghana were perceived as investment pari-
ahs; now most people knew that they were doing well. But if
you went to a posh dinner in 2006 in London or New York
and mentioned Angola, Rwanda, Ethiopia, Mozambique,

Algeria, Libya, Sudan and Sierra Leone, everyone would dismiss them because there were wars going on there.

There were indeed wars going on, but they weren't the cliché 'tribal wars' of fevered Western imagining but conflicts which could be traced back to the Cold War. When the British and the French, the Belgians and the Portuguese withdrew from their colonies in the 1960s the new powers, the US and Russia, hastened to helicopter in their tame dictator before the other side did. Hello, Lumumba; *bonjour*, Mobutu.

The new superpowers were even more ignorant about Africa than the retiring colonialists but they perceived every country in Africa as having strategic importance. That gave us the big African wars of the 1980s, as the US and its proxies, usually the apartheid-era South Africans, with whom the Americans were theoretically not on speaking terms, and the USSR and its henchmen, the Cubans, Czechs and East Germans, fought for supremacy in countries like Angola and Mozambique. In 1990 the Cold War ended, and the USSR lost interest in Africa. The US, which had only been there to thwart the Russians, also lost interest. For the first time in a century the Africans were left to their own devices without interference from the white nations. The US and Russia had poured so much weaponry into the continent that it took a few years for things to calm down, but pretty soon they did and the terrible civil wars came gradually to an end.

When I went travelling in 2006 and 2007 there was, for the first time in recorded history, no war taking place in Africa. Whenever I said this to Westerners they greeted it with disbelief and told me about Darfur, Eritrea, Somalia, Côte d'Ivoire and the Congo. There were terrible things happening in those places, but there weren't actual wars going on, as there had been in 1990. And these were but five of fifty-three countries.

The more I travelled around the more excited I got. Countries like Angola, Mozambique and Ethiopia which people thought were at war, were in reality peaceful and stable. What was more, these were the fastest-growing countries on earth and nobody wanted to invest in them. All three were growing faster than China. If the old truism about the gap between perception and reality held true, this was the widest gap on earth, and these were the places to invest.

Perceptions of Africa were uniformly negative, largely thanks to the aid organisations and people like Bono and Geldof. Their mantra ran something like this: 'Africa is locked in a vicious cycle of poverty. There's no way the Africans can find their own way out of the poverty trap. Their only hope is for us to give them handouts, monitor the way they govern themselves, and teach them how to farm and fish.' This was startlingly inaccurate. Far from being locked in a cycle of poverty Africa had become the fastest growing part of the world, and its fishermen and farmers, thanks to being more attuned to the natural world than their Western equivalents, were among the most efficient in the world. Some years ago I was quoted in a Sunday paper as saying that Bob Geldof had done more harm to Africa than Bob Mugabe. Mugabe, I said, had destroyed one country economically; Geldof had dissuaded people from investing in fifty-three.

The opportunity that had led me to start Blakeney was the discovery that there were stock markets throughout Africa and the Middle East that no one was paying attention to, with the result that many of the companies quoted on them were selling far too cheaply. The opportunity I saw now was that there were whole countries like Ethiopia and Angola that no outside investors were paying attention to, thanks to the Bonos and the aid people, but that were growing faster than anywhere else in the world. That had to provide an opportunity.

There was a problem: me. I had proved during the Blakeney strategic investing period that my skill lay in identifying wrongly priced companies listed on stock markets. I was a listed-stock investor. But most of the countries about which I was now getting excited did not have stock markets on which to list. Investing there would mean buying large chunks of privately owned companies, going on the board and getting involved in their management. This was private equity investing and involved a process similar to strategic investing, at which I had already demonstrated my incompetence.

That did not stop me. At a meeting with the management of an African bank in which Blakeney had a holding I met a Bangladeshi-American woman called Runa Alam. She was far better prepared than I and asked a number of brilliant questions. I was intrigued and talked with her afterwards. I discovered she was running a successful African private equity fund but was feeling itchy because she had no stake in the company she worked for and was ready to move. I told Runa my plans and she got almost as excited as I was. She agreed to leave and join me in setting up a new private equity company to invest in Africa.

There are many things wrong with England, but it is probably the easiest place in the world to start a business. Open a bank account, go online with Companies House, and twenty-four hours later you have a new company. Runa and I formed Development Partners International (DPI) in 2007, with her as chief executive and me as chairman, and off we went. We resolved that we would do our best to hire only Africans and that DPI would be owned entirely by the people who worked for it.

In 2008, when the financial world went into meltdown, we were out trying to raise money to invest in Africa, a challenge for a new firm. However, Runa and I had made a lot of people a lot of money at our previous firms and many of them were ready to give us a chance in our new venture. By bits and pieces we managed to raise over $500 million, much of it from people we already knew.

Suddenly DPI had become a real company, and we were in business and ready to start investing. What gave me particular pleasure, as someone who despises the self-righteous nanny-ism of political correctness, was that our new firm was half women, half black, half Muslim and, with the exception of Runa and me, all African.

26

Ambushed in Abyssinia

I met Teddy many years ago at a wedding in Switzerland. 'Teddy' is an English rendering of Tewodros, his Ethiopian name. He is one of the most charming men I have ever met; thanks to his charm he is also a brilliant salesman. I have never been certain what his trick is, but he is one of those people that when they start talking, others leave whatever conversations they are having and creep over to listen to him.

Teddy had started an oil exploration company in his native Ethiopia, a very large country which, ever since the Queen of Sheba trotted off to see King Solomon, has been reputed to be rich in oil and minerals, though most of these treasures have yet to be found. Teddy had licences to prospect in an area somewhat larger than Belgium in the Ogaden in south-eastern Ethiopia. He also had sixty-five people in a camp in the middle of the wilderness who had been doing seismic tests in the hope of identifying the best places to drill for the billions of barrels of oil that Teddy was confident lay under his vast concessions.

Such was Teddy's skill as a salesman that twenty minutes after I had met him at the wedding I was agreeing to invest personally in his oil company, an oil company which so far had no oil. However, according to the seismic work, said Tewodros, there could be literally billions of barrels of the stuff. Teddy asked me to go on the board of directors. I accepted because Ethiopia is a fascinating country and his invitation gave me the opportunity to get involved in it. The board comprised five other old white men, all investors in the company, and Teddy as chairman. We normally had our meetings in Paris or some other European city convenient for the majority of the directors.

Not long after I joined the board Teddy suggested that we went to Ethiopia and had our meeting there. We would spend a couple of days in Addis Ababa, Ethiopia's elegant capital, with its tall Orthodox churches, its Merkato, reputed to be the biggest market in the world, and its tree-lined boulevards. We would meet important members of the government, including Mr Meles, the prime minister. Then we would get in a small plane and fly to our camp, where we would stay overnight in shipping containers, watch the seismic crew at work and hold our board meeting around a table in the desert. Apart from our crew the only other inhabitants of the Ogaden, a vast and arid wilderness, were migrant Somali herdsmen with their cows and camels.

The Somalis, a warlike lot who have long thought of the more numerous and more powerful Ethiopians as their enemies, maintained the Ogaden belonged to them. If there was oil to be found there the Somalis regarded it as Somali oil, not Ethiopian oil. A century ago the Ethiopians incorporated the Ogaden into greater Ethiopia after Queen Victoria generously ceded it to the Emperor Menelik as a present. The Somalis like to point out that it wasn't hers to give, but this trifle did not bother Her Majesty's Colonial Office. It was as if the Somalis announced today that they were giving Scotland to Norway. From time to time the Somalis issued threats against Teddy's company and anyone else considering drilling there, warning them they were stealing Somali national resources.

Regardless of all this, we liked the idea of a board meeting in the Ogaden, so a date was set, visas were obtained and inoculations given against the exotic and fatal diseases which Western doctors believe are prevalent in the darker parts of Africa. Most of us had been to Ethiopia before; it is a country older than the United Kingdom with a rich culture and few diseases. We were looking forward to spending time there again and hanging out at the Sheba Bar of the Addis Hilton, one of the great liberation-era hotels of Africa. The Sheba Bar was where everyone met. There was a newer and more expensive hotel, a white wedding-cake Sheraton, but the Ethiopians couldn't afford to go there so it was peopled only by UN and NGO workers spending aid and charity dollars.

Ten days before we were due to leave for Ethiopia the board members received an email from Teddy. 'Gentlemen,' it said. 'Bad news. I was in a plane crash yesterday. I was returning from Gambella in western Ethiopia to the capital. We were in a small Cessna. There were three of us: the pilot, Muhammad my friend and oil mentor who used to work for Petronas, and I. The engine failed fifteen kilometres short of Addis and we crashed in open country. Muhammad was killed outright, the pilot is on life support and I am unharmed.' Teddy attached a photograph of the Cessna. It looked like a crumpled beer can and was in two halves. How Teddy had survived without injury was a mystery. 'However,' the email continued, 'the show must go on. We will continue with our board meeting plans in the Ogaden in ten days' time.'

I sent Teddy an email in reply, copied to the board.

Dear Teddy,

Perhaps as the oldest guy on your board I can voice a few personal thoughts about this terrible happening. You are a brave and resolute man but don't underestimate the shock you have suffered. You have had a double trauma: a near-death experience yourself and the death of a close friend and mentor. I suspect it will take time for the impact of these to be fully felt.

Under the circumstances I would favour postponing our trip for a few months. We have all been looking forward to it but there is no pressing business need to do it now. Perhaps you should take some time out, go off with your wife, and let the impact of this sink in.

You are right that the show must go on but I'm sure the board would be happy to have tickets for a later performance in a few months' time. We could maybe have the April board meeting in London and then go to Ethiopia for the next meeting.

Thinking of you,
Miles

Teddy replied to the board:

Thanks, Miles, for your wise advice. I must admit, as we were going down, the first thing that flashed through my head was my young children and wife.

I realise that the shock will take some time to subside, but I still feel like ploughing through. However, I have always believed in listening to people wiser and more experienced than myself such as my grandfather, now in his nineties, and you because you are almost as old as he. I will heed your advice. We will postpone the trip to Ethiopia.

'There is a destiny that shapes our ends, rough hew them as we will,' Shakespeare.

Warmest regards,
Teddy

So we postponed the meeting.

Ten days later, when we had planned to be in the Ogaden for our meeting, 400 members of the Ogaden National Liberation Front, Somalis armed by the Eritrean government, swept through our camp when everyone was asleep and murdered all sixty-five of our employees. None escaped. Two weeks later we learned from Ethiopia's military intelligence service – people who have a way of finding out what needs to be found out – that the reason the ONLF had attacked our camp was that the Ogaden grapevine had told them that the board of the oil company would be there on that date. They had planned their attack with the intention of killing the chairman and five white directors of the company conducting oil exploration in the Ogaden. The sixty-five employees were incidental.

The Somali are imaginative and experienced people when it comes to killing. If Teddy had not had his plane crash, I and my fellow directors would probably have watched our entrails being barbecued in front of us as we died slow and imaginative deaths.

I am happy to say that today things are much better. The oil company and the Ogadenis have made peace, and the company has embarked on a successful programme of school- and clinic-building for the locals. Meanwhile the ONLF is a spent force, and, just in case, there are units of the fearsome Ethiopian army making sure that nothing nasty happens.

27

Return from the Madagascan Tomb

Angela Fisher and Carol Beckwith have spent thirty years taking photographs of the ceremonies, dress and customs in Africa that they fear will not be around much longer. Their *African Ceremonies* books and companion volumes are a unique archive. Today Africans are casting off traditional robes and putting on baseball caps, and in forty years' time their children will want to look at what they have abandoned. Angela and Carol's photographs will be the best record of what they will have lost.

They go off unsupported and by themselves into places where white people are seen less often than eclipses of the sun. Carol, in an attempt to get some close-ups, once spent two years as the second, or it may have been third, wife of a Ouadabi chief in Niger. Their work involves going to places where things that sensible travellers like me regard as the essentials of adventurous African travelling, such as air conditioning, ice-cold Martinis and beds, are unknown.

They had asked me along as their baggage carrier on a trip to photograph the Betsileo tribe's grave-wrapping ceremonies in the Madagascan highlands. Traditional Betsileo families take the corpses out of the family tomb every few years, lay them down in the sun, drink litres of cane spirit, tell them the news, introduce grandfather, dead and wrapped in silk, to grandson, and then pop them back in the tomb with a new wrapping of white silk.

Madagascar is a unique country. The encyclopedias may say it is part of Africa, but it isn't really as it split away about 150 million years ago along with India when they parted from the supercontinent of Gondwana. Part-way across what is now the Indian Ocean the Indian land mass dropped Madagascar in the sea behind it like a large turd four times the size of England. India of course kept on moving until it hit China and gave us the Himalayas. Madagascar, on the other hand, remained stationary and uninhabited by anything other than baobab trees, forty-three species of lemur and some strange bats, until a bunch of enterprising Indonesians, whose cousins were busy colonising the South Seas from Tahiti to New Zealand, turned the wrong way out of Sumatra. Consequently the native people are Asian in origin and speak an Asian language which involves words having uncountable syllables all but one or two of which are swallowed. Antananananarivo, the capital, is Tana, and Ambositra, where the Betsileo live, is Mbusht.

After a few delays and an expedition to the port of Antsiranana, formerly Diego-Suarez, where thousands of Vichy French died in an attempt to prevent the island falling to the British in 1942, we returned to Tana and left

the next day in a four-by-four with Herry, our dashing
chain-smoking driver, and Ramillisson, a diminutive retired
university anthropologist Angela and Carol appeared to have
kidnapped and taken along in the mistaken belief that he
could explain what was happening. In the event Ramillisson
sat in the car putting on anoraks and complaining of the cold
while Herry the driver filled our ears with tales of famous
famadihanas he had seen. We had a six-hour drive through
red-earth mountains rising behind rivers threaded with
paddy fields to Ambositra.

We arrived exhausted at 10 p.m. to find that le Motel des
Violettes had sold our carefully booked rooms to a higher
bidder. Our confirming fax was denounced as a forgery. The
best hotel in town, the Mania, where I longed to stay if only
for the name, was also *tout complet*. Herry finally found us
a Malagasy B & B with squeaky-clean rooms and ventila-
tion provided by the wind sighing gently up through the
floorboards.

Next morning was the grave-wrapping. We went first to
meet the main members of the family. Our invitation had
come through Martine, a Belgian woman who had been
married to a Betsileo. Her husband's body would be one of
those to be brought out and rewrapped, although Martine
herself was not able to be there. The husband's sister met us
at their little red-brick village house, where twenty family
members had already gathered. Before setting off there was
food to be eaten, permissions to be sought from the ancestors
and cane spirit to be drunk.

The food was being cooked in huge iron cauldrons on open
fires when we arrived. We, honoured foreign guests, were fed
first. Two tin plates, one of rice and one of well boiled chunks

of pig fat, were given to each of us while twenty hungry faces looked on waiting for us to eat so they could start on their own pig fat. Carol and I were already suffering from dysentery brought on either by prawns (Carol's theory) or the dirty fingers of the chap pawing the sliced tomatoes as he formed a pattern on top of our morning fried eggs (mine). With convincing vehemence I was able to say, *'C'est formidable, mais j'ai un terrible mal à l'estomac.'* Carol then passed out, and it was left to Angela to tuck into three huge globs of poached pig fat on behalf of the foreign delegation. But then she is Australian.

Ramillisson took off his anorak and spooned several helpings of pig fat into his tiny body, as did Herry. The speechmaster, who had already made five or six ten-minute speeches of welcome to us in a language which later turned out to be French, then made an even longer speech to the ancestors, who seemed to be inhabiting the upper left-hand corner of the room.

I was meanwhile sitting on the edge of the bed of the chief, a man so old and infirm that he could not even eat pig fat. I thought it an even bet that he would be an ancestor before nightfall. Finally, when *les ancêtres* had given permission, a litre bottle of near-toxic cane spirit was passed round. Despite *mal à l'estomac* I managed to choke down enough of this to make my eyes run.

Then off to the forest, our party and the speechmaker in Herry's four-by-four, the rest of the family, now some 150 strong, on foot. It took us twice as long to get there in the car, and when we arrived there was a group already on the roof of the tomb hammering and chiselling. The tomb door was sealed closed, and to open it you had to remove a keystone from the roof. We were told to keep our distance. For us to be there before the opening would be *fady*. *Fady* is Malagasy for taboo. Just about everything is *fady* somewhere some time on Madagascar. The mood of the *famadihana* was unlike that at any Western memorial service or funeral, the grown-ups laughing and joking, the children larking around. No solemn faces, counted minutes of silence or hushed reverence in the face of death.

Finally the keystone was removed, and two people lowered themselves into the tomb. A minute later the door was opened and we were summoned but told to walk around the tomb and enter from behind. To approach it from the front was *fady*. I did not know what to expect. My contact with dead bodies has been limited and personal. I'm extremely squeamish, and the thought of confronting a platoon of wrapped corpses that had been maturing in tropical heat for the four years since the last rewrapping was not one I was relishing.

Carol, Angela and I were invited to go in first. Everyone was excited at the prospect of the two world-famous photographers immortalising the family *famadihana* in the next volume of *African Ceremonies*. The girls crept into the tomb, their necks bent under Nikons and foot-long lenses, while I trotted behind trying to make my tiny Ixus look important.

The tomb was carved out of limestone and sunk two storeys into the earth. Inside the air was as cool and odourless as a cloister. On three sides were chambers each containing two to six white-wrapped corpses of different branches of the family. They were surprisingly thin, but it was easy to make out the human shapes within, the heads and the feet and the crossed arms. I assumed that the bodies had been embalmed.

Photographs taken, we backed up the steps out of the tomb and joined the 150-strong semicircle outside. The master of ceremonies then read out the contents of an important-looking piece of stamped paper. Herry informed me that this was the municipal permission to open the tomb. And then, as everyone burst into what sounded like a Malagasy version of 'The Wild Colonial Boy', two people appeared carrying the first corpse. Straw mats had been laid in front of the tomb. The body was put down at the far end of the mats and they went back down for another. Close family members knelt by the wrapped body and stroked it and talked to it. They moved aside as the next one was laid down. Everyone was laughing and joking and telling stories.

It was only when the fifth body came up that the corpse's widow threw herself on it and went into a fit of sobbing and keening. I expected her to be comforted by other family members. Not at all. Some women pulled her almost roughly off the corpse as the next body was put down alongside and took her over to sit under a nearby thorn tree, where she was left keening by herself until such time as she could come back and have a good laugh. In the course of twenty-seven bodies coming out of the tomb, only she and one other woman showed any signs of grief, and their doing so was clearly not appreciated by the rest of the family.

From what we were told, the Malagasy make little distinction between life and death. Dead people are thought of as being in the next room, and I suppose that taking them out of it for a chat every few years underlines the lack of a barrier between death and life. The ancestors are involved in everything. To do things without the ancestors' permission is to court trouble.

It was an afternoon like no other I have ever had. While the last bodies were being brought out, the first were being rewrapped in fresh sheets of white silk. The women did the wrapping. Sheets were tightly bound around the corpse and the ends tucked in neatly, following which silk cords were tied around the neck and the ankles to keep everything in place. One woman to whom I had been chatting in pidgin French said, '*Photographe, photographe,*' and knelt down beside her husband's freshly wrapped corpse, put on a big grin and gave the body a hug while we snapped her with her man. The fact that he was now an ex-man was irrelevant. Her smile would have been exactly the same if he had been alive standing next to her rather than lying wrapped in a shroud.

At the best traditional *famadihanas* after the bodies have been brought out they are walked seven times round the tomb with, said Herry, a shot of cane spirit being consumed by the walkers on each circuit. Dancing then takes place with the corpses balanced uneasily on people's shoulders. After each circuit everyone gets more and more incapable, and by the end corpses are flying all over the place. Sadly, our family was a sober lot. As Herry told me, 'Bah, they are too Christian.' Once the rewrapping had taken place, the bodies were hoisted aloft one by one and gently marched back into the tomb, face down if they had been face up and vice versa, to give them a different view for the next four or five years.

I suddenly found myself much moved, the more so because everything was so happy and full of joy. The Betsileo seem to have found a way of making humour, fun and laughter transcend dying.

28

Georgie's Last Adventure

The visit to the tomb in Madagascar stirred and moved me. Death is such a final and miserable business in the West while to the Betsileo it is but a hiccup on a longer journey. I was deeply affected by the way that the living Betsileo would chat to their dead loved ones and tell them the news.

There are two people I would particularly like to do that with. One is my mother. She had a life full of interest and adventure and I like to think she would want to know about mine.

The other is my daughter Georgie. She was the real adventurer of our family. She spread laughter and light around her but could never quite light up the dark place in her own soul. She took her own life when she was twenty-seven. I wrote a letter to her godparents telling them how we, Tasha, Guislaine, and I, went to Los Angeles where she had been living for the previous five years to say goodbye to her.

July 2004

Dear Godparents,

Georgia would like you, as her godparents, to know how
her friends in Los Angeles said goodbye to her. She had
a great sense of occasion. The four days we spent in Los
Angeles taking our leave of her were days like no other,
imbued with her special spirit.

She died in the early morning of Wednesday July 21st.
Her funeral was three days later in the chapel at Pierce
Brothers. Pierce is a patch of lawns and palms and funny
Californian trees with red and orange blossoms hidden
amongst the glass and granite of Century City. Marilyn
Monroe's grave is here. Georgie had had a thing about
Marilyn Monroe from the time she was six years old.
Perhaps she sensed what they had in common, the elec-
tric, sudden, smile, the grace, the natural ability to please
and, behind that smile, the inner darkness that made life
so difficult for both of them. Georgie would have liked
the thought of saying her last goodbye next to Marilyn
Monroe.

I had arranged the funeral by telephone from London
at a day's notice and, because of that, had thought it would
just be us, Guislaine, Tasha and I, together with a few close
friends. I had had quite a battle with Pierce Brothers to
arrange the funeral at such short notice. When we arrived
there, Georgie was lying in the chapel.

I had ordered a dignified beech coffin but in true
Georgie style, she had turned up at Pierce Brothers a bit

late, something to do with not getting her release permit from the coroner in time, and they never had time to put her in a proper coffin, so Georgie was there in a cardboard box. At first, Guislaine, Tash and I were horrified but then we softened and realised how little Georgie would have cared. She was nearly always late, usually because she had forgotten something vital, and you forgave her for it, even if it meant no beech coffin. We draped a towel and a bit of blue cloth round the box, Guislaine picked a rose and I a lily from the flower arrangements and laid them in the coffin alongside her.

The three of us went up privately to say goodbye to her before anyone else came into the chapel. We had asked Pierce not to make her up but to leave her as she was. She did not look in death as she did in life. Her face was mottled and her complexion was different but she looked at peace, like a deep sea diver who had held her breath too long and then has surfaced in a calm and peaceful place. I held each of her little curled up hands in turn, tucked the lily in one and gave her a kiss.

Then the doors to the chapel were opened and people began to step in from the garden in their ones and twos. Some we had met before, most we had not. She had a gift for forging close relationships; every one of the more than a hundred people who came in to the chapel, who hugged us, hugged each other and then went up in their ones and twos to say goodbye to Georgie, felt like her family.

Jim Miller, the peaceful, compassionate, priest whom Georgie had met in AA [Alcoholics Anonymous, the fellowship that played such a big part in Georgie's life as

someone who had had a cocaine addiction and had with
great courage got herself clean] and who had written his
own service when he married her and Derick in the Joshua
Tree National Park said a few words about Georgie's spir-
ituality. She was not a conventional Christian but she had
a very definite God and she believed fiercely in an afterlife.
Guislaine, Tasha and I then spoke for a minute or two each
about what Georgie had meant to us. I thanked people for
coming and said how Los Angeles had become her home
and how the people in the room had become her family. I
talked of her gift for bringing sunshine and laughter into
other people's lives but how she could not light up the
dark place in her own soul.

I told them that when Tasha came to tell me in the middle
of the night that Georgie had killed herself, because it was
Tasha who got the news first in England, I drove out to
Oxfordshire, where Guislaine lived, to tell her. I arrived at
three in the morning. Guislaine and I walked out into her
garden and we looked up and the clouds cleared and we
could see the stars and feel Georgie's presence all around
us. It brought to mind the lines from Romeo and Juliet –

And when she shall die,
Take her and cut her out in little stars
And she will make the face of heaven so fine
That all the world will be in love with night
And pay no worship to the garish sun.

One by one people came up to talk about Georgie. Jeff
Young, whose wife, my old and dear friend, Annie, was

our Los Angeles mother hen during these difficult days, was first:

'I have been to too many funerals in recent years, and said goodbye to too many friends but I have never been to something like this, something where there is so much feeling, so many people affected and so much emotion in the room.'

Derick, the warm and gentle man to whom she had been married for two years, had driven down from San Francisco where he now lives. He walked to the front of the chapel and, with a quiet, remembering, smile on his face said, 'I'm not much good at writing but when Georgia and I split up I wrote a story. I've never shown it to anyone. It told how this beautiful little bird would fly around singing every day until it got tired and came to rest on a stumpy old tree with long roots deep in the earth. "Look at those roots," said the bird, "can you show me how to make roots?" "I'll try," said the tree, "if you can teach me to fly." And for two years the tree tried to show the little bird how to make roots, and the little bird tried to teach the tree to fly . . . But it was not in their natures. The tree could never get into the air and the little bird tried but could never put down roots.'

The next day there was a celebration of Georgie's life in a hall next to a church in Westwood. In view of the short notice we had thought that only a handful of people would be at the celebration. The hall was the size of a tennis court. By the time her old friend and mentor, Andrew McCullough, whom she had met in AA got up to speak, all the chairs had been taken and people were standing three deep at the back and sides. There must have been three hundred in the room. I hugged more people in that afternoon than I had done in my life before. Guislaine, Tasha and I spoke to nearly all of the people in the room. We were so proud and so moved by the stories we heard.

Most of us go through life with close relationships with a dozen or so other people outside their families. Here were three hundred, all of whose lives had been intimately touched by Georgie.

Andrew talked first. He told both of the magic Georgie had and also of how difficult she had found the everyday business of living. He then called people up to speak one by one, after which others came up to speak spontaneously, each for a minute or two. The stories they told had common threads. First, although many of the people had to choke back tears as they spoke, just about every one of the stories left us laughing. So many of those who spoke had felt themselves in despair through addiction; Georgie had come into their lives and had dropped everything to help them; so many had stories of how Georgie had taught them how to enjoy life and have fun and had shared her own very special style with them. Whether it was shopping for shoes, and that came up more than once, camping in the desert, singing in the street, driving down Sunset with six people crammed into her most precious possession, her battered old VW, or dancing on the beach, all the stories had laughter and fun in them. Above all the stories told of Georgia's generosity; she had no meanness in her. There was not one person in the room to whom Georgie had not given of herself.

And then her sister Tasha rose to her feet to sing Georgie's signature song and as she sung there was not a person who could not hear and feel Georgie there in the room with us. And then one or two others picked up the song with Tash and by the time she ended three hundred people, tears flowing down their faces, were singing –

Delta Dawn what's that flower you have on?
Could it be a faded rose from days gone by?
And did I hear you say he was meetin' you here today?
To take you to his mansion in the sky-y.

Georgie had left a long and lucid goodbye note behind her telling of her lifelong battle with depression. Throughout the note spoke her belief that she was going to an after-life – its last words were 'I can't wait to see Granny' – and she would see us again. It had been found on her compu-ter in the motel where she had killed herself and the coroner had passed it on to us. It began: 'First of all let's get one thing straight: I am doing the right thing. I asked God to help me do this and he said OK . . . Everyone always says how suicide is the most selfish thing you can do and I agree in the sense that someone else is going to have to clear up my stuff and I'm sorry, but, beyond that, I think it's more selfish of people to go on demanding that I live in this much pain.' She went on in the note to talk individually to people she had loved and with whom she had shared experiences.

'Well,' she said, 'I have intensely experienced life, that's for sure. And I think like in "Like Water for Chocolate"

I have burned all my matches at once.' And she said she would like to be cremated and to have her ashes scattered in the Joshua Tree National Park, the place where she and Derick had been married.

Two days later, thirty of us, family and friends, drove the three hours from Los Angeles to Joshua Tree. We met for lunch in the Twenty-Nine Palms Motel, the funky oasis, all purple and orange, in the desert where we had stayed the night before Georgie's wedding.

After lunch we drove together into the Park. The Park is a place of solitude and quiet; it stretches to the horizon on all sides. It has a few roads leading between the small round hills that rise from the scrubby desert but most of all you remember it for the great rocks and boulders scattered everywhere, some the size and colour of elephants, some twice that. Tasha found a quiet and hidden place. We got out of our cars and walked for a few hundred yards. I was carrying Georgie's ashes in a wooden box. No one spoke. We stopped on a great flat sand-coloured rock. I walked on a further thirty yards or so, placed the box on another rock, opened it and returned to join the others. We stood in silence for a few minutes thinking our own thoughts while the wind blew about us. Then Guislaine, Tasha and I walked together over to the box. After a few moments of private prayer we each took a handful of ashes and threw them to the sky. Andrew, who was watching, said it was as if the ashes danced away on the hot desert wind. They did. We returned to the others and then one by one or in small groups Georgia's friends walked over to the rock and gave her ashes, dancing, to the wind.

We had brought with us a frayed old overnight bag that I had given Georgie many years ago and that she took everywhere. Inside was her wedding dress, a filmy, yellowy-pinky thing, and two empty packets of Marlboro Red that I had taken from Georgia's car when I went with Jeff Young to collect it from the motel. Guislaine, Tash and I walked the hundred yards or so to the nearest Joshua tree. A Joshua tree is like a stumpy palm tree with a spiky haircut. Where a palm tree has fronds, a Joshua tree has spiky leaves sticking out. Tasha tied the wedding dress to some of the upper spikes; Guislaine freed one end so the dress streamed out in the wind. I stuck the two Marlboro Red packets on the top spikes and left the overnight bag at the bottom of the tree so she could arrive at her destination with her usual luggage.

We walked back to join the others. We stood together all of us and hugged and cried and even laughed as Georgia's wedding dress danced and floated in the desert wind. Now she was free.

To me, Georgia had an incredibly full life. Many people who live to eighty experience little and touch few. She was the same age as Janis Joplin and Jimi Hendrix when they died, a year older than Keats and two years younger than Shelley. Her poetry lay in the way she led her life.

29

Breakfast in Baghdad

Baghdad had so many memories for me. Walking up partridges in the date groves, skidding two and a half tons of ancient Rolls-Royce round desert mud pans, splashing in the pool at the Alwiyah Club, and the many evenings when Iraqis would sit around Ma's dinner table laughing and telling us jokes as if the good times would never end. For them the good times had ended abruptly in 1958, and for the country as a whole the good times had never come back. Saddam had seen to that. What I remembered most were the Iraqis themselves, the gentlest and most civilised of the Arabs, in contrast to their big-talk cousins the Egyptians.

Despite an abhorrence of what Saddam was doing to his own people, with the near-extinction of the Marsh Arabs and the persecution of the Shi'ites, I had followed the build-up to the American-led invasion of Iraq with dismay and had been out in the streets demonstrating against Bush and Blair and their plans. But by 2010 Iraq had ceased to occupy much of a place in the Western media, in contrast to the blanket coverage of the invasion and its immediate aftermath, so I thought I would go and have a look for myself. I went there in January at a time when everyone assured me Baghdad was 'more or less back to normal'. Maybe I could have another swim in the Alwiyah Club pool.

The flight to Baghdad left Istanbul at 3.30 a.m. The only other planes leaving around that time were going to Afghanistan and Islamabad. Lady Gaga was singing 'Bad Romance' on the airport video. One third of the passengers were tired and cowed middle-aged Iraqis loaded with sacks of duty-free goods and two thirds were shaven-headed English-speakers in jeans, grey sweatshirts and desert boots carrying rucksacks – fit, muscled men with ripples of flesh at the backs of their bare necks.

'Hi,' I said to the man next to me in shake-down. 'What's taking you to Baghdad?'

He looked at me as if I were a five-year-old. 'Security. We're all security.'

I thought about an alternative universe in which a plane from Zurich to New York contained one third cowed Americans with shopping bags and two thirds musclebound shaven-headed Arab youths on their way to America to make New York 'secure'. . .

After an uneventful flight I met Bartle and Zaab, my friends and lookers-after, who had set up an investment company, Northern Gulf Partners, in Baghdad. Bartle Bull was a journalist who specialised in riding across deserts and embedding himself in rebel armies, while Zaab too had a knack for popping up at the crossroads of history. Everyone said they worked for the CIA. I doubted it.

'Hi, guy,' said Bartle as I came out of customs. 'Welcome to Baghdad.'

Surreal did not begin to describe it. I'd been in Lebanon and Sudan in immediate post-war times, but they had been nothing like this. I was ushered outside to where three cars were waiting. Bartle got into one armour-plated four-by-four; Zaab and I clambered into the one behind. A third car followed as 'chaser'. Six khaki-clad hard men sporting pistols, ammunition pouches and automatic rifles eased their way into the cars with us, clones of the people who had just got off my plane.

'Hi, Miles, I'm Pete,' said the boss clone, whose shaven head had sinister creases in it. 'Flak jacket?' he offered just as you might say, 'Gum?'

'Um, no thanks.' I was already sweating, and the jacket looked heavy and hot. I noted that Bartle and Zaab were not wearing jackets.

'Your call,' he said, buttoning up his own and barking, 'OK, roll,' at the driver. I noted as we passed through the fifth checkpoint on the way out of the airport that there were almost no other cars on the road.

'This used to be a bad ride,' said Zaab, 'twenty minutes of white knuckles. A lot of the top Ba'athists lived in the big houses along the airport road and would fire rockets and guns at you. You had to go at 120 mph. But now it's the safest road in Baghdad.'

This was good news indeed, but, just in case, Pete turned on the siren to alert any local breakfasting Ba'athists that we were on our way.

After half an hour of high-speed driving we penetrated three security gates and drew up at a pile of shipping containers in the secure Green Zone. The stack of containers was our hotel. I was originally going to stay in the Palestine, the old Meridien, but a car bomb outside the hotel a week earlier had closed off that option. My bedroom was a partitioned-off part of a container. No windows.

Bartle, Zaab and I checked in and met for sweet black tea on plastic chairs in a dusty parking lot full of bulletproof four-by-fours bristling with electronic equipment. In the background was the constant clatter of US helicopters and the *duh-duh-duh* of machine-gun fire. I asked a passing American what the chopper noise and firing was about.

'Sir, that is the sound of freedom.'

'They're just practising,' said Zaab.

At 6.30 p.m. Bartle, Zaab and I hopped into a four-by-four for a short trip through empty Green Zone streets to the biggest US embassy in the world: 1,200 personnel behind the kind of walls the Israelis use to bottle up the Palestinians. The embassy was utterly sealed off from the outside world. We were dropped at the wrong gate and had to walk 300 yards to the right one.

'Watch out for incoming,' said our driver as he left us.

'Incoming what?'

'Rockets and mortars.' Of course. Silly me.

I had steeled myself to run the passage of US security thugs at the gatehouse and was puzzled when three uniformed Incas carrying guns almost as big as they were asked politely in fractured English for our IDs. Inside the blockhouse more courteous Incas smiled and chattered incomprehensibly as they waved us into the metal detectors with elaborate courtesy.

'What's up?' I asked Zaab, pointing at the Incas.

'Oh, the Americans outsource everything. The guards used to be Nepalese and Fijians, but they got too expensive. Peruvians are cheaper, so they use them now. And cheapest of all are Ugandans. The Americans put the Ugandans on the outside of the wall in the most dangerous positions. They used to use Chileans too, but then the Chileans and the Peruvians had a football game that ended in a gun battle inside the embassy compound.'

In the twilight years of the western Roman empire Rome outsourced everything to barbarians. And that was the end of them. The biggest embassy the world's most powerful country had ever had was guarded by rented Incas. The embassy itself had been built by a Kuwaiti company.

Our host at the embassy was an eager fresh-faced financial attaché – let's call him Joe – who had arrived three weeks earlier from Moscow and couldn't wait to get on with the job.

We ate a memorably disgusting meal in the hangar-like mess hall washed down with iced tea, after which Joe gave us a tour. Fort Bragg must look like this: a giant indoor swimming pool, basketball courts, gyms, office blocks. Two differences from Fort Bragg. Between the buildings here were duck 'n' dives, concrete shelters to dodge into when you saw an incoming rocket. And between the duck 'n' dives were young, decidedly non-American girls in tight jeans loitering and chattering to each other.

'They're cute,' said I to Joe. 'Who are they?'

'Uh, contract interpreters.'

'Ah.'

I asked Joe how he was enjoying Baghdad and what he thought of it.

'It's great. Such opportunity. I'm working with people who need investment.'

'That's great. And what do you actually think of the city?'

'What, Baghdad?'

'Yup.'

'Oh, well, I haven't been outside the embassy yet. There's not much reason to do that. We like to stay behind the walls.'

The next day we would visit the stock exchange, a couple of companies and lunch with a banker at the Alwiyah Club, where I had last been in 1957. I wondered how businesses in Baghdad would compare with the hundreds of companies I had visited elsewhere in the Middle East and Africa. And I wondered what the Alwiyah Club would be like, more than half a century since my previous visit.

Waking up in the container was difficult with no natural light, so it was a shock to step outside at 8 a.m. and find myself in a cool-blue-sky Baghdad morning. After breakfast we were going to leave the Green Zone, with its high walls and gun towers, and go into Iraq proper: Baghdad, the Red Zone.

I asked Bartle if we really needed Pistol Pete and his five Testosterone Tommies to accompany us. 'Well, usually we cruise around with a driver in a little Toyota, and we're fine. In four years we've only once come close to being blown up and that was when the car ahead of us was vapourised by a bomb on the airport road. But following the car bombings last week and with the elections coming up everyone's edgy. The Sunnis and the Ba'athists will do their best to derail the election.'

So at 9 a.m. our convoy of three cars crossed the muddy Tigris, which I had last seen fifty-three years before, when King Feisal II was on the throne, and arrived in Karada, the Kensington of Baghdad. Here there were people actually walking on the streets – not many of them, and almost as many Iraqi soldiers and policemen sitting on their brightly painted armoured cars – but life was going on. Half the shops were boarded up, and most trade was happening on the pavements, where boxes of air conditioners from Turkey and microwaves from Dubai were piled building-high. A few cafés had a few people in them, but there was none of the bustle and buzz of Cairo or Damascus. The buildings were as shabby as those of Lagos, but how nice it was to see life on the streets after the neutron-bomb emptiness of the Green Zone.

We pulled up at the stock exchange. Our five bodyguards jumped out and deployed, backs to the vehicles, scanning the streets and waving their weapons in best Bruce Willis fashion. 'Don't touch the doors, don't touch the doors,' Pete screamed at us. Like five-year-olds we could only get out when Pete told us it was safe and we were let out. A half-hour stand-off then took place while our guards argued with the Iraqi stock exchange guards, who wouldn't let them inside with guns.

Finally we went in past a table-mounted machine gun pointed at our belly buttons by a smiling stock exchange doorman, who *salaam alekhoum*ed us as his finger massaged the safety. Two de-gunned bodyguards accompanied us, sulking.

We were welcomed by the ex-chairman of the exchange.

The place was packed with old men gossiping in airport-style seats looking at display screens. I suspected that they were there for the gossip and the air conditioning more than the trading. The brokers sat yawning next door. I asked our broker about company accounts. 'Mr Miles, you don't understand. Accounts not important. Here you need information.' He tapped his nose. 'In Baghdad you must know what is going to happen before it is announced. That is how you make money.'

I was delighted to find a market where it appeared that insider trading was still obligatory, but I was assured that insider trading was not tolerated and our friend would certainly never have anything to do with it.

Lunch was with Mowafaq Mahmood, a courtly retired Iraqi businessman, at the Alwiyah Club. I remembered the Alwiyah as the Hurlingham Club of Baghdad. It was founded by the British in 1926 and hadn't changed much since – apart from the fact that the last splash of paint had gone on in the 1970s. The rules remained strict. Just as in a London gentlemen's club you had to leave your briefcase at the door and couldn't get your phone out, at the Alwiyah you had to leave your bodyguard at the door and couldn't get your pistol out.

Lunch was interrupted by Muhammad, the club manager, who rushed up babbling. Pistol Pete, our cranium-creased bodyguard, had forced an entrance to the club so that he could guard us, saying to Muhammad, 'Fuck you and your fucking club and fuck your fucking pisspot country.' Muhammad became so emotional while telling us this that all the good ol' Iraqi boys in the Members' Bar of the Alwiyah put down their Johnnie Walkers to listen. He switched to Arabic so they could understand better. Zaab calmed the manager and returned ten minutes later having dealt with Pistol Pete.

Back home in the Green Zone, after taking a short siesta in my container, where I was lulled to sleep by the music of machine guns from the embassy firing range, we dined in the dining container with Mazim, owner of the hotel. During dinner we talked. The one thing everyone agreed on was that the Americans had been broadly welcomed when they arrived in Baghdad in 2003. If, said Mazim, they had put a provisional Iraqi government in place with the US providing support and assistance, it might just have worked. But the Iraqis woke up and found they had been occupied. The Yankee liberators had become humiliating American occupiers.

Talk of American occupiers reminded me of visiting Babylon over fifty years earlier, when I had been in Baghdad with Tom. Babylon was then just being dug up, the Tower of Babel and the Hanging Gardens arid sites in the desert, starved of water since the Euphrates changed its course 3,000 years earlier. More recently Saddam had decided that Babylon, the city of Nebuchadnezzar, would make a fitting monument to Saddam the Great, so he set teams to work 'rebuilding' it. Work began to create a modern Babylon on top of the painstakingly excavated old city. Bricks were fired stamped with the legend, 'This was built by Saddam Hussein, son of Nebuchadnezzar, to glorify Iraq,' but before work could really get going the invasion of 2003 put an end to construction.

The 'son of Nebuchadnezzar' was replaced in Babylon by the delegate of Dubya, General James T. Conway of the 1st US Marine Expeditionary Force. It took him only a matter of weeks to build Camp Alpha, a US military base, right on top of Babylon, parts of which were levelled to the ground by

US Marine bulldozers to make a helicopter base and a parking lot for equipment. Tanks crushed 3,000-year-old roads of ancient bricks, and a number of walls and gates were knocked down to permit military vehicles to pass.

I asked Bartle what he, as an American, thought of this.

'Miles, you know, I betcha Conway thought that Babylon was just somewhere in the Bible.' He went on to tell me that while General Conway was flattening Babylon, Bartle had been the first and only Western journalist to be embedded into Muqtada al-Sadr's Mahdi Army, usually portrayed as being the most homicidal of the Shi'a militias. The Mahdi Army wanted its story to be known in the West and agreed he could spend six weeks with them. This resulted in two long articles by Bartle in the *New York Times* and longer ones elsewhere.

Bartle later learned from his interpreter that while he was calmly tucking into his evening rice the conversation around him had once gone like this:

Mahdi soldier (in Arabic): 'This Bartr Boo must be a spy. When shall we kill him?'

Bartle to interpreter: 'What's the guy saying?'

Interpreter to Bartle: 'He say that Chelsea won today.'

Bartle: 'Good. What about the Red Sox?'

Interpreter in Arabic to soldier: 'Mr Bartr no spy. Is independent reporter.'

Mahdi soldier: 'He Christian dog. Shall we shoot him now or cut his balls off first?'

Interpreter to Bartle: 'He say the Red Sox lost.'

Bartle: 'Damn.'

Bartle knew nothing of this debate until his interpreter told him two years later.

Next day we sacked Pistol Pete and the TTs for general lack of humour. To replace them we acquired the Baghdad Bazooka Boys, eight moonlighting Iraqi soldiers in two pickup trucks. These were hired from the retinue of Mr Chalabi, the man whom the Americans unsuccessfully tried to impose on Iraq as prime minister, who had since become their strong critic. He was, as was everyone, a cheek-kissing friend of Zaab's.

Mounted on the back of each truck was the finest ordnance that Mr Chalabi's deep pockets could buy, a machine gun manned by a uniformed Iraqi in balaclava, helmet with built-in telescopic sights and the obligatory wrap-around Ray-Bans. The gunner sat in a swivelling chair constantly rotating and pointing his gun at anything with two legs. Next to him in the armoured post on top of the pickup were two other guards with automatic pistols and assault rifles. One truck went in front of our armoured vehicle, the other tail-gunned us. Everyone wore balaclavas, helmets and black wool gloves. Who would have thought that 1980s IRA fashions would have taken such root in Baghdad?

The Bazooka Boys had wild grins on their faces and no regard for the rules of the road. We scorched down divided highways on the wrong side forcing oncoming cars into ditches; we drove headlong into blocked intersections and watched the stationary traffic part like the Red Sea for Moses at the wave of a black glove and the swivel of a machine gun. Policemen actually saluted. We spent the morning trying to locate different offices. Addresses meant nothing. We were told, 'Wait by the statue and I will send a boy.' Getting to our destinations involved driving over roundabouts and traffic islands, along pavements, shunting other cars out of the way, and finally coming to rest in front of the welcoming weaponry of our hosts' door staff. Unlike with Pistol Pete and the TTs, the door staff welcomed the Bazooka Boys. Greetings were shouted, weapons admired and stroked, balaclavas doffed; and we were soon ushered into dark buildings where only a lunatic would take the lift.

The meetings were all similar. We went up dark stairs to sit in unlit offices on tilting chairs with worn seats. Courteous Iraqis plied us with sweet black tea in tiny glasses and talked about the rebuilding of the country. Everyone was charming. The shares of all the companies seemed expensive relative to their current business, but, it was explained by all we met, were a steal valued on their bright future prospects. I did not ask who would be stealing from whom.

We all agreed that the potential of Iraq was boundless. It had more oil than Saudi Arabia, the exploitation of which would provide money for the rebuilding of the country. We also all agreed that Iraq would end up in a sunny place. It was getting from the present to that place that required an act of belief.

We made a trip to the Palestine Hotel, where I had been meant to stay. One of the three giant car bombs that had gone off in Baghdad a week earlier had been detonated between the Sheraton and the Palestine. The force of the bomb had destroyed a large part of the lower floors of both hotels together with many of their upper windows. Everywhere you had to pick your way through shattered glass and twisted metal. The general manager showed us around. Bartle and Zaab and a local partner were potentially interested in a scheme to rebuild and rebrand the Palestine, the site of which, right on the Tigris in the middle of downtown, was one of the best in Baghdad.

'When will you be open to guests again?' I asked the GM, looking around at the devastated entrance.

He looked puzzled: 'But we are open. Occupancy, I regret, is low, only 20 per cent.'

We then did what I regard as the only truly risky thing I did in Baghdad. Forget roadside bombs, improvised explosive devices, snipers and suicide bombers; we did something insane. We took the lift to the top of the Palestine. The lift was twenty-seven years old and I doubted if the Schindler maintenance man had been to call since the turn of the century. We survived. The view from the eighteenth-floor Panorama Hall Bar, windows all blown in, the room a mess, took in the whole of Baghdad. It looked surprisingly normal apart from the presence everywhere of the white and grey concrete fortifications surrounding every building of size. And then we had to take the lift down again.

One major pleasant surprise of Baghdad was the absence of American troops on the streets; by then they were billeted in giant bases outside Baghdad. Worse than the troops had been the hated mercenary contractors such as Blackwater. The parting act of the disastrous US viceroy, Paul Bremer, had been to give all foreign troops and contractors total immunity from Iraqi law. The US troops were under orders to be nice to the locals in the later days; the mercenaries never were. They despised the Iraqis and showed their contempt.

Every Iraqi I spoke to had stories of Blackwater mercenaries breaking into houses, shooting suspects, violating women and wantonly destroying property.

When the Americans were still on the streets, Iraqis were not allowed to get closer than within a hundred feet of a US vehicle; for an Iraqi car to attempt to overtake a US military or mercenary vehicle was literally fatal. Blackwater vehicles would fire lethal bursts at random cars that offended them. Even now that they were off the streets their malign presence was felt. We had stopped for a photo session by Saddam's ten-storey-high crossed-swords monument. Overhead a Blackwater helicopter was screaming around at little more than treetop height in a deafening and threatening manner. 'Some yee-hah from Texas showing off to a visiting biggie,' said Zaab.

I had an introduction to Michael Christie, Reuters bureau chief in Baghdad, so Zaab, Bartle, I and the Bazooka Boys went to visit him. Reuters inhabited three or four collapsing houses in a secure compound filled with other collapsing houses, which housed Associated Press, the BBC, Agence France-Presse, the Japanese press agency and a few others. Most of the time the expatriate journalists stayed in their compounds because getting around Baghdad was so difficult. Iraqi staffers were employed to do the legwork. One reason everyone reporting from Baghdad seemed to echo everyone else may have been that they all messed in together, with the chief entertainment being the compound parties, where duty-free booze was drunk and stories swapped.

I asked Michael about the risks of being a reporter in Iraq. 'Reuters has lost seven people since the invasion,' he said.

'Good God,' I said. 'Roadside bombs?' 'No, all shot.' 'Don't they have bodyguards?' 'All shot by Americans. Every one.' 'On purpose?' 'Who knows? The Americans say it's easy to mistake a camera lens for a gun, but their vision equipment can read a watch at a hundred yards.'

High point of our afternoon was tea with His Royal Highness Sherif Ali, pretender to the throne of Iraq. 'Sherif' means he is a direct descendant of the Prophet. In the Kassem revolution of 1958 King Faisal II and the royal family were butchered. Our man was the son of Faisal II's uncle, the all-powerful but not all-popular regent, Abdul'illah, also murdered in the revolution. Our host had been out of the country at the time of the revolution or he too would have been butchered.

Zaab was, of course, a buddy of the Sherif. The Hashemite family, of whose two branches Sherif Ali and the current King of Jordan were the heads, had been careless in the throne-keeping department. They'd lost three. The Hashemites started off as kings of most of Arabia including Mecca, but a warlord called Saud booted them out in the 1920s and attached his name to most of the Arabian peninsula. Churchill, annoyed at the loyal Brit-loving Hashemites being ousted by an unwashed Bedu, put one of the deposed king's sons on the throne of a country he had just invented, Jordan, and the other, Feisal, on the throne of Syria. In the latter matter he had failed to consult the French, who thought they were ruling Syria, and Clemenceau in turn booted Feisal out of Syria, leaving Churchill, who was getting short of Arab thrones on which to seat members of the unlucky Hashemite family, to make him king of another country he had just invented, Iraq. So the ex-king of Syria woke up as King Feisal I of Iraq, the grandfather of the butchered Feisal II and great-grandfather of the man ushering us into his spacious villa on the banks of the Tigris, a villa which Saddam had built to house Yasser Arafat.

Sherif Ali sat on a near-throne while we sat audience-style in front of him. He had one immaculately tailored leg languidly crossed over the other. He spoke melodious English and looked as if he were one of the better-dressed members of a St James's Club, which for all I knew he was. The Sherif gave us the most objective overview of Iraqi politics I had had. Things were complicated. At the time of our meeting he, a Sunni and a descendant of the Prophet, was running for parliament as an MP on the ticket of the Shi'a SCIRI party. A Lebanese friend had said to me in Beirut a year earlier, 'If you think you understand Lebanese politics, then they haven't been properly explained to you.' That was even more true of Iraq.

Talking to the Sherif, I was reminded how civilised most Iraqis are, particularly when compared to their Babylon-smashing Yankee occupiers. Iraq needed a government that could take decisions and get things done so that it could start to use the country's potentially huge oil income to rebuild. Talking to the Sherif I almost believed that this was possible.

30

Doing the Hand Flap

I have been back to India many times since the Morland family left it in 1949. And every time, as I leave the airport and smell the smell of India, something deep within me tingles and says, 'This is my birth land.' A few years ago I was idly surfing the Internet when I saw something that made my pulse gallop, something that would allow me to combine India with motorbiking: Extreme Bike Tours.

A man called Zander Combe took small groups of bikers around India on Enfield Bullets. You could go either to the Himalayas, where, Zander's website noted, he was hoping to get in the *Guinness Book of Records* for cooking the world's highest prawn masala – although what the prawns would smell like after being carried to a Himalayan peak on an ancient motorbike I did not like to think – or you could do the South India Tour, starting in Cochin and finishing in Goa. For me India is about its people. There would be few people in the Himalayas and many in South India. It was an easy choice. I signed up. If I had known then what I know

now I would have stayed at home. Well, perhaps. Driving in the wake of Zander through the towns, hills and jungles of southern India is the nearest thing I know to assisted suicide.

A bare six weeks after finding Zander's website, my diary cleared of grown-up London appointments, a Cochin taxi dropped Robert and me off at a tiny hotel in a back street. Robert had been a friend since Oxford. While still a happily married man, he did, at the occasional moment of stress, like to go a-biking.

I am spoilt and used to staying in five-star hotels. On this trip we would be staying in two-star hotels. I had looked some of them up on TripAdvisor. The features the hotels we were booked in had in common were an abundance of sewage, little of it going down the right hole, and cock-roaches the size of rats. Here's what TripAdvisor reviewers had to say about the Royal Retreat in Munnar, a tea town up in the Western Ghats, where we would spend our first night on the road.

Mr Ankur Tewari: 'The biggest problem which I faced in the hotel was of fooding. The food quality is very poor. Most of the time the service is not available. Even the menu items are also not available. So if you want to stay make sure you eat out.' Coimbatore Sam had this to say: 'It was an awful trip in my life ever . . . Which was run by totally unprofessional people . . . I started facing problem since I checked in. It's absolutely an worst trip and I never suggest this hotel and absolutely not for honeymoon couples. Please stay away . . .'

Outside our Cochin hotel were seven shiny Enfield Bullets, a 1956 English bike still made in India, its advertising tag line,

'Built like a gun, goes like a bullet' – presumably because it exploded frequently. I was told we had 'full Indian insurance'. 'What does that cover?' I asked. 'Oh, $150 of damage to the bike.' 'And what about if I run someone over?' 'Ah, that's a cash transaction,' said Zander. He added that if you ran someone over in a village, you didn't stop because if you did the village people would beat you to death. And if there was an accident it was important to settle the matter in cash before the police turned up as bribing the police was far more expensive than buying off the person you had hit.

Cochin was lovely, all fishing nets, crumbling churches and Dutch forts, but we had business to do and little time for sightseeing. We were introduced to the other 'extreme bikers'. We were seven in all. I was curious as to what our companions would be like. Ravers? Biker babes? Karma seekers? Ganja-istas? No. We had Bill, Ian and Charles, three lads from Newcastle, who had, I suspect, spent many a Friday night out-talking Yorkshiremen in the pub, and two blokes from Derby, Terry and Dave, both ex-army. Terry was a fruit and veg man while Dave drove the high-speed train to London. They were almost as old as Robert and me.

Our leader and the founder of Extreme Bike Tours, Zander Combe, a forty-ish Englishman with a ponytail, I took an instant liking to when I learned he had been expelled from Radley for misbehaviour with women. He had been based for the last sixteen years in Anjuna Beach, Goa's Hippy Valley, the place that made the world safe for ganja in the 1960s and our final destination on this trip. Team mechanic was Vijay, a gentle, smiling Goan and the only person who understood our bikes.

The Mighty Bullets

We were taught how to ride them. Unlike a normal bike, the Bullet's gear pedal was on the right, where you normally found the brake, and to change gear you had to click the gear pedal down, not up. And there was a false neutral between each gear. The result was that when you wanted to do an emergency stop because of a fast-looming holy cow you stamped on the gear lever, which is where years of biking had told you the brake was, which promptly changed you up from third to the false neutral between third and fourth, while the bike sailed on at undiminished speed.

'The bikes are like women,' Zander had told us. 'Treat them gently but with firmness, and they'll do anything you want.' Zander was unmarried.

Starting required pushing the kick-start gently down while pressing the decompression lever, at which the ammeter dial went to the left a bit; then you pushed the kick-start down a bit further and the dial centred, at which brief but critical moment you let the kick-start come up and then quickly, gently but firmly kicked the starter down. After doing this ten times the bike was silent and the heat inside your helmet and your reinforced ventilation-proof biker jacket had built to Chernobyl levels. Vijay would then shimmy up, give the starter a nonchalant prod with his left foot, and the bike would roar into action. What a noise. The Bullet had none of the vulgar gargle of a Harley or the scream of a Ducati, it was the deep-throated *ta pocketa pocketa* of a civilised English engine which had spent a life in the tropic Indian sun.

We went on a fifteen-kilometre ride through Cochin traffic to get used to the bikes. 'Only one thing is vital,' said Zander. 'The horn.' We were to sound it at all times. And if the horn broke we were to stop immediately and await Vijay, as we would be invisible without a horn on an Indian road.

The ride was a qualified success. We stalled frequently and found ourselves stationary in the middle of scrambles of traffic, all using their horns at us. Each of us would then gently but firmly depress the kick-start while trying to watch the ammeter dial as the sweat cascaded in rivulets down the inside of our helmet visor. After a bit my bike did begin to exhibit its Katherine Hepburn qualities and glided along throatily *ta-pocketing* while I changed from third to fourth with no neutral in between, the coconut palms flashed by and the fragrance of Cochin's sewer-canals was left behind.

I was glad to get back to our hotel, a teetotal establishment, have a long shower, put on my new Cochin linen trousers and saunter off with Zander and Vijay to the Brunton

Boatyard, a five-star hotel, where we sat on the terrace by the sea, watched the fishing boats set out on the evening tide and rehydrated with a number of the most delicious mojitos I had ever tasted.

We then set off. After a day on the road from Cochin to Munnar I had learned Indian hand signals. Well, hand signal. There was only one. A brown hand would come out of the driver's window and flap lazily in a Wildean manner. This meant one of seven things:

1. Please overtake; the road is clear.
2. A cement truck is hurtling towards us; you will be killed if you pull out.
3. I am about to turn right.
4. I am about to turn left.
5. I'm hot and bored and feel like flapping a limp-wristed arm out of the window.
6. Look, children, there's Auntie's house.
7. I have just picked my nose.

Now that I knew all this, driving was much safer.

Misty Munnar with its lakes, tea plantations and forests with canopies 200 feet high was left behind, and we swooped down to Madurai in the hot and dusty plains. The road from Munnar was a biker's dream, curve after tightening curve gliding through the mist-shrouded mountains, but the road was narrow and the Indian buses filled it from edge to edge. Dodging the buses was tricky and required a detour into the dirt while avoiding the ditch. B.A. Bill, ex-747-pilot, didn't. The bus forced him into the ditch, his bike whip-tailed, and poor B.A. Bill was flat on his face in the road.

Half an hour later Bill and bike were repaired by Vijay's wizardry, and we sailed on till Charles, another of the Newcastle lads, caught a patch of sand on a hairpin and he was off. Little serious damage, and on we went.

We hit the plains and accelerated, now doing 80 kph (Indian kph are like dog years – multiply by two for normal equivalent), an unheard-of speed. Robert was *Easy-Ride*ring along just ahead of me – the gum trees were whistling by, buffaloes tossing their heads, tuk-tuks keeping clear as seven mighty Enfields bulleted along – when he hit a reverse-camber patch on a high-speed bend, the bike fishtailed violently and I watched in slow-motion horror as the bike skidded on to its side and went down on top of him and came to rest in the ditch. I skidded to a halt and rushed back. Robert was motionless under the bike. I sat him up gently and he croaked unconvincingly, 'I'm OK.'

Before he could say anything else, platoons of Tamils appeared from the undergrowth and started fighting over which bit of Robert they would administer first aid to. Legs and arms were seized and worked up and down; Robert's head was rotated and wobbled. I fought them off, and we found that Robert was bruised but functioning apart from possible cracked ribs. Zander gave him powerful 'muscle relaxants' from the first aid bag and promised Goan medicinal 'herbs' if that didn't work. Robert's bike was hammered back into rideable shape by Vijay and we cruised on with Vijay, clad in flip-flops and flappy shirt, on the bike and poor, sore Robert in the support van.

When we arrived in Madurai, Robert was gasping with pain whenever he raised his right arm. He and I, escorted by

Shirath, went off to a hospital. Madurai had hospitals where normal cities had bars. Its stupendous temple made it a place of pilgrimage, and what more natural than after a trip to the temple but that you should have your spine fixed at Dr Ram's Spinal Intervention Clinic or your boobs boobed at the Sunny Days Cosmetic Surgery Centre.

We however headed for the Apollo. This was one of a chain of private hospitals throughout India. A central casting doctor in spotless whites sat Robert on a bed, pushed and pulled his arms, listened gravely through the stethoscope, asked four or five questions, said, 'Probably a rib fracture.' Twenty minutes later, after an X-ray and a consultation with an even more senior doctor in spotless whites, Robert was sent on his way with some strapping and the knowledge that over time his rib would mend. Riding a motorbike would delay that process by weeks. All this cost the equivalent of eleven pounds including the X-ray. Robert took the powerful painkillers they gave him and ignored the advice about not riding a motorbike.

Not only are Indian distances and speeds like dog years, equivalent to at least double their value in the normal world, Zander had started to lie about them. When we finally reached the end of the boulder-strewn watercourse that passed for the Mudumalai Forest Reserve road after eleven draining hours, we had covered 310 kilometres of mountain hairpins (thirty-six of them winding down a precipice between Ootacamund, the famous 'Snooty Ooty' British hill station, and here), mentally disturbed traffic, roads closed by landslides, and random attacks by homicidal buses. Zander had promised us a journey of 200 kilometres. 'Oh, was it really 300 clicks?' said

Zander, and I could swear he was adopting the Indian head nod. 'I had no idea it was so far . . .'

Talking of head nods, having mastered Indian traffic indications (the hand flap) I was now studying Indian personal intercourse. We had crossed from Kerala into Tamil Nadu, the heart of south India, home of the Tamils, the most bloody-minded people on earth after the Northern Irish (remember the Tamil Tigers in Sri Lanka), where the signs were written in indecipherable squirly-bits script and the locals refused to speak not only English but also Hindi so they did not have to lower themselves by communicating with outsiders. Consequently communication with lesser races (English, other Indians, Martians) was done by means of the Tamil head nod.

Indians do of course tend to nod their heads like metronomes, but in Tamil Nadu it was the sole means of communication. If you asked a Tamil a question the head oscillated from left to right, picking up speed until it was almost a blur. The Tamil nod, often accompanied by a patronising smile as if to say what a stupid question, meant, 'No, but it's more fun if you think I'm saying yes.' Some examples:

1. Thank you for ordering a sweet lime soda. It will be here immediately despite the fact we have no soda and the last lime was used in the curry.
2. Of course there are no knives and forks: what are your fingers for?
3. All our ice is made from purified water.
4. The hot water comes on at 6 p.m.

5. The road to Ooty is straight ahead. (Zander had warned us
   that asking the way was fruitless as the answer was always a
   vigorous slicing gesture with the forearm pointing straight
   ahead.)

Because from time to time we did need to communicate
with the Tamils, Zander had captured one, Shirath, and hired
him to drive the support van, which picked up fallen riders
and bikes. Being a Tamil he refused to admit to speaking
English, but luckily Vijay had discovered a common tongue
with him although most of their conversation was done
by head nodding vigorous enough to power a wind farm.
Shirath's main purpose was to leap out of the car in the event
of an accident, negotiate a cash pay-off with the flattened
Tamil and then drive off at speed before a policeman arrived
and the villagers beat us to death.

The Mudumalai Forest Reserve was splendid. After five
days staying in hotels where the fooding had been vegetable curry on a banana leaf, the drinking a disaster ('Sir,'
head nodding so fast it appeared ready to separate from the
shoulders, 'not having bar.') and the loo paper a myth, it was
wonderful to be in a place equipped with these luxuries.
Better yet, before dinner a smiling man shimmied out of the
jungle and positioned himself behind the bar with a cocktail
shaker in his hand, the first man for five days who did not say,
'Bless you,' when you said, 'Mojito'.

The biking had everything. At its best, as you slalomed
through sweeping bends under a canopy of mangoes, gum
trees and acacias, seven bikes in full song making the noise
a Harley would make if it had had a proper education, you

could not imagine anything finer. At its worst, fighting to follow Zander and the five other bikes ahead of you, stay upright and not to stall in the maelstrom of Madurai traffic while tuk-tuks closed in on you like Messerschmitts from either side as you attempted to overtake a bus painted as the Juggernaut while another bus proclaiming itself to be under the command of Lord Ram came thundering towards you, you just said thank you as your Bullet somehow found a hole between you and the converging buses and popped out in time to see Zander heading off in the opposite direction.

And then there were the adrenalin moments, such as on the 6,000-foot climb from the plains up to Ooty, when it seemed that every bus and lorry in the subcontinent had chosen to make the climb at the same time. You had the choice of going up at 5 kph choking on the exhaust of a lorry, or overtaking the bus that was overtaking the lorry as you entered a blind bend (there were few sighted bends on the road to Ooty) with a ditch on one side, a 1,000-foot drop on the other and a keen awareness that if a lorry was coming downhill only the Lord Vishnu could save you. Zander, as lead bike, normally waited till just before the blind bend before throwing his bike on to the wrong side of the road and accelerating fearlessly into the unseen. If you were riding third or fourth you followed – heart a-thump – as by that time the open and visible space ahead had shrunk to nothing. I felt every chamber of my heart fibrillating away every time we overtook.

Before lunch in the reserve I walked around with Robin, the German Parsee camp botanist, who told me how, two weeks earlier, he and another camp worker had had to pull a cobra out of a hole in the wall of No. 4 bungalow (mine).

Eight new check-ins had stood around holding their luggage while Robin and his co-worker attempted to get the snake, which had followed a frog into a hole and got stuck, out. Eventually they succeeded, and Robin's mate was left holding a furious cobra by the tail while it attempted to climb up its own body to give it a platform for a strike, giving it a flick every few seconds to straighten it out. Robin meanwhile was holding a sack open, terrified the cobra would bite his hand as it was dropped in. The new arrivals stood round catatonic with horrified fascination. Finally the snake was bagged up and next day released into a distant part of the garden.

I carefully checked the hole leading into my bathroom for wiggly things. 'Please, not to worry,' said Robin. 'Cobra gone.' 'Phew. Thank heavens. Any other livestock in my room?' '*Nein, nein.* Vell, just in der roof.' 'Yes?' 'Only a flying snake. They flatten ze body and can glide a hundred metres on a good wind. But only mildly venomous.'

For anyone like me who came of age in the 1960s, all Indian journeys end in Goa.

After ten days of sweat, terror, adrenalin, excitement, exhilaration, pain (like most of us, I had a 'Goa tattoo' of red weals on both calves from being barbecued by a smoking Enfield exhaust pipe) and sheer hard work (eleven continuous hours from Mysore to Udipi left you drained), we were now on Agonda Beach. Ten palm-thatched huts with thick, soft mattresses (what joy after ten nights of hard boards and concrete platforms); a friendly bar crammed with substances forbidden in Tamil Nadu and Kerala: rum, whisky, vodka, even a case of Sula Indian Sauvignon Blanc; a kitchen turning out spice-marinated grilled fish, crab masala, fragrant coconutty curries; and, fifty feet from the huts, a mile of powdery white sand dotted with slender outriggered fishing boats.

We were at the White Sands in Goa. We had survived everything Zander had thrown at us and had come to love our quirky old bikes, their funny false neutrals and strange decompression levers that you had to tickle if you wanted to start them. After ten days on the road I sat at midnight giggling like a nine-year-old under a beach palm having had one mojito too many and one puff too far of whatever it was that the rickshaw driver had sold us in Mysore. This was the world as we liked to think it had been in the 1960s but was it ever this good? Life here was at its simplest and best. It was twenty pounds a day for the White Sands and another six for the best seafood dinner you had ever eaten.

I ripped off my clothes and threw myself into the sea followed by a stroll down the sand. Indians are naturally clean people and do not like to dirty their own doorsteps. It had soon become apparent why we needed to rechristen our night stop Turdle Beach. Every forty yards or so along the beach was a squatting Indian, pants around ankles, not dirtying his own doorstep in the beachfront village. Not a good place for an after-dinner walk in the dark.

I had learned at dinner the night before that Zander had more steel in his body than bone. I was glad not to have known this earlier as I had been comforting myself over the 3,000 very Indian kilometres of our trip that if he had been risking his life on the subcontinent's roads for sixteen years and was fine, then we should be too. If I'd known earlier that one forearm was titanium (a cow, which walked placidly away with hardly a moo after Zander had demolished his Enfield colliding with it), a foot was steel (a fast-moving palm tree), and various other bits were held together with pins and bolts after miscellaneous encounters with the flotsam and jetsam of the Indian road, I would have been even more terrified than I was.

A day later we arrived safe and sound at the Joly Julie, a group of startlingly red and white bungalows in the forest a mile or so from hippy heaven – Anjuna Beach. I felt flat that the trip was over – no more reason for the adrenalin to pump – but apart from the Goa burn tattoos and a cricked back from the concrete mattresses, I had also seldom felt more content. Ganesh had delivered us safe.

Zander proposed a bike trip to a deserted beach 'only thirty clicks away'. I remembered *Das Boot*, the wonderful German film about a U-boat that survives everything from depth charges to ruptured pressure hull on an Atlantic hunting trip. As the boat chugs serenely into Brest, its home port, sun shining, mission accomplished, with the crew on deck celebrating, the submarine is wiped out by an RAF bomb. No one voiced it, but we all felt that one more outing on our brave Bullets could be throwing providence one offering too many in the way of temptation.

Instead I spent the last morning drinking mojitos at the Rock On Cafe, 'Where You Rock' on Ozran Beach between Little Vagator and Anjuna. The beach was busy. Half the population of Moscow was there. Every rock and stretch of white breaking-surf sand was peopled with near-naked pairs of Russian girls being photographed, bodies entwined in sapphic poses, by pot-bellied Russians with extending lenses.

I sat entranced trying to catch the action on the zoom of my inadequate little Panasonic.

India and Zander's mystery tour had been grand. I, who lived a life of five-star spoiltness in England, had spent two weeks in conditions that would at times have made an eighteen-year-old backpacker blanch. Our standard meal was vegetable curry on a banana leaf and *dosas* cooked on a hot stone in a tiny roadside shacklet with a tin cup of *chai* – hot, syrupy, milky tea. Yet for the first time I had survived a trip to India without Delhi belly.

As I sat sipping my cocktail, a newly bought wooden-chunk bracelet adorned with tantric signs on my wrist, looking at a cow chewing contentedly at the edge of the surf, I thought back over the longest 3,000 kilometres I had ever travelled and knew there was only one thing to say.

'Om.'

31

Vroom Vroom

Zander's Extreme Bike Tour around south India was, in retrospect, extreme. Extremely dangerous. I had been calmed into a sense of security by the other bike trips I had made, trips where you did not find a cow in the middle of the motorway acting as a traffic-calming device, trips where buses and tuk-tuks did not come at you as if you owed them money, and trips where you did not find yourself following a man with titanium limbs around blind hairpins with a 1,000-foot drop half a foot away on your right.

My first big trip had been the London to Istanbul odyssey on the Beast. Nothing would ever match that because I set off in ignorance of what lay ahead, never having ridden a motorbike before. If ever a trip represented a loss of virginity that was it. Some time elapsed following that before the next big bike journey. I had a succession of BMWs like the ones the police ride. I rode them around London, and big though they were they were adept at dodging in and out of the traffic. Being hampered by traffic jams was a thing of the past. I was free to scoot past lines of stationary cars. I took these bikes to Europe, twice across the Pyrenees to Spain, twice across the Alps and on to Italy, and many times to France, biker heaven, be it Brittany, Normandy, the Loire and the Atlantic coast, or Provence and the Côte d'Azur.

Then I saw *Motorcycle Diaries*, the film of a 1952 bike trip made by two young Argentinian medical students, Ernesto and Alberto, who set off from Buenos Aires on a Norton 500, *Il Poderoso* – the Powerful One. They career laughing across the limitless Pampas, climb the Andes and cross the pass into Chile, make their way down to Valdivia on the Pacific and up the Chilean coast through the port of Valparaiso and on through the desert to Peru, where they are going to work in a leper colony. *Il Poderoso* gives out long before they get there; the second half of the trip is done by hitching.

By the time they get back to Argentina, having visited Bolivia, Colombia and Venezuela on the way, Ernesto and Alberto have been radicalised by seeing the inequalities of South America where the poor are little better than serfs. Ernesto takes himself off to Cuba to join Fidel Castro who is hiding out in the Sierra Madre and conducting guerrilla operations against the dictator Batista. Castro always called Ernesto by his nickname, Che, *che* being Argentinian Spanish for 'mate'. Soon everyone else did too.

I watched the film with my pulse racing. What a thing to do. I lay in bed that night, my brain going round and round and thinking about their journey. Why couldn't I do that? No, seriously. But I didn't speak Spanish and I knew noth-ing of motorbike mechanics . . . A few days later I had found Rentamoto in Buenos Aires on the Internet and arranged to rent a 1,200 cc BMW GS Adventure, the same giant steel-panniered off-road bike that Ewan McGregor had been riding round the world.

A short month later, Spike* and I were barrelling across Che's pampas, plains which I had expected to be as boring as the American Midwest but which turned out to be a place of impossible beauty. The road undulated under a sky the light blue of the Argentinian flag as it curved through marshy salt pans flecked with egrets, ducks and black-necked swans, and on through county-sized fields of fluffy-tailed pampas grass flickering in the brilliant sun. Hawks, harriers and eagles hovered along the edge of the road. I saw an eagle snatch a dove in full flight. There were the times floating at a cruising speed of just under 90 mph across the limitless pampas, Chuck Berry on the iPod, a blue sky bigger than any I had ever seen, and the Andes a smudge on the horizon, when I felt nothing could touch me.

Spike and I left the plains behind, spent Christmas Day with friends in the Andes, and on Boxing Day, following in Che Guevara's tyre treads, survived seventy kilometres of rip-rap – iron-hard corrugated mud that can shake anything but the strongest bike to shreds – and crossed the Bariloche Pass into Chile, passing down to the Pacific and the roaring sea lions of Valdivia. We followed Che to Valparaiso with its sherbet-yellow houses, Madonna-lipstick-purple cathedrals and Oxford-blue and paisley-orange schools. We left Valpo just in

---

* Bikes are meant to be feminine; mine, with its steel panniers, finned engine and handlebars that belonged on an ox, was anything but. I named her Spike after a well muscled personal trainer who looked after a friend of mine in Key West.

The road to Chile

time to avoid the annual New Year's Eve massacre, when the students get drunk, dance the samba and throw each other into the icy harbour.

Here we parted from Che. He went north to the Atacama Desert, while Spike and I headed east and made our hairpin way up the Andes towards its highest crossing, Portillo Pass, 11,000 feet above sea level, a bare-cliffed place of heart-stopping wildness and grandeur where the screaming wind all but lifts your bike into the void and vegetation is a stranger, mountains a million years older than the Alps.

Three days later, a continent twice-crossed, as Europe had been on my virgin bike ride, Spike and I were nosing our way once more into the outskirts of Buenos Aires through fields forked with lightning from a summer storm of terrifying strength. I was feeling a combination of exhilaration at the enormousness of where the faithful bike had taken me, relief that some higher power had brought me back safe after the challenges of the Argentinian roads – few moments in the past two weeks had passed when I had not been conscious of the hair's breadth of a wandering cow or careless truck driver that separated me from quadriplegia – melancholy that the trip was as much history now as was the ride of Che and *Il Poderoso*, and heaviness that it was time to get back to being a grown-up.

Non-bikeys don't realise how physical biking is, quite unlike driving a car. Steering is done with the weight, as in skiing, not by turning a wheel as in a car. You slow for a corner, pick the best line, being careful not to trespass over the mid-line for a left-hand bend as you do not want to be decapitated by an oncoming bus as you lean into it, throw your inside knee out to lead you into the turn and bank the bike – the sharper the turn, the steeper the bank – and then as you go into the turn and just as the weight of the slowing bike is coming close to making it fall, you wind the throttle up to pour on power, and the bike starts to move back to the vertical as the centrifugal force of the added power pushes it upright and back towards the outside of the bend. And as soon as you come out of the bend out goes the other knee, and you are picking your line for the next corner, the bike rising and falling for corner after corner, much like a slalom skier throws her weight from left leg to right as she flips through the poles. After a few minutes of a long swooping run through the Andes the adrenalin is pumping so hard you are gasping. The rhythm of a high mountain road turns makes you feel that heaven is just one hill away as you throw half a ton of screaming machine into bend after bend.

Part of the intoxication comes from the knowledge that if you pick the wrong line going into a bend because you have underestimated its sharpness you do not have the option of braking halfway round – as you do in a car. Hitting the brakes on a sharp bend would throw the bike upright and send you straight ahead and off the road. All you can do if a corner unexpectedly tightens into itself is to force the bike even further over on its ear and pray it too will tighten into the turn.

Then, two years later, South America and Zander's Enfield adventure both behind me, I was in a London restaurant and an ethereal Japanese waitress was slipping a plate of sashimi in front of me with a graceful dip, and it hit me.

Japan. Of course.

Through the web I found Japan Bike Rentals. They turned out to be run by Jonathan, an Aussie who lived in Tokyo. He agreed to rent me a BMW 1200 RT, the exact twin of one of my bikes in London. Better yet, he could devise an itinerary which he would load on a satnav, and he would book me into hotels along the way. I said I wanted to go off track and spend nights in *ryokans*, country inns in fishing villages and up mountains, which I had read up about. Jonathan plotted a trip around south Japan, about which I knew as much as I did about Mars. I'd been to Tokyo twice, for a day each time, but never ventured outside the centre. I didn't speak a syllable of Japanese and I couldn't use chopsticks.

A day after I landed in Tokyo the rented BMW – or Beemer-san as I had already christened my bike – and I were lost in a ferry port. The good news was that there were lots of port signs; not so good was that not one was in English. A ferry port marshal suddenly leaped from behind a giant truck waving the kind of light baton that five-year-olds favour for birthday parties. He ran ahead of the bike. Everyone in Japan ran everywhere.

Waiting to board I noted the bike was almost blown off its stand by the screaming wind. This did not look good for the ferry-boaters about to spend nineteen hours in the open Pacific. I had a 'special cabin' on the top deck. Everyone else, male and female, was in a giant deck-wide hamster cage on the deck below. We tootled off into the dark down Tokyo Bay past Yokohama. Just as I finished the picnic I had bought earlier in Tokyo we left the shelter of the bay and nosed out into the open Pacific. The boat reared like a startled horse. Everything flew everywhere – salad on the walls, salami on the sheets. If this was not a typhoon it was its best friend.

Within fifteen minutes waves were crashing green against my window five decks up. I lay on my bed gripping the sides. Walking about was literally impossible. For the first two hours I was terrified as I was sure we would sink, but by and by I realised that Japanese boats were built to withstand tsunamis. The madness went on for fifteen hours until we found the shelter of Tokushima Roads. And funnily enough, when I'd got over the fear, being confined to bed for fourteen hours was strangely relaxing. And by some miracle I never felt sick. At last, drained but grateful, we disembarked at Tokushima on Japan's southernmost big island of Shikoku. Despite the typhoon, we were only two minutes late.

After the ferry Beemer-san and I had four hours through twisty mountain roads, mist, bursts of sun, vertiginous gorges, pine forests and everywhere the froth of cherry blossom. Next day, brilliant sun, tiny roads dodging pagoda temples, an hour following a wild river through valleys and fields, and later skirting Provençal beaches with umbrella pines and hawks overhead.

Before dinner, my first night after the ferry, I had my first Japanese bath. The hotel staff, who seemed to regard me in an affectionate way as a giant pink joke, had found an outsize kimono. Wearing this and slippers, I nervously made my way to the baths led by a giggling girl. There were three Japanese men inside squatting on tiny stools like sumo wrestlers. I threw off my kimono and joined them, all four of us naked. Lonely Planet had told me that you must scrub yourself for at least fifteen minutes before presuming to enter a public bath. Baths were for relaxation, not washing. Desperate not to give offence, I sluiced and soaped and sprayed. Finally, after fifteen minutes of sluicery, I joined the three men in the large communal bath. They ignored me. Perhaps I was too pink and strange to contemplate.

Half an hour later I was back in my room, pink as a valentine and ready for dinner, of which the highlight was two monster fish heads, one cooked, one raw.

Southern Japan is a combination of Corsica and Scotland, a place of wildness, jagged hills and pines. The high point was a night in the Takafue *ryokan* on the slopes of the mighty Mount Aso-San, a grumbling and far from extinct volcano whose bubbling crater I was going to circumnavigate the next day. *Ryokans* are places of luxurious simplicity. You sleep on a mat on the floor; you have your own private *onsen* – a rock-carved outdoor bath – and teams of smiling maidens bring you thirteen courses of *kaiseki*, a traditional Japanese dinner.

At the Takafue *ryokan* I went to bed feeling like a god. I woke next morning with the realisation that a far more powerful god, the Japanese forest and mountain deity, was bent on revenge. I opened the blinds to a monsoon. And a thunderstorm. And a banshee wind. And cold. It was a day to bring a smile to the face of Lady Macbeth.

By 9 a.m. I had put on rain gear, five layers of clothes, and trudged up the hill to Beemer-san, where five smiling maidens under gaily-coloured paper umbrellas gave me the kind of farewell the banzai boys in the white scarves used to get as they prepared to fly their Zeros into US aircraft carriers.

My satnav was programmed for the sights of Mount Aso and determined that I should see them, but to have followed its bidding would have sent me plummeting, fog-blind, over the caldera's edge into the bubbling lava. I switched off the satnav. My only map was one of the whole of Japan, quite useless for navigation. Purely by chance I located an expressway and nosed on to it. I didn't know where I was, but it had the wonderful words FUKUOKA 132 KMS on it.

I was frozen, soaked and terrified. The wind blew the wind socks rigid and horizontal at motorway bridges, and then suddenly the gale would switch direction and hit from the other side. It was so strong that its force distorted the plastic of my helmet visor if I stuck my head far enough above the windscreen to see where I was going. My knowledge of physics was insufficient to work out how a bike, hit by a 100-kilometre-an-hour side wind, could stay upright. Why wasn't I blown flat into the fast lane? Something to do with momentum because of speed? Did that mean I had to go as fast as possible just to stay upright? Every nerve and instinct was alive and working to keep the bike upright and straight ahead, trying not to tense too much, crouching for a smaller wind profile and ignoring the rain bullets penetrating my neck and my visor. The adrenalin pumped.

I stopped for half an hour to regain my senses at a service area. I stripped off layers of clothes and got my most precious stuff out of the tank bag. Soaked, all soaked. Puzzled Japanese slurping noodles stopped to look at Pinko-san sorrowfully separating sodden 1,000-yen note from sodden 1,000-yen note while he munched a cold Japanese pastry.

Back on the bike the satnav graciously pointed the way through the storm to the Fukuoka Grand Hyatt. Never had a hotel been so welcome. The rain had stopped and Fukuoka was a buzzy town. I was dry and tomorrow the sun would shine. Next morning I almost choked on my Fukuoka croissant when I saw the front page of the English-language *Japan Times*: FREAK STORM WREAKS CHAOS NATIONWIDE. MANY KILLED, AIRPLANES AND TRAINS DISRUPTED. ANA CANCELLED 83 FLIGHTS. TYPHOON-STRENGTH WINDS OF 143 KPH RECORDED.

If I'd known what was in store I would have been mad not to have stayed put in the Takafue *ryokan* happily grunting in my bath while the storm raged outside, even if it did disrupt my itinerary. As it was, Beemer-san and I had set off into the maelstrom in cheerful ignorance. I was glad I had. I would not forget that day's biking. Better to have travelled ignorantly and to have arrived than not to have travelled at all.

Two days later, I found myself on the road to Hiroshima.

Hiroshima . . .

I had tried to stop myself thinking about it in advance. Humankind's biggest single act of violence against humankind. Executed at the order, not of a Hitler or a Genghis Khan, but a mild-mannered homespun haberdasher from Missouri, Harry S. Truman. What we *gaijin* remember of Hiroshima is the image of a mushroom cloud. Auschwitz, Pol Pot, 9/11 were terrible events in a catalogue of the massacres of the innocent, but Hiroshima was different. Hiroshima was the opening of a door to the end of our world. The dead were civilians, not combatants. Nevertheless I would try to arrive there with an open heart and an open mind to stand below the place where *Enola Gay*'s bombardier had pulled a lever to send Little Boy, as the USAF called the first A-bomb to be dropped in wrath, hurtling to earth, detonation and death.

We puttered in through squally clouds, the tail end of the unseasonal typhoon that had behaved so badly two days earlier, and found not a monotone Armageddon but a city as cute, colourful, stylish and appealing as a Macbook Air. Young people were everywhere, shiny shops, a buzz in the air, laughter, courting couples, youth, fun, giggling. A torrent of positive energy. Good-looking, chic people.

I was on the thirtieth floor of a stylish hotel. No trades-
man's entrance for the travel-worn biker. Beemer-san, now
honourably road-stained, was parked immediately next to
the main hotel entrance for the admiration of visitors. It was
strange how in the country that made more motorbikes than
everyone else put together there were so few bikers. Beemer-
san and I were a rarity.

I had a tea-time sake in the thirty-third-floor Sky Lounge
and looked out to the south. Hiroshima is on the coast of
Japan's Inland Sea and has many rivers and canals running
through it. Less than a mile away, in the arms of two rivers
between the neat Toronto-style street grid of sparkling
modern buildings, was the green and gravel of the Peace Park,
the area over which the bomb went off.

Half an hour later I walked over to it. The bomb detonated
600 metres above where I was now standing and directly
above a hospital. The entire centre of the city was, with the
exception of three buildings, vapourised. The first people to
go in after the blast remarked that everything was covered in
thick talc-like dust – all that remained of the buildings, the
people, their possessions and their toys. I had seen the same
dust covering downtown New York on 9/11, the remnants of
the vapourised Twin Towers.

In the words of the Memorial Museum leaflet, 'At the
instant of detonation, the temperature at the centre exceeded
a million degrees Celsius generating an enormous fireball . . . The blast pressure 500 metres from the fireball was
19 tons per square metre. Buildings were crushed. The heat
rays and blast burned and crushed nearly all buildings within
two kilometres of the centre. In an instant the city was almost
entirely destroyed.'

Counting the dead was difficult. Some 80,000 were thought to have died instantly. But, said the pamphlet,

The special characteristic of atomic bombs is nuclear radiation, something which conventional weapons never produce. The acute effects that appeared immediately after the bombing manifested in a wide range of symptoms, including fever, nausea, diarrhoea, bleeding, loss of hair and severe fatigue. After-effects began to appear about two years later and continued appearing for more than ten years. These include keloids [huge bumps under the flesh], leukaemia, and various cancers that continue to plague survivors to this day.

By the end of 1945 a total of 200,000 people had died as a result of the bomb. Many more had died since and others were permanently crippled in body and in mind.

The Peace Museum displayed narratives, photographs and objects from 6 August 1945, but unlike, say, the Saigon US War Crimes Museum in Vietnam, it made no judgements and took no sides. It stated its abhorrence of nuclear weapons but indicted no one. That made it the more powerful.

After a minute looking at the photographs of blistered bodies and torn school uniforms I was crying. An hour later I walked out into the Peace Park of fountains, water, trimmed evergreens, blossom and an air of tranquillity and peace. Every minute a deep gong sounded. I would follow the example of the Peace Museum and make no judgements. Did the end justify the means? How many lives were saved by shortening the war? Was the murder of 200,000 civilians, most of them living wretched lives in the last days of the Japanese empire, justified?

Following the dropping of the second bomb, on Nagasaki, Emperor Hirohito, whose voice had never before been heard by his subjects, went on the radio for the first time ever. 'This war has not necessarily been going to our advantage . . .' is how what he said is normally translated. A ceasefire was declared a week later.

It was 6.30 p.m. when I left the Peace Park. I walked for an hour through mid-town Hiroshima, had a snack and a couple of sakes.

Every time I make one of these trips I wonder if it will be the last. Long bike rides are not like long car journeys. In a car you don't think of getting hurt. If you have an accident the car may get damaged, but unless you're unlucky you should be fine. If a biker has an accident he gets hurt. I've had two accidents in twenty-three years of biking, and although I was trickling along at 20 mph both times when an idiot car driver (to a biker all car drivers are idiots) decided to turn right across the road without looking, I broke bones while the driver hardly noticed the dent.

I've never hunted foxes, but biking and hunting seem to me to have much in common, although we bikers try not to kill things we can't eat at the end of our jaunts. Both are very physical sports in which the cost of an accident is high. The physicality and the thrill is why I ride. Banking 1,200 cc of BMW a-scream into corner after corner for two hours of sweat-drenched mountain riding gives me a high I never get in a car, but might on a horse. I wouldn't know; I'm scared of horses.

If you are my age, you pray that if one of those mountain bends leads you into the flank of a turning petrol lorry you will fly off into the sayonara, not the paraplegic ward. Bikers are always aware of it. That's why biking makes you appreciate being alive.

Acknowledgements

I am always struck by the length of Acknowledgements at the end of books. It's worse than Oscar night. I have much that I can thank my parents, children and ex-wife for, not to mention thanking other friends along the way, but this book is not one of them. For me writing is a wonderful but solitary occupation.

If you want to know the best places to do it I would suggest the north Norfolk coast and a hotel in a fishing village in Brittany where much of this book was written. A big thank you to Norfolk and Brittany.

There are however two people to whom I owe a huge debt. Caroline Moorehead and Michela Wrong. They are both terrific writers. Google them and buy their books. When I thought I had finished this book I gave it to them to read. 'Put a tick by the bits you like and a cross by the bits that bore you. Oh, and any comments would be welcome.' They did. I followed their recommendations to the letter. They did not hold back but the book is the better for it.

Thank you, Caroline. Thank you, Michela. You both rock.